The Sociology of Literature

Diana T. Laurenson and Alan Swingewood

The Sociology
of Literature

SCHOCKEN BOOKS · NEW YORK

Published in U.S.A in 1972
by Schocken Books Inc.
200 Madison Avenue, New York, N.Y. 10016

Printed in Great Britain

Contents

Preface

This book has been written in the hope that it may serve to introduce the idea of a sociology of literature both to those who believe that social science is simply the study of *facts*, and to those for whom literature is a unique subjective experience which defies scientific analysis. The remarkable widening of interest in sociology at all levels during the last few years has been largely confined to those areas of inquiry already well cultivated – education, social stratification, religion, race relations, deviance – to the exclusion of other, less traditional, and more ambiguous subjects. The sociological study of literature has not developed, either in terms of its theory or in its methods of analysis, but has remained in some kind of limbo, suspended between literature as literature and sociology as social science. In the English language there is no adequate guide to the social analysis of literature in the past or in the present and no published attempt to relate theory to research. In this book we have tried to fill this gap and to argue strongly for the development of a literary sociology.

The book has been divided into three parts. In Part One we discuss the theory of literature as a social product linking the problems involved in the sociological analysis with past and with contemporary writers; some degree of intellectual continuity is suggested. In Part Two we examine the social situation of the writer himself, and try to relate the specific economic, political, and social influences to the structure of his work. Part Three puts forward some tentative analyses of proven literary texts in an attempt to relate theory to practice. Parts One and Three were wholly written by Alan Swingewood, while Diana Laurenson wrote Part Two. Although there are some differences of emphasis on a number of points between the two writers, it is hoped that the result is not too contradictory and will help to encourage the development of the sociology of literature.

In France the sociological study of literature has not lagged behind the development of other specialisms. Many of the ideas in this book stem directly from French writers: in particular, the Rumanian-born scholar Lucien Goldmann. It was with sadness that we heard of his sudden and relatively early death at the age of fifty-six, shortly after this book had been completed. Perhaps more than any other writer during the past twenty years, Goldmann positively *developed* the sociological study of literature through his writings on drama and on the novel. Without his work this book would have been that much more *imprecise*.

November, 1970

Part One:
Theory
by Alan Swingewood

1 Introduction: Sociology and Literature

For the literary critic literature is seen as a largely self-enclosed, self-sustaining enterprise. Works of literature must be approached primarily in terms of their own inner structure, imagery, metaphor, rhythm, delineation of character, dynamics of plot, and so on. Only occasionally is the external society allowed to intrude and then merely descriptively, as a necessary background. The modern literary critic, absorbed as he is in wholly textual criticism, in the intrinsic qualities of literature, would almost certainly be hostile to any claim that his subject could be illuminated by an approach which would be largely extrinsic. To suggest that sociology (defining it for the moment as one example of the extrinsic approach) would not merely cast light on certain literary problems, but that without it there could not be a complete understanding of literature – such a view would be rejected, and with feeling. After all, as the literary critic would doubtless point out, the study of literature and the study of society imply wholly different methods and orientations. What possible bridge can there be between the worlds of imagination and science?

These objections should not deter the prospective literary sociologist. At the most basic level, that of content, sociology and literature share a similar conspectus. Sociology is essentially the scientific, objective study of man in society, the study of social institutions and of social processes; it seeks to answer the question of how society is possible, how it works, why it persists. Through a rigorous examination of the social institutions, religious, economic, political, and familial, which together constitute what is called social structure, a picture emerges, not always clearly, of the ways in which man adapts to and is conditioned by particular societies; of the mechanisms of 'socialization', the process of cultural learning, whereby individuals are allocated to and accept their respective roles in the social structure.* This aspect of sociology is related to the concept of social stability, of continuity within different societies, the ways in which individuals come to accept the major social institutions as both necessary and right. But, of course, sociology is concerned also with the processes whereby society changes, gradually, or cataclysmically as in revolution, from one type of society to another – from feudalism to capitalism for example – and the effects which these changes have on social structure. Social processes also refer to small-scale internal change: the means, for example, whereby social and political authority are 'legitimized', that is, come to be accepted as right by the majority of the population; the ways in which conflict between classes, between groups, or simply between individuals is either successfully or unsuccessfully regulated by social institutions, allowing some form of consensus to be achieved.

As with sociology, literature too is pre-eminently concerned with man's social world, his adaptation to it, and his desire to change it. Thus the novel, as the major literary genre of industrial society, can be seen as a faithful attempt to re-create the social world of man's relation with his family, with politics, with the State; it delineates too his roles within the family and other institutions, the conflicts and tensions between groups and social classes. In the purely documentary sense, one can see the novel as dealing with much the same social, economic, and political textures as sociology. But of course it achieves more than this; as art, literature transcends mere description and objective scientific analysis, penetrating the surfaces of social life, showing the ways in which men and women experience

---

* The psychological approach to literature rarely employs these sociological concepts, being more concerned to relate literary creativity to specific psychological conditions. It is frequently reductionist in that the literary text is seen as merely a reflection of the author's psychological history, as a peculiar *individual* phenomenon. This is not to deny that certain events in the socialization of writers, such as Dickens's experience of the blacking factory, will express themselves in a writer's work, through his choice of characters, plots, use of symbols, metaphor, etc., but this in no sense supplants explanation and understanding of literature in terms of social structure and, as we suggest later, of values.

society as feeling. 'Without the full literary witness,' writes Richard Hoggart, 'the student of society will be blind to the fullness of a society.'*

Although, then, it would seem that literature and sociology are not wholly distinct disciplines but, on the contrary, complement each other in our understanding of society, historically they have tended to remain apart. Early sociologists, such as Comte and Spencer in the nineteenth century and Durkheim and Weber in the twentieth, while making the occasional reference to imaginative literature, on the whole subordinated it to the study of social structure. The sociological study of literature is thus a fairly late arrival, for although there are today well developed sociologies of religion, education, politics, social change, even of such an imprecise area as ideology, there is virtually no established corpus of knowledge called the sociology of literature. It is also unfortunate that the small amount of knowledge and research which does exist is on the whole exceedingly dubious in quality, lacking in scientific rigour, banal in the quality of its sociological 'insights', and frequently consisting of the crudest correlations between literary texts and social history.†

At the present time it is possible to characterize two broad approaches to a sociology of literature. The most popular perspective adopts the documentary aspect of literature, arguing that it provides a mirror to the age. This mirror image approach has a long and distinguished history: the French philosopher Louis de Bonald (1754–1840) was one of the first writers to argue that through a careful reading of any nation's literature 'one could tell what this people had been', while Stendhal, in a celebrated passage in *Le Rouge et le Noir*, wrote of the novel as a 'mirror journeying down the high road', sometimes reflecting 'the azure blue of heaven, sometimes the mire in the puddles'. On this view literature is a direct reflection of various facets of social structure, family relationships, class conflict, and possibly divorce trends and population composition.‡ As one of the

* R. Hoggart, 'Literature and Society', in *A Guide to the Social Sciences*, ed. N. Mackenzie, London, Weidenfeld & Nicolson, 1966.
† For this conception of a literary sociology, see G. Watson, *The Study Literature*, London, Allen Lane The Penguin Press, 1969, ch. 10, 'Sociology'.
‡ Cf. M. C. Albrecht, 'The Relationship of Literature and Society', *American Journal of Sociology*, vol. 159, pp. 425–36.

more distinguished writers in the sociology of literature has well expressed it: 'It is the task of the sociologist of literature to relate the experience of the writer's imaginary characters and situations to the historical climate from which they derive. He has to transform the private equation of themes and stylistic means into social equations.'*

This 'transforming' of the private world of literature to specific social meanings, the extrinsic approach to literature, has frequently come under severe criticism. It is argued against it, for example, that the method tends to use literature solely as a quarry of information to be sociologically 'ransacked'; that literature is being 'turned over from the outside' by those lacking the necessary critical apparatus for understanding and evaluation.† Implicit too in this method is the danger that the literary sociologist might not have sufficient skill to unravel the historical details of particular periods. After all, since the literary document has to be analysed in terms of the world it supposedly represents, then 'only a person who has knowledge of the structure of a society from other sources than purely literary ones is able to find out if, and how far, certain social types and their behaviour are reproduced in a novel in an adequate or inadequate manner'.‡ But the real problem arises over the question of what literature actually reflects. If the novel, for example, is the mirror of an age, then this raises the question of whether or not purely literary devices may distort this portrayal; too often in the past an artistic fidelity to historical and social truth has been assumed, with wholly disastrous interpretative consequences.§ There is, too, the question of generalization: to what extent are the fictional characters and situations typical of a specific historical period? Can any useful sociological generalizations be drawn – for example, from the novels of Charles Dickens and Mrs Gaskell – on such social issues as

* L. Lowenthal, *Literature and the Image of Man*, Boston, Beacon Press, 1957, p. x.
† Hoggart, op. cit.; F. R. Leavis, 'Sociology and Literature', in *The Common Pursuit*, London, Chatto & Windus, 1952.
‡ E. K. Bramsted, *Aristocracy and the Middle Classes in Germany*, *Social Types in German Literature, 1830–1900*, Chicago, University of Chicago Press, 1964, p. 4.
§ Thus Taine (see chapter 2 below), in his study of English literature (1864), forgot that in the Elizabethan theatre feminine roles were played by boys and thus argued for the essential masculinity of Elizabethan heroes and types.

nineteenth-century management–labour relations, the role of trade unions or working-class consciousness? What useful sociological material is there in the Victorian novelist's conception of the English working class, which is not far more accurately conveyed from a close reading of contemporary journals, factory reports, government inquiries, crude health, and mortality statistics? And these latter sources are free to a very great extent from the Victorian novelists' middle-class perspectives and ideology.

The conception of the mirror, then, must be treated with great care in the sociological analysis of literature. Above all else, of course, it ignores the writer himself, his awareness and intention. Great writers do not set out simply to depict the social world in largely descriptive terms; it might be suggested that the writer by definition has a more critical task, of setting his characters in motion within artificially contrived situations to seek their own private 'destiny', to discover values and meaning in the social world. For society is more than an ensemble of social institutions that make up social structure: it contains both norms, the standards of behaviour which individuals come to accept as right ways of acting and judging, as well as values which are consciously formulated and which people strive to realize socially. Literature clearly reflects norms, attitudes to sex by the working class and middle class, for example; it reflects, too, values in the sense of the writer's own intention, and it might be suggested that it is on the level of values where literature is seen to reinforce and illuminate purely sociological material. This is particularly noticeable in literature which chooses itself as subject. Thus although both Balzac in *Lost Illusions* and George Gissing in *New Grub Street* (1891) provide a fairly accurate picture of the increasing commercialization of literature during the nineteenth century, the novelists' real aim lies more properly within the realm of values. The essential theme of both novels is the conflict between the genuine literary consciousness of poet and novelist on the one hand and the practical, wholly calculative and mercenary dictates of the industrialized literary market on the other – the tension between literature as art and literature as trade. Both Balzac and Gissing are using specific historical features of the nineteenth century as the background for their main theme: the devaluation of values, the sacrifice of the artist on the altar of profit. It could be argued, then, that the 'true' meaning of great literature and the social groups involved in its production lies precisely in the quest and the struggle of both for 'authentic values', the values of a genuine human community in which human needs, aspirations, and desires are mediated through social interaction. If this is so, and it will be defended later in the book, then the task of the sociologist is not simply to discover historical and social reflection (or refraction) in works of literature, but to articulate the nature of the values embedded within particular literary works, what Raymond Williams has called 'the structure of feeling'.* Thus Lowenthal has suggested that the main purpose of any viable sociology of literature must be to discover the 'core of meaning' which one finds at the heart of different works of literature and which expresses many aspects of thought and feeling on subjects as varied as social class, work, love, religion, nature, and art. In his own work Lowenthal shows how Cervantes' hero Don Quixote can be understood sociologically as a structure of sentiments and behaviour indicative of 'extreme personal insecurity' which ranges from fears of starvation and loss of social status to philosophical uncertainty. Such sentiments, he argues, can be seen as a direct result of the rapid increase in social mobility which followed the decline of Spanish feudalism with its stress on fixed social position, and the development of a much more fluid and open commercial society in which social status depended more on achievement than on ascription. Don Quixote is thus seen as an essentially isolated individual dominated by an apprehensive rather than optimistic view of the world.† For Lowenthal, this kind of analysis will succeed in revealing the 'central problems with which man has been concerned at various times, permitting us to develop an image of a given society in terms of the individuals who composed it'. We learn both of the nature of society and the ways individuals experienced it, through the fictional characters who see and record 'not only the reality around them, but their hopes, wishes, dreams and fantasies . . .'. The social meanings of this inner life of characters, Lowenthal concludes, are related to problems of social change. Thus literature, as a reflection of

* R. Williams, *Culture and Society*, London, Chatto & Windus, 1958.
† Lowenthal, op. cit.

values and of feeling, points both to the degree of change occurring in different societies as well as to the manner in which individuals become socialized into the social structure and their response to this experience. Literature, because it delineates man's anxieties, hopes, and aspirations, is perhaps one of the most effective sociological barometers of the human response to social forces. It has to be said, however, that while literature will reflect social values and feelings in the way that Lowenthal has argued, it is highly probable that as society grows more complex in its modes of socialization, change, and social structure, it will become increasingly difficult to analyse literature solely in terms of reflection. In the eighteenth century it was still possible for Fielding in *Tom Jones* to portray a whole society, a totality, in terms of its values and feelings through his rich gallery of characters; as, indeed, had Homer living in a more homogeneous and smaller society. But with the beginnings of industrialization and the development of a complex social structure involving a multiplicity of class and status positions, together with the growth of mass communications and the so-called mass society, 'no one could possibly attempt anything along the same lines . . . if only because no single individual can have personal knowledge of more than a minute fraction of it'.* If the novel, whose rise parallels the emergence of industrial society, reflects social structure, then it has done so in portraying the problems of *society in general* in terms of a restricted milieu which functions as a social microcosm: Balzac's nobles, bourgeoisie, and artists, Proust's decaying aristocracy, Aldous Huxley's upper-class intellectuals, reflect the particular historical crisis of society in general.

The second approach to a literary sociology moves away from the emphasis on the work of literature itself to the production side, and especially to the social situation of the writer. A leading authority in this field, the French sociologist Robert Escarpit, has tended to concentrate exclusively on this aspect.† Patronage and the costs of production replace the literary text as the centre of discussion. Thus the writer's relationship with his patron,

* I. Watt, 'Literature and Society', in *The Arts in Society*, ed. R. N. Wilson, New Jersey, Prentice-Hall, 1964.
† R. Escarpit, *Sociologie de la Littérature*, Paris, 1958. Cf. R. Williams, *The Long Revolution*, London, Chatto & Windus, 1961, part 2.

often oblique and unsavoury, is traced in some detail, from the patronage of the medieval courts to that of the eighteenth-century aristocracy. With the rise of cheap publishing and a mass market the patronage system gives way to the autocracy of the publisher and booksellers. The growth, too, of a specifically middle-class audience in the late eighteenth century helped to shift the writer's position from one of dependence to one of profession. This gradual democratization of culture, as the German sociologist Karl Mannheim has called it, is especially significant for the rise of the novel, a pre-eminently middle-class literary genre, and the emergence of modern 'sensibility' or modern psychology. The cultural triumph of the middle classes can be seen as foreshadowing mass culture and the virtual commercialization of literature. The writer's position in a mass society is extremely important as a contrast to his earlier social situation, and clearly likely to affect his creative potential in many ways; the links between this historical background and the development of literature constitute a key area in any literary sociology. It involves a major problem, namely the precise linkage between the text and its background – how do literary production and consumption affect the form and the content of particular literary works? It must be noted, however, that although this approach is essential for any thorough understanding of literature, as crucial support for textual analysis, great care has to be exercised in order to avoid the extremely crude forms of reductionism so obviously inherent in it. The work of literature must never become a mere epiphenomenon of its surrounding environment.

A persistent theme of this particular sociological approach is the emphasis on the increasing alienation of the writer from his society and the consequent impact on literary style and content. This social fragmentation has frequently been traced to the decline of patronage in the late eighteenth century and the writer's emergence as a member of a 'free floating intelligentsia'.* In pre-industrial society, it is argued, a relative harmony existed between the author and his audience; in Periclean Athens, Aeschylus, Sophocles, and Euripides were more or less inte-

* This is a well-worn cliché of modern sociology. It can be traced to John Stuart Mill, but its more recent use derives from Karl Mannheim. See especially his *Ideology and Utopia* (1936).

grated into society and not regarded as members of a separate class. In Augustan Rome, on the other hand, the glorification of the regime by Horace and Virgil can be seen as a direct result of the system of patronage.* With the decline of Rome and Athens courtly patronage became the writer's main support, for example, in Renaissance Italy and in seventeenth- and eighteenth-century France; patronage of the court was then frequently followed by that of the rich, with needy authors vying with each other for food and money.† Patronage and the limited audience of pre-industrial and early commercial society clearly conditioned the writer's response: there existed between the author and his audience a congruence of values, of mutual understanding. But with the rise of a specifically middle-class reading public, lending libraries, and cheap publishing, writers were forced more and more to depend on the system of royalties for their living: literature, as already observed, turned into a trade. For the genuine creative writer the late nineteenth and early years of the twentieth century completed his alienation from society and strengthened his identification with largely intellectual groups. The point which divides the period when it was still possible for the writer to identify with the middle class and express its values through literature, pre-eminently social and rational, from the period of doubt and uncertainty with its emphasis on the psychological and subjectivist state, has often been cited as the year of revolutions – 1848 – when Europe was convulsed with conflict. After this date, in most Western European countries the middle class had either attained political power or were in the process of doing so. The creative writer, with his critical function turned in now on the class from which he usually derived both his paternity and income, becomes 'problematic'.‡

These, then, are two of the major orientations to the socio-logical study of literature, the one buttressing the other in terms

* It has been suggested that pastoral poetry reflects the 'taste for a fashion-able kind of escape which arose in the latter days of Greece and Rome among certain urban and leisured audiences' (Watt, op. cit.).

† Bramsted tells of one nineteenth-century German prince who was in the habit of dispensing a somewhat rustic patronage to his authors, namely produce from his farms, ducks, geese, eggs, etc., which the needy writer could sell or consume depending on his needs (Bramsted, op. cit.).

‡ Cf. A. Hauser, *A Social History of Art*, London, Routledge & Kegan Paul, 1961, vol. 4, ch. 1. See also below, chapter 3 (I).

of total understanding. But, as with many subjects, a pernicious division of labour has tended to separate them so that research either concentrates on the social context of writing or on the literary text and its social meanings. Those sociologists whose starting point is the text frequently regard the social prerequisites of writing as largely irrelevant for a literary sociology. Thus Lucien Goldmann has argued that in the case of great writers (and for him these are the only writers worthy of study) the purely sociological conditions of writing are surmounted and transcended so that the meanings within the texts are unrelated to the market conditions of authorship. He suggests that second-rate writers can be defined precisely as those who do not succeed in freeing themselves from the dictates of the social-economic context, so that sociological conditions penetrate their work, dominating its structure and content and giving it a purely temporal significance. Goldmann's point is contentious: most eighteenth- and nineteenth-century authors wrote for a specific audience, creating character and incident that would conform with its values, especially the attitudes towards sex. In both Dickens and Balzac the structure of the novels hinges on the requirements of serial publication, and Balzac's peculiarly dramatic elements (criminal characters, sudden and violent dénouements) are obviously connected to the development of French magazine-publishing in the 1830s and the 1840s. Goldmann's point is probably more apposite in the case of modern literature. Great writers no longer publish in serial form, this being mainly the prerogative of the second-rate and pulp writers. More significantly, it has now become exceedingly difficult to connect the audience, publisher, social group nexus with great literature in any meaningful way. Is it at all possible, for example, to connect sociologically Virginia Woolf's stream of consciousness writing technique with the general social conditions of authorship prevailing in the early twentieth century? Is it not rather a question, as Goldmann insists, of tracing through the linkages between the writer's social group affiliations and connecting both their structure and values with the literary texts? The publisher–author–audience relationship is thus, on this view at least, no longer sociologically determinate.

While the study of literature as a form of social reflection as well as its study in terms of the social context of authorship constitute the two major modes of study, they by no means exhaust the sociological approach. A third perspective, one demanding a high level of skills, attempts to trace the ways in which a work of literature is actually received by a particular society at a specific historical moment. Thus Guy de Maupassant's literary reception in England during the 1880s and the 1890s helped to effect the transition from an English literature penetrated by a naïve or oblique sexuality to one distinctly modern in outlook. In the novels of Thomas Hardy and George Moore, for example, sex is treated more directly than in the novels of Dickens and George Eliot, and this change serves to illustrate the conflict of values, in late Victorian England, between the traditional literary practitioners and the innovators.* Lowenthal has shown how in Germany between 1880 and 1920 the middle and upper classes successfully assimilated Doestoevsky into their own peculiar ideology. The dominant theme in German literary criticism, Lowenthal's main source, in this period was an emphasis on Dostoevsky's irrationalism, which Lowenthal suggests is connected with the rapid contemporary growth of big business and a fully capitalist society.† 'If giant economic and political structures were to be accepted by the people, the ideal of competition among men through the development of reason and will had to be replaced by a veneration of non-rational ideals removed from the forum of critical verification.' To the German critics Dostoevsky appeared as anti-intellectual, mystical, otherworldly, and implacably hostile to the ideas of socialism; his novels could be used as 'intellectual weapons against efforts to reorganize society' such as those proposed by German socialism. This reception of Dostoevsky, Lowenthal suggests, illustrates the profound crisis of consciousness which afflicted the German nation during these forty years and which was to

* B. Slote, *Literature and Society*, Lincoln, University of Nebraska Press, 1964.
† Lowenthal's method of research was to read 'nearly all' the books, magazine articles, and major newspaper articles written on Dostoevsky during the forty years after 1880 (L. Lowenthal, *The Reception of Dostoevsky's Work in Germany, 1880–1920*, in Wilson, op. cit.).

culminate in the extreme irrationalism, anti-intellectualism, and anti-socialism of the Nazis.

Lowenthal's choice of Dostoevsky points to a problem we have not yet really touched upon: the choice of writer for study and analysis. It is interesting to note that on this point most sociologists of literature and literary critics are agreed: one studies great writers and their texts precisely because their greatness implies deep insights into the human and the social condition. Thus for Leo Lowenthal, the artist 'portrays what is more real than reality itself', while for Richard Hoggart, great literature penetrates more deeply into human experience because it has the capacity 'to see not only individual instances but deeper and more long-term movements below the surface detail' and the ability 'to unite dissimilars, to reveal a pattern out of a mass and a mess, like a magnet placed into iron filings'.* The great artist portrays 'the whole man in depth'.†

The problem of choice cannot be resolved here but it clearly involves the question of criteria; and the specific criterion seems here to be simply that of persistence, that great literature *survives*. If this is so it brings into doubt the nature of any sociology of mass culture, popular culture, and so on, which, on this view, does not have a message for posterity or contain deep insights into man's social and human condition. But if the basic purpose of sociology is to understand the nature and the workings of all societies and men's position within them, then popular culture must surely claim a reasonable status. If the argument of Lowenthal is accepted, that literature embraces the fundamental values and symbols which provide cohesion to the different groups within society, then popular culture could be used as a 'diagnostic tool' for analysing modern man, especially since it has become so widely produced and assimilated.‡

In the chapters which follow we shall attempt to provide evidence of the mutual needs of both sociology and literature, and to suggest that no student of human society can ignore the 'literary witness' and the literary consciousness.

* Hoggart, op. cit.
† Lowenthal, *Literature and the Image of Man*. Cf. F. R. Leavis, *The Great Tradition*, London, Chatto & Windus, 1948.
‡ Lowenthal, *Literature, Popular Culture and Society*, New Jersey, Prentice-Hall, 1961. See also B. Barber and D. M. White, *Mass Culture*, New York, Macmillan, 1957.

2 The Social Theories of Literature

Like many areas of sociology, the sociology of literature has a distinguished as well as uncertain history. It is fashionable nowadays to treat the history of any discipline, especially if it reaches back beyond the nineteenth century, as a somewhat irrelevant and unrewarding academic exercise, a mere display of erudition, unrelated to the immediate problems. Too often the history of ideas has tended to conform to this indictment, that it is no more than 'interesting', possibly even 'stimulating', but nevertheless a scholarly luxury. It is, of course, more than this: the study of the past as theory, as speculation, can tell us not only of the ways in which early predecessors struggled with the same kinds of problems that face the modern researcher but, more particularly, it can clarify the methods used: social science cannot possibly be understood solely in terms of what it does today, and any theory of literature and society can be shown to have a lineage which continues to exercise an influence on present work. We shall argue that the history of the sociology of literature has, at different times and in different writers, posed precisely the major questions of its subject, and that the various responses can be seen to be as much the result of ideology as of scientific immaturity.

I

The first really systematic treatment of the relationship between literature and society belongs to the French philosopher and critic, Hippolyte Taine (1828–93). He was not the first, of course, to grasp the social implications of the imaginative arts: Plato's conception of imitation implies a view of literature as a reflection of society. But prior to Taine the social analysis of literature was in the main sociologically thin in content, lacking in scientific rigour. Indeed, up to the beginning of the seven-teenth century, literature had rarely been thought of in material terms and it was not until the collapse of the medieval world with its static social structures and all-pervasive religious values that men became really aware of society and its institutions as secular forces. The view that literature was socially conditioned, a 'conventional wisdom' in the seventeenth and eighteenth centuries implied both a chain of historical and social causation as well as a developed critical awareness. The seventeenth-century debate in England and France over the respective merits of the Ancients and the Moderns, the question whether contemporary European literature was comparable with that of Greece and Rome, serves to illustrate the increasing critical and comparative perspective.* The chief discovery of the debate, that epic poetry fitted a particular type of society, 'rude' rather than 'polished', clearly shifted attention to environment as an important causative agent. Seventeenth-century writers con-ceived environment as a complex of certain physical factors, especially climate and geography, plus the somewhat ambiguous notions of 'national character' and 'liberty'. These fragile corre-lations received relatively little development during the course of the next century, writers for the most part being content to state the truly absurd and the obvious, while others forged the most ingenious connections. The chief factor was usually cli-mate, its extremes conducive to the development of a 'national temper' which in turn produced social and political institutions that could either favour or retard literature, institutions em-bodying peace or war, liberty or despotism.†

* The discussion in the first part of this chapter is greatly indebted to R. Wellek's *The Rise of English Literary History*, Chapel Hill, University of North Carolina Press, 1941, especially chs 2 and 3. It has also drawn on the same author's *A History of Modern Criticism*, Vol. 1, *The Later Eighteenth Century*, London, Jonathan Cape, 1955. W. K. Wimsatt and C. Brooks, *Literary Criticism*, New York, Knopf, 1957, was also helpful.
† Thus William Temple in his *Of Poetry* (1690) argued that English comedy's superiority over others was due to 'the native plenty of our soil, the unequal-ness of our climate, as well as the ease of our government, and the liberty of professing opinions and factions – plenty begets wantonness and pride; wantonness is apt to invent and pride scorns to imitate. Liberty begets stomach and heart, and stomach will not be constrained. Thus we have more originals, and more that appear that they are: we have more humour, because every man follows his own and takes a pleasure, perhaps a pride, to show it. 'Quoted in Wellek, *Rise of English Literary History*.' p. 32.

Seventeenth-century writers did grasp, however, the documentary value of literature. In 1699 a certain James Wright declared that 'old plays will always be read by the curious if it were only to discover the manners and behaviour of several ages and how they altered. For plays are exactly like portraits drawn in the garb and fashion of the time when painted'.* This perspective is strongly echoed in one of the first genuine works of social science, Vico's *New Science* (1725). Vico grasped clearly the social aspects of the world and of history, that the social world was largely the work of man, not of divine providence, and that therefore its institutions as well as its art could be analysed in material terms.† Vico related the *Iliad* of Homer to the north-east of Greece, since it describes the Trojan Wars and the period when 'Greece was young and consequently burning with sublime passions such as pride, anger, and vengeance'. The *Odyssey*, on the other hand, was written by Homer much later, and in the south-east, since it 'celebrates Ulysses, who reigned there', during a period when the passions 'were already somewhat cooled by reflection'.‡ The so-called 'mechanical materialism' of the seventeenth and eighteenth centuries – mechanical in the sense that it implied a simple one-to-one relation between culture and the material basis of society, and thus underrated the active function of human consciousness, that change is above all social and that it is men who change the world – although emphasizing the effects of climate and national character on the development of literature increasingly gave more weight to geographical factors.§ In the writings of Herder (1744–1803) and Madame de Staël (1766–1817), this strong empirical, anti-metaphysical strain was brought to its logical summation.

* Quoted in Wellek, op. cit., p. 33.
† This became a common postulate of eighteenth-century writers, and is most marked in B. Mandeville, *Fable of the Bees* (1714) and Montesquieu, *Spirit of the Laws* (1748), both early examples of proto-sociology.
‡ Vico, *The New Science*, trans. from the third edition (1744) by T. G. Bergin and M. H. Fisch, New York, Cornell University Press, 1948, Book III. For a discussion of Vico's theory of literature, see E. Wilson, 'The Historical Interpretation of Literature', in *The Triple Thinkers*, London, Penguin Books, 1962.
§ Thus the Abbé du Bos, in his *Critical Reflections on Poetry and Painting* (1719), a widely popular and critically acclaimed work, reduced artistic genius to a mere matter of physical environment and physiology. See Wellek, *The Later Eighteenth Century*, pp. 32–3.

Herder, in opposition to the *a priori* aesthetic of his fellow German philosopher, Immanuel Kant, who argued that a sense of beauty could result only from a purely 'disinterested judgement', proposed a wholly empirical aesthetic based on natural science, history, and psychology. Herder argued that each work of literature was rooted in a certain social and geographical environment where it performed specific functions and that there was no need for any judgement of value: everything is as it had to be. Literary history is thus cultural history, and for Herder the main question, which he continually poses, is why certain literatures develop in particular areas and why they sometimes decline to establish themselves elsewhere.* His explanations are disappointing, for although employing factors such as variable climate, landscape, race, customs, and political conditions, they rarely move beyond the vague generalities of earlier writers and the exact relationship between literature and social structure is hardly grasped; literature is analysed with reference to history and then used as a means of understanding history. Herder, in fact, is even loath to use his own professed method: instead of the concepts of race, climate, and concrete social conditions he frequently generalizes from the generic and sociologically meaningless terms 'spirit of the time', 'spirit of the nation', the implication being that literature bears a direct causal connection to these dubious concepts.†

Like Herder, Madame de Staël relates literature to climate, geography and social institutions in a generally muddled manner. She opens her book on literature and society with the claim that her purpose is no less than an examination of 'the influence upon literature of religion, custom and law', since 'the

* René Wellek has produced an impressive list of eighteenth-century writers who made genuine attempts to grasp the social foundations of literature. The French author, Marmontel, for example, in his *Poétique Français* (1763), attempted to consider 'poetry as a plant and discover why, indigenous in certain climates it rises and flowers as of itself; why in other climates it flourishes only by cultivation; and in others cannot be made to bloom in spite of all efforts; and why even in the same climate it has sometimes flowered and borne fruit and sometimes withered'. Quoted in Wellek, op. cit., pp. 65–6. Like many others, however, Marmontel singularly failed to realize his project.
† J. C. Herder, *Outlines of a Philosophy of Man*, trans. T. Churchill, London, 1800. On Herder, see Wellek, *The Later Eighteenth Century*, ch. 9; R. T. Clark, *Herder – His Life and Thought*, Berkeley, University of California Press, 1955; J. K. Fugate, *The Psychological Basis of Herder's Aesthetics*, The Hague, Mouton, 1966.

social and political influences that affect the nature of literature have not been frequently analysed'.* But her intentions are rarely realized and her work contains few valid sociological insights. Her conception of literature is somewhat broad: 'everything that involves the exercise of thought in writing, the physical sciences excepted'. Both metaphysics and fiction are then related to a varied number of factors, especially climatic conditions, which are seen to demarcate quite neatly the literatures of the South and the North. 'Melancholy,' she writes, 'that fertile sentiment in works of genius, seems to belong almost exclusively to Northern climates.' Northern nations are 'dark and moody', with an independence of mind and an indifference to life made possible only by the 'harshness of the soil and the gloom of the sky', and their literature is dominated by a 'passionate sadness' that comes from living in a 'foggy climate'. Southern literature, on the other hand, is characterized by 'coolness, dense woods and limpid streams', with its descriptions of love combining with the 'benevolent shade that protects them from the burning heat of the sun'. Not that climate is all-pervasive. National character, which, she argues, is a result of a complex interaction between religious, legal, and political institutions, is equally important. The Italians, for example, do not write novels because they are too 'licentious' and have little respect for women. Madame de Staël has an interesting observation here, arguing that the novel form could develop only in those societies where women's status was fairly high and where a strong interest in the private life existed. Women, after all, she adds, know nothing of life 'but the capacity to love,' and although England has a poetry full of 'gloomy imagination' it is the country 'where women are most truly loved'.†

Here at least there is a positive step forward in the social interpretation of literature. An awareness of the role of women in creating the novel as a literary genre represents a significant advance on the simplistic correlations of her predecessors and is

* Madame de Staël, *De La Littérature* (1800), Paris, Minard, 1959, vol. 1, p. 3.
† Cf. I. Watt, *The Rise of the Novel*, London, Penguin Books, 1963, who acknowledges Madame de Staël's anticipation of many elements of his analysis of the growth of the eighteenth-century novel. See especially ch. 2.

truly *social*. Madame de Staël grasps, too, the importance of a strong middle class for the growth of literature, arguing that it produces liberty and virtue, two important prerequisites of art. 'Happy the country,' she writes, 'where the writers are gloomy, the merchants satisfied, the rich melancholy, and the masses content.' But overall her work suffers from the constant invocation of direct causality: too often she states that literature is the expression of the national character which seems to mean simply the 'spirit of the time'.*

By the beginning of the nineteenth century, then, the social analysis of literature had hardly progressed beyond the crude formulations of the seventeenth-century materialists. No method had been devised for analysing the relationship between social structure and its art; there were few genuine insights. There were no mediating factors, and literature was simply the outgrowth of climate, soil, and national spirit. Thus the sheer arbitrariness of the explanations, and while Madame de Staël did at least propose the modifying influence of the political and legal framework on a society's literature, her final analysis would always revert to the indefinable spirit of the nation. It would be wrong, however, to dismiss these early attempts at a proto-sociology of literature, for there was another aspect to the question apart from the emphasis on climate and national character.

During the last years of the eighteenth century a new theme announced itself: the increasing trend to various forms of literary and artistic fragmentation, a theme, of course, which has persisted to this day. Thus for Adam Smith (1723–90) the arts of poetry, music, and dancing were originally a unified whole, with the tribal chiefs, for example, combining the art of legislator with those of the poet and the musician.† Another Scot, Adam Ferguson (1723–1816), accepting this so-called 'primitivistic' view of man, argued that by nature man was a poet since poetry expressed his innermost sentiments. 'The early history of all nations,' he wrote, 'is uniform in this particular. Priests, statesmen and philosophers, in the first ages of Greece,

---

* Similarly, the German philosopher, Hegel, in his lectures on the philosophy of history in Berlin, 1822–3, argued that national literatures fully expressed their societies, societies conceived as organisms continually transforming themselves under the influence of the dominant spirit.

† A. Smith, *Lectures on Rhetoric and Belles Lettres*, ed. J. M. Lothian, Edinburgh, Nelson, 1963.

delivered their instructions in poetry, and mixed with the dealers in music and heroic fable.' But this was a precarious unity which gradually dissolved in the face of growing economic and social differentiation – both Smith and Ferguson were among the first to grasp fully the social significance of the division of labour, for while it had the effect of producing great wealth and abundance it was also instrumental in breaking the organic structure of pre-industrial society, turning men into the objects, not the subjects, of the historical process. Eighty years before Marx, Adam Ferguson observed:

Many mechanical arts require no capacity; they succeed best under a total suppression of sentiment and reason ... Manufacturers, accordingly, prosper most where the mind is least consulted, and where the workshop may, without any great effort of imagination, be considered as an engine, the parts of which are men.

A developed division of work, while essential for commodity production, has the unintended effect of turning literature into the specialized function of a separate social group and, with the growth of commerce, into a trade, a commodity:

The talents of men come to be employed in a variety of affairs, and their inquiries directed to different subjects ... The science of nature, morals, politics and history, find their several admirers; and even poetry itself ... appears in a growing variety of forms.*

There is here a suggestion of the process which Marx would call 'alienation'. Both Ferguson and Smith were suggesting that as society becomes increasingly commercial and industrial, man and his arts are unintentionally torn away from a living organic relation with society itself. Ideas such as these find expression in the philosophies of Frederick Schiller (1759–1805) and Hegel (1770–1831). Schiller argued explicitly that labour, through the soul-destroying agencies of economic specialization and the commercial spirit, acted as the chief destroying agent of 'aesthetic civilization'. Against labour he proposed the concept of play (*Spiel*), the spontaneous and aesthetic contemplation of nature which would act in healing the split between man and nature, between intellect and sense. Art, Schiller suggested, will provide the civilizing element reuniting

* A. Ferguson, *An Essay on the History of Civil Society* (1767), ed. D. Forbes, Edinburgh, University of Edinburgh Press, 1966, part IV, sections 1–2.

man and returning his wholeness to him.* Hegel, like Schiller, stressed man's divorce from 'living nature', from other men. Accepting de Bonald's maxim that literature was an expression of society, he argued that while the epic was the perfect expression of 'heroic ages', a kind of national spirit, the modern world with its specialization and individualism tears man away from the deep relationship with nature on which epic action rests. The contemporary world, Hegel suggested, with its systems of bureaucracy, its police forces, its extended division of work, finds a substitute for the epic in the novel, 'the middle class epic' as he calls it. Hegel talks of the novel as a form of consciousness, with each age possessing its own 'prevailing mental attitude', its own 'specific outlook on the world', which produces its own particular artistic forms. Thus the consciousness of the contemporary world is the 'prosaic mind' expressed in the novel form, faithfully reflecting that world's fragmentation and loss of unity.†

One can trace, therefore, during the latter part of the eighteenth and the beginning of the nineteenth century, two approaches gradually developing in the social study of literature. There was the movement which became known as positivism,‡ the search for material, scientifically ascertainable causal connections between 'facts' such as climate, geography, and race, and literature, which was generally defined to include philosophy and politics. Literature itself was as much a fact as the others and with a similar status in scientific research. As such the approach implied the absence of absolute standards: artistic evaluation was wholly dependent on time, place, and function; it was completely relative. Against this strictly empirical attitude was ranged the argument that literature was much more

* F. Schiller, *On the Aesthetic Education of Man* (1795), ed. and trans. E. M. Wilkinson and L. A. Willoughby, Oxford, Oxford University Press, 1967. On Schiller, see Wellek, *The Later Eighteenth Century*, ch. 11; G. Lukács, *Goethe and His Age*, London, Merlin Press, 1968.
† G. W. F. Hegel, *Philosophy of Fine Art*. Much of Hegel's analysis of literature and society is embedded in the early work of G. Lukács and through him, Lucien Goldmann (see chapter 3 below).
‡ The term 'positivism' became synonymous with scientific method during the nineteenth century. In the social sciences it was a doctrine which made an appeal to the facts the only viable foundation of sound knowledge, facts which should support observable laws of society; its aim was to apply the methods of natural sciences to the study of human society.

than a simple or indeed a complex reflection of society as a whole: it was rather the embodiment of man's essential strivings for a sense of community and 'authenticity', an attempt to grasp the meaning of a world which was being emptied of genuine values through the progressive incursions of the division of labour. On this view values become the all-important aspect of the study of literature, and a literary sociology becomes primarily the study of those values by which the individual and his society should live. There is here a strong critical conception, as distinct from the wholly scientific descriptive tendency of positivism.*

In the course of its development during the nineteenth and twentieth centuries, the sociology of literature would tend to keep these two differing perspectives separate – positivism through the writings of Taine, and the critical tendency through Marxists such as Lukács and Goldmann.

2

Taine – philosopher, historian, politician, and essayist – is generally regarded as the founder of the sociology of literature. Although largely ignored and forgotten outside France, Taine's work on literature and society, specious though most of it is, does contain an awareness of the basic and perennial problems which face any literary sociology.

Like his predecessor Auguste Comte (1798–1857), who coined the word 'sociology', Taine strove to develop a completely scientific outlook, to submit literature and art to the same research methods as those employed in the physical and natural sciences. 'Vice and virtue,' he once wrote, 'are products like vitriol and sugar', and thus subject to the same research status. For the scientific observer morality becomes merely a question of precise scientific formulas; Taine was constantly attacking novelists and critics who emphasized the moral intent of their work as against the purely descriptive. It would be wrong, however, to see Taine as a genuine positivist, for underpinning

* We are not suggesting, of course, that this latter critical tendency is less scientific than positivism, only that it brings values to the centre of its research. This distinction is in any case purely schematic, ignoring the many overlappings, and is merely intended to highlight the later discussion of Lukács and Goldmann.

much of his writings is a strong Hegelian element which in a paradoxical way perhaps links him with Goldmann and the Marxist tradition.*

For Taine, as with Madame de Staël and Herder, literature is traced to the material foundations of society. In the Introduction to his study of English literature†Taine wrote that a literary work was no 'mere individual play of imagination, the isolated caprice of an excited brain, but a transcript of contemporary manners, a manifestation of a certain kind of mind'.‡: Literature reflects certain ascertainable facts and emotions: Taine categorizes the novel, for example, in terms similar to Stendhal, as a 'portable mirror which can be conveyed everywhere and which is most convenient for reflecting all aspects of life and nature'.§ As the dominant literary genre of industrial society the novel shows what is, and represents no more than an 'accumulation of data which through the operation of scientific laws would fall into inevitable patterns'. Clearly any literary sociology which bases itself on such clear-cut positivism as this – literature as source of information, as documentation – can and must be prepared to study all types of literature, good, bad, and indifferent, since the problem is simply one of objective material causation and reflection. But like many sociologists Taine is loath to draw this conclusion. Literary works, he argues, 'furnish documents because they are monuments'. Different historical periods succeed in producing a harmonic relationship between genius and the age; the more deeply an artist 'penetrates into his art, the more he has penetrated into the genius of his age and race', while the mediocre artist, although his work might seem equally valid a social document,

---

* The Russian Marxist, George Plekhanov, who wrote extensively on literature and art, thought highly of Taine's work, arguing that his theories, although largely inaccurate, nevertheless marked a decisive advance on those of de Staël and Herder (*Essays in the History of Materialism*, London, Martin Lawrence, 1934).

† H. Taine, *History of English Literature*, trans. H. van Laun, 4 vols., London, Chatto & Windus, 1906. On Taine, see Wellek, *History of Modern Criticism*, vol. 4, *The Later Nineteenth Century*, London, Jonathan Cape, 1966, ch. 2; S. J. Kahn, *Science and Aesthetic Judgment: A Study of Taine's Critical Method*, London, Routledge and Kegan Paul, 1953; H. Levin, *The Gates of Horn*, New York, Oxford University Press, 1963, ch. 1.

‡ Taine, op. cit., vol. I, p. 1.

§ Quoted in Levin, op. cit., p. 19.

is both unexpressive and unrepresentative. Only the really great artist is capable of fully expressing his time, and by 'representing the mode of being of a whole nation and a whole age, a writer rallies round him the sympathies of an entire age and an entire nation'. Art is thus the collective expression of society, with great literature embodying the spirit of the age in a manner close to Hegel's conception. The problem for Taine is to determine the causes behind the emergence of great art and literature.

Taine proposes the use of three concepts, race, moment, and milieu, arguing that they comprise the material foundations exhausting all 'real causes' and all 'possible causes of movements', and claiming that 'if these forces could be measured and deciphered, one could deduce from them . . . the characteristics of the future civilization'. The interaction of race, moment, and milieu produces either a practical or a speculative 'mental structure', and this leads to the development of the 'germinal ideas', characteristic of certain centuries and epochs, which find expression in great art and literature. The significance of this formula is not so much the statement on material causation, common enough during the nineteenth century, but rather its suggestion of the precise connections between a literary work and its society. In the history of the sociology of literature Taine's is the first real theory, far more systematic than those of de Staël or Herder, and constituting rather more than a collection of haphazard and random insights. The question is how successful was he in applying the theory?

Like any social scientific approach which sets up a number of causal, determining factors, Taine has both to differentiate between them, and to assign some kind of causal sovereignty either to one or to a clustering of these factors. Taine argues, however, that his three factors are interdependent: at some times the racial element is emphasized, at others, moment and milieu. In his study of English literature, for example, race is seen to perform a major causal role.

Taine defines race in terms of innate and hereditary characteristics, temperament, body structure, and so on, and suggests that although the many human races have been widely dispersed through the world and live in situations very different from their original habitats, 'the great marks of the original model remain'. A race acquires its characteristics from 'the soil, the food and the great events that it underwent at its origin'.* Thus the history of English literature is seen partly as a protracted struggle waged by the original 'primitive stock' of Angles and Saxons against the imposed and alien Norman culture.

The subjugated race is not a dismembered nation, dislocated, uprooted, sluggish ... It grew very feebly ... it increased, remained fixed in its own soil, full of sap: its members were not displaced; it was simply lopped in order to receive on its crown a cluster of foreign branches. True, it had suffered, but at last the wound closed, the sap mingled.†

The English civil war, in this interpretation, is the culmination of these racial antagonisms: the 'original stock' once again became the masters, a fact which the literature of the following centuries faithfully reflects. Post-civil-war literature is 'solid and practical' with a strong bent towards political satire; it is thoroughly empirical and wholly opposed to speculation. A naturally Protestant people, imbued with a 'sunny, sombre, and passionate' imagination, blessed with large feet (both sexes) and rosy-cheeked children, the Anglo-Saxons have a culture very different from the elegant and philosophically superior Normans. Having thus rewritten in racial terms what many contemporary historians had thought to be a class struggle between the aristocracy and a rising middle class, Taine consistently muddles his analysis. At one moment the Normans are described as a 'light and sociable race', with 'facile', 'abundant', and 'curious' minds, while elsewhere they are characterized as a race entirely lacking in the 'madness and genius of imagination'. Taine's slipshod methodological approach is especially marked in the distinction he makes between nation and race: on the one hand racial elements are said to 'persist through all circumstances in all climates', while on the other hand a nation has its 'original qualities ... transformed by its environment and history'. Thus in his discussion of Dutch art Taine combines both inherent and environmentally induced factors such as marriage customs, religion, and eating habits in his analysis. Race as an explanatory factor in the analysis of literature tends to be used indiscriminately by Taine, with differences of epoch, class, and region wholly ignored. It is a simple blanket term, and

* Quoted in Wellek, op. cit., vol. IV, p. 29.
† Taine, op. cit., vol. I, p. 138.

34

one popular during the nineteenth century. It has little relevance to Taine's theory or indeed to any sociological theory of literature.

The second element, moment, Taine defines in a variety of ways. Its most frequent meaning is in terms of the age, the epoch, the spirit of the time. Each epoch, says Taine, has certain 'dominant ideas' and contains at least one intellectual pattern capable of surviving for centuries. Moment in this sense can thus refer to periods in which one particular conception of man prevailed, for example, the knightly ideal of the Middle Ages or, in the modern age, 'the courtier and the man who speaks well'. Moment can also mean 'literary tradition', the effect of literature on literature. Thus, discussing French tragedy in the sixteenth and eighteenth centuries, Taine argues that while both centuries employed in their drama the same human types and dramatic situations, the eighteenth-century writers had the great advantage of working with the models of the sixteenth century. What a writer makes of the tradition which he inherits is quite clearly a major part of a literary sociology and Taine was one of the first to grasp this. But for the most part he makes only the most mundane observations, spiced with specious biological analogies which, like the concept of race, were highly popular during the nineteenth century.*

Taine, however, was mainly concerned with his third element, milieu or environment. The term was in no sense a new conception: Balzac, in the Introduction to his *Human Comedy*, had made use of it in the sense of the habitat of animals, a natural-science term derived from the writings of the zoologist Geoffrey St Hillaire. But Taine's theory of milieu has pretensions to provide a complete causal explanation of literature. Like his other concepts, milieu can mean many different things. Climate and geography naturally exercise an important influence, for in this respect Taine had hardly advanced beyond the simplistic

---

* 'Thus it is with people as with a plant; the same sap, under the same temperature, and in the same soil, produces, at different steps of its progressive development different formations, fruits, seed vessels, in such a manner that the one which follows must always be preceded by the former and must spring up from his death' (Taine, op. cit.). This evolutionary conception of literature is one which many French critics after Taine accepted, especially Ferdinand Brunetière, for whom literary tradition was the key element in literature's growth (see chapter 4 below).

formulations of the eighteenth-century writers. Thus we find him virtually repeating Madame de Staël's climatic clichés: cold, moist countries induce a variety of ills, ranging from 'melancholy and violent sensations' to gluttony, drunkenness, and warlike personalities; an excessive amount of rain has the further consequence of providing thought with a sinister element, especially in England. A 'bright and pleasant sea coast' on the other hand, one which incorporates some advance in commerce and navigation, will produce 'settled social organizations' characterized by oratory, science, and literature. Madame de Staël's melancholic Nordic personality haunts the discussion. Thus Taine disparages Restoration comedy and the humorous writings of Dr Johnson on the grounds that to a sophisticated Frenchman they were wholly dull and insipid.

Taine's search for a simple cause and effect relationship between elements of the milieu and literature frequently leads him to make the most absurd and crude analyses. Thus in his analysis of Dutch art, for example, he constructs the most banal correlations:

... water makes grass, grass makes cattle, cattle make cheese, butter, and meat; and all these, with beer, make the inhabitant. Indeed, out of this rich living, and out of this physical organization, saturated with moisture, spring the phlegmatic temperament, the regular habits, the tranquil mind and nerves, the capacity for taking life easily and prudently, the unbroken contentment, the love of well being, and, consequently, the reign of cleanliness and the perfection of comfort.*

The point is, of course, that climate and geography are fully deterministic and there is never any question of the individual freeing himself from these conditions, no conception of self-consciousness. Man is entangled in Taine's broad climatic truth: the North is sad, the South is joyous.†

On the other hand, when Taine analyses literature more closely he tends to shift his arguments, making a more determined effort to relate particular literature to social and political conditions. But again he is disappointing. Each separate dis-

* Quoted in Wellek, op. cit., p. 33, from *Philosophie d'Art* (1865).
† The influence of sunshine on literature, Albert Guerard has remarked, 'seems to be mostly moonshine' (*Society and Literature*, Boston, Lothrop, Lee, and Shepherd, 1935, p. 52).

cussion is prefaced by a preliminary sketch of the social and political background of the literature under discussion, which is no more than potted superficial history and, like Madame de Staël, full of empty rhetoric. It is only when Taine writes on the literary audience that a more serious contribution to a sociology of literature is suggested. He notes, for example, the fact that 'literature always adapts itself to the taste of those who can appreciate and pay for it'. Thus, comparing Tennyson and the French poet Alfred de Musset, he observes that while the former wrote for his family circle, sportsmen, wealthy and cultivated businessmen and lovers of the countryside, Musset was appealing to intellectuals, Bohemian artists, and women of leisure, two distinct audiences which supposedly conditioned the form and content of their work. Similarly, Taine argues that seventeenth-century French drama was essentially the 'child of the courtly nobility', a fact reflected in its excessive stylization and choice of heroes.*

While Taine was clearly aware of the strong economic pressures on literary production, he rarely went beyond crude correlations. He made few serious attempts to link the economics of writing, the economic aspects of milieu, which had become so marked during the commercially-minded nineteenth century, with the literary text itself. As with the other parts of his conception of milieu, his tendency is always to explain the literary work mechanically, as a response to external conditions. There is nothing in any of his analyses of actual textual criticism, of linking specific parts of the text with specific external facts. Thus in his essay on Balzac, which Wellek describes as the 'high point' of his criticism, Taine argues that the whole basis of the *Human Comedy* rested on Balzac's failure to realize his ambition and greed for money in the world of commerce. Balzac's novels, Taine concluded, flowed from one simple truth: he was a businessman, and a 'businessman in debt'.

All this, then, suggests a profoundly mechanical form of materialism. But as was suggested earlier, Taine's peculiar hotch-potch system of causation has blended with it a curious Hegelian flavour. It almost seems that Taine was determined to refute his own theory for, dissatisfied with his three major

* Cited in Wellek, op. cit., vol. IV, p. 34.

determining elements, he reinforced the formula with a psychological dimension.

Man, forced to accommodate himself to circumstances, contracts a temperament and a character corresponding to them; and his character, like his temperament, is so much more stable, as the external impression is made upon him by more numerous repetitions, and is transmitted to his progeny ... So that at any moment we may consider the character of a people as an abridgement of all its preceding actions and sensations; that is, as a quantity and as a weight ...*

But this is the deterministic Taine. In his actual analyses of literature he frequently remarks that literary achievement is essentially a 'problem of psychological mechanics', of the artist's dominant ruling passions.† Indeed, the fundamental cause of all art and literature, of every kind of 'human production', is the 'moral disposition' of the artist; the key is the artist's 'master faculty'. Taine had no wish, it seems, to dissolve literature into a matter of simple material terms, for like any good nineteenth-century bourgeois he clearly wishes to retain the magic, the genius, of the individual artist in the process of cultural creation. Thus, after discussing the material facts which lead to the emergence of Shakespeare he remarks that, notwithstanding his analysis, 'all comes from within – I mean from his soul and his genius: circumstances and externals have contributed but slightly to his development'.‡ And of Dickens:

It is not through the accidental circumstances of his life that he belongs to history, but by his talent ... A man's genius is like a clock; it has its mechanism and among its parts a mainspring ... This inner history of genius does not depend upon the outer history of mankind; and it is worth more.§

Taine has quite clearly abandoned his materialistic scheme in favour of a more shadowy, non-empirical, psychological ex-

* Taine, op. cit., vol. I, p. 18.
† Wellek has pointed out that Taine held a profoundly irrational view of man. Taine himself wrote of man as 'a nervous machine, governed by a temperament, disposed to hallucinations, transported by unbridled passions, essentially unreasoning, a mixture of animal and poet'. Thus artists are conceived as monomaniacs with one dominant ruling passion, that of imagination (op. cit., vol. IV, p. 46). Taine thought in terms of types in his analysis of literature, and one definition of the type which he used was as ideal, the hero, 'the powerful, elemental passionate man', whom he finds in Shakespeare and Balzac (ibid., p. 40).
‡ Taine, op. cit., vol. II, p. 50.
§ ibid., IV, p. 117.

38

planation. All great change, he argues, is rooted not in social structure but in man's soul: 'The psychological state is the cause of the social state.' His revision of materialism is thus complete.

This brings us to our final point on Taine's literary sociology. His rejection of an all-pervasive materialism allows him to choose great literary works for analysis. He has, like Hegel, equated artistic greatness with historical development and progress, arguing that particular ages crystallize in great works because the great artist's superior 'moral state' enables him to grasp the essence, the truth of reality. Taine's obvious dilemma was the contradiction, generated by his materialist theory, between its application to literature and art and his desire to allow some measure of autonomy to the creative spirit. There is here one of the major and persistent problems in the sociology of literature: from Taine to Lukács and Goldmann there has been a tendency to accept the traditional literary critics' view of the superiority of great literature because of its supposed monopoly of crucial social and human insights. At the same time, it must be noted that Taine frequently uses literature as a document,[*] and throughout his writings there runs a strong and persistent reductionist element. He has no conception of the *literary text* as the focal point of research.

But his concepts and general outlook made their impact. Academic research became dominated by the positivistic method which Taine very largely enshrined, to the extent that it concentrated so 'heavily upon the backgrounds of literature that the foreground was all but obliterated'.[†] As the Danish critic George Brandes, an ardent champion of Taine, expressed it, the artist 'is nothing but a good observer who by a happy accident has also the capacity to give shape to his observations'.[‡]

Taine, then, had developed a theory but no method of applying it systematically. The theory itself was largely specious and,

[*] Thus he uses one definition of type as a source of information on social structure, especially class structure. But this is a very general application.
[†] Levin, op. cit., p. 12.
[‡] Quoted in O. Seidlin, *Essays in German and Comparative Literature*, Chapel Hill, University of North Carolina Press, 1961, ch. 1, 'George Brandes'. For Brandes, as for other positivists, the literary work was used to illuminate the author's life, and the life to support and determine the work. Life and work were seen as dual entities causally related, requiring only research to compare and mutually clarify.

perhaps because of Taine's lack of rigour, other writers turned to a new theory which, by defining milieu in terms of economic factors and social class, appeared to provide a more realistic as well as a more rigorous sociological approach.

3

In 1848 two young German revolutionaries, Karl Marx (1818–83) and Frederick Engels (1820–95), published a document which was to make a lasting impression on the history of mankind. The *Communist Manifesto*, in many ways a summation of previous materialism, argued that the social history of man was the history of class struggle; that history possessed a discernible pattern defined as stages of development, antiquity, feudalism, and capitalism, with socialism to follow, each one characterized by a particular mode of production and class structure. Capitalism represented the most advanced stage of social production, based on commodity production and wage labour and employing an extensive division of labour and sophisticated technology. In the sense of revolutionizing the means of production, that is, in breaking the static feudal social relations and stagnant system of production, capitalism represented a progressive social formation. As far as literature was concerned this implied the impossibility of 'national one-sidedness' since capitalism develops the 'numerous national and local literatures' into a 'world literature'. The paradox is obvious: while capitalism creates a profoundly unequal and conflict-ridden society, it unintentionally builds a literature which transcends class, region, and nation, speaking out to men everywhere.

Taine, as we have seen, argued that literature was largely the expression of environment, heredity, and creative genius: Marx and Engels, although couching their analysis of literature equally in terms of its material foundations, were more concerned with purely economic factors and the important role played by social class. Unlike Taine, they provided no systematic account of a theory of literature and society, and it was left to their followers to create a specifically Marxist sociology of literature. The results were poor. In many cases an extremely one-sided and mechanical explanation was put forward, dogmatically defining literature as a mere epiphenomenon of the social structure. Lunacharsky, the first Soviet Minister of Culture under Lenin, could thus write that the role of the Marxist critic was to provide 'a complete picture of the entire social development of an epoch', since 'literary work always reflects the conscious or unconscious psychology of that class which the given writer expresses'. To assess accurately any work of literature, Lunacharsky went on, one must begin with its content, its 'social essence', seeking to link this with specific social groups. Literary form is especially important: when detached from its content it shows a tendency to acquire an 'isolated, elusive character', characteristic of 'class tendencies which are devoid of content, which fear real life, and which try to hide from this life behind a screen of verbal gymnastics of a high flown, pompous or . . . facetious and frivolous nature'.* These quotations may serve as an illustration of the ways in which many Marxist writers approached the study of literature and society, and which has moved one recent critic to term it the 'dogmatic theory of social criticism'.† In interpretations such as Lunacharsky's the causal nexus is wholly explicit: form is defined by content and content by the historical alignment of class forces. It must be said, at once, that the founders of Marxism, although ambiguous in many of their comments, were rarely as dogmatic as this.

As a student at the university of Bonn, Marx much preferred literary composition to attending formal lecture courses; the university records attest to his greater concern with purely aesthetic problems than those of law.‡ He composed poetry, ballads, half a novel (subtitled *A Humorous Tale*), and the first act of a Gothic tragedy. But by the early 1840s Marx's interest in literature had waned, replaced by a passion for philosophy, economics, politics, and history. Under the influence of German philosophical idealism, especially Hegel, French socialism, notably Fourier and Saint Simon, and English political economy, Marx moved towards a complete materialistic explanation of the social world. Together with Engels he fashioned a dialectical and historical interpretation of social development, one which

---

* A. Lunacharsky, *On Literature and Art*, Moscow, Progress Publishers, 1965.
† L. T. Lemon, *The Partial Critics*, Oxford, Oxford University Press, 1965.
‡ Details on Marx's early life have been drawn from P. Demetz, *Marx, Engels and the Poets*, Chicago, University of Chicago Press, 1965, especially ch. 3.

41

gave priority to the contradictions and conflicts endemic in all social processes, arguing that social change results in the main from conflict between antagonistic social classes.*

Two themes dominate the early writings of Marx and Engels, the all-pervasive social influences of ideology and the division of labour. The concept of ideology pointed to the social conditioning of all thought, that different kinds of thinking, whether philosophical, economic, or historical, represented no more than a perspective related to the writer's class position, a one-sided, distorted view of the world.† They argued that it was only under 'definite historical conditions' in specific social contexts that the 'ideological reflexes' developed:

The production of ideas, of conceptions, of consciousness, is at first directly interwoven with the material activity and the material intercourse of men, the language of real life. Conceiving, thinking, the mental intercourse of men, appear at this stage as the direct efflux of their material behaviour. The same applies to mental production as expressed in the language of politics, laws, morality, religion, metaphysics, etc., of a people. Men are the producers of their conceptions . . . real active men, as they are conditioned by a definite development of their productive forces . . . We set out from real, active men, and on the basis of their real life process we demonstrate the development of the ideological reflexes and echoes of this life-process. The phantoms formed in the human brain are also, necessarily, sublimates of their material life-process, which is empirically verifiable and bound to material premises. Morality, religion, metaphysics, all the rest of ideology and their corresponding forms of consciousness, thus no longer retain the semblance of independence. They have no history, no development; but men developing their material production and their material intercourse, alter, along with this their real existence, their thinking and the products of their thinking. Life is not determined by consciousness, but consciousness by life.‡

* Marx's and Engels' theory of history has been called historical and dialetical materialism, since it borrowed from Hegel the concept of dialectics – that all phenomena have their opposites and their contradictions, that everything is in a constant state of flux and that change is both sudden and gradual, qualitative and quantitative. From French socialism it absorbed the idea of social class as the motor force of change, as well as the notions of socialism and communism. From Ricardo and Smith, Marx and Engels derived their emphasis on economic factors in social life and in social change. The pivot of their theory is perhaps contained in the famous statement of the *Communist Manifesto*: 'The history of all hitherto existing society is the history of class struggles.'

† This conception of ideology plays an important part in the sociology of Goldmann (see chapter 3 below).

‡ Marx and Engels, *The German Ideology* (1846), part 1.

One sees here an important difference between the method of historical materialism and the positivism of Taine: if social life is the determinant of all thought then the psychological dimension which is so crucial for Taine is relegated to the status of a minor influence. Marx and Engels, following Smith and Ferguson, were convinced of the crucial role exercised by the division of labour for social life which, as it became widespread with the development of commerce and industry, had the effect of removing certain individuals and groups from the sphere of material production to that of mental production. The division of labour, they argued, produced what they called 'pure theory', that is thought which was unsullied by mere material considerations, such as philosophy, theology, and, by implication, art and literature. Under the brutal economic dictates of the capitalist market, the need for profit, literature was being progressively 'industrialized'.* Writing becomes a specialized trade like any other.†

These trends are reflected in literature. As we have seen, the notion of literature as a reflection of society was a popular nineteenth-century conception, and Marx and Engels are no exceptions in adhering to this view. They frequently refer to literature as reflecting reality in various ways, although it must be noted that important differences distinguish their analysis from that of Taine and others. For example, in his comments on Shakespeare's *Timon of Athens*, Marx pointed to the play as reflecting the social function of money, its 'divine power' controlling men and constituting its social essence, its social character. Marx, however, adds a further dimension to his discussion: money is not merely the means of controlling men but embodies man's

* At roughly the same time that Marx and Engels were noting the social significance of the division of labour, the great French critic Sainte-Beuve, in a celebrated essay, *On Industrial Literature* (1839), pointed to the encroaching commercialization and the trend towards a conception of literature as trade. Unlike Marx and Engels, however, the division of labour was not the pivot of his analysis.

† Marx and Engels often compared modern man unfavourably with Renaissance man, arguing that the division of labour had led to a largely fragmented social type. Renaissance man, for example, possessed mastery in many languages, travelled extensively, and had wide-ranging intellectual interests: modern man was by comparison a mere shadow. Their point was, of course, that the former 'wholeness' could be recaptured only through socialism and communism.

43

'estranged being', his alienation from himself and society, and as such represents the 'alienated ability of mankind'.

My own power is as great as the power of money. The properties of money are my own properties and faculties. What I *am* and *can do* is, therefore, not at all determined by my individuality. I *am* ugly, but I can buy the most beautiful woman for myself. Consequently I am not *ugly* for the effect of ugliness, its power to repel, is annulled by money . . . What I as a *man* am unable to do, and thus what all my individual faculties are unable to do, is made possible for me by *money*. Money, therefore, turns each of these faculties into something which it is not, into its *opposite*.*

Marx praises Shakespeare for describing the essence of money as a thing standing outside man, controlling his social behaviour yet created by him for his use. This 'externalization', this 'objectification' of things, the concept of 'reification',† means an important philosophical accretion to the solely descriptive. Linked with the argument of the division of labour, capitalist society in Marx's and Engels's terms can thus be seen as a system which creates an alienated and reified world where man has lost his spontaneous connections with others, where he has become a partial, a fragmented being.

These early comments suggest a somewhat deterministic conception of literature: economic forces condition the structure of ideas within society and these coalesce into an ideology which reflects the 'false' consciousness of a social class. Thus in *The German Ideology* (1846) the relationship between literature and the economic structure of society is conceived simply in terms of strict economic causality: art as ideology has no autonomy.

Following the failure of the 1848 revolutions and the subsequent lull in political activity, Marx had begun working on his vast economic and sociological study of capitalism. His absorption in economic sociology meant fewer comments on literature than before. But they do exist. In 1857, in a preface written for his *Introduction to a Critique of Political Economy*, Marx posed the intriguing problem of the apparent contradiction between

* Marx, *Economic and Philosophic Manuscripts* (1844), third manuscript.
† The notion of reification as a tool of analysis in literature is used by Goldmann in his discussion of Robbe-Grillet and the French New Novel (see chapter 3 below). For a general discussion of the concept, see P. Berger and S. Pulberg, 'Reification and the Sociological Critique of Consciousness', *New Left Review*, January/February 1966.

the largely backward material culture of Ancient Greece, and its advanced art, 'the unequal relationship of the development of material production . . . to artistic production'.

It is well known that certain periods of the highest development of art stand in no direct connection with the general development of society, nor with the material basis and the skeleton structure of its organization. Witness the Greeks as compared with modern nations or even Shakespeare.*

The real source of Greek art lay in its system of myths: its material foundations, therefore, are to be found in the religious superstructure, and not directly within the economic substructure. As for the timeless appeal of Homer and Aeschylus, Marx's answer is similar to Vico's: Greek civilization was man's 'natural childhood', and not, as Hegel had supposed, his adolescence, with its innocence, vitality, and spontaneity carrying an aesthetic appeal across the centuries. This non-sociological account, with its emphasis on psychology rather than on economic structure, contrasts sharply with Engels's later formulation of the *Iliad* as a textbook of economic analysis and a simple mirror of the age.† Marx's manuscript, however, was left uncompleted and the problems he had raised were seemingly forgotten. But two years later, in 1859, in the Foreword to the *Critique*, the thesis of strict economic causality is again invoked:

In the social production of their life, men enter into definite relations that are indispensable and independent of their will, relations of production which correspond to a definite stage of development of their material productive forces. The sum total of these relations of production constitutes the economic structure of society, the real foundation, on which rises a legal and political superstructure and to which correspond definite forms of social consciousness. The mode of production . . . conditions the social, political and intellectual life process in general.‡

* Marx and Engels, *Literature and Art*, New York, International Publishers, 1947, p. 18.
† Engels declared that the *Iliad* reflected population increase 'with the expansion of herds and agriculture, the beginnings of artisanship', while the Homeric poems reflected development in metalworking, shipbuilding, and architecture (cited from *The Origin of the Family, Private Property and the State*, in Demetz, op. cit.).
‡ Marx and Engels, *Selected Works*, Moscow, Foreign Languages Publishing House, 1958, vol. 1, pp. 362–3. During the 'thaw' in the Soviet Union this pronouncement was liberally quoted, while in the 'freeze' periods the more ambiguous passage from the 1857 *Preface* was used (Demetz, op. cit., p. 242).

45

It would be wrong, however, to infer from this that Marx had settled his views on the relationship of art with society. He was clearly concerned with stating a general methodological principle, that on the whole the economic structure of society will largely condition its mode of thought; it could still leave room for a certain degree of artistic autonomy.

From the scattered comments he made on literature after this pronouncement it is clear that Marx was no economic dogmatist. In 1869 he wrote caustically of the crude sociological analysis which the French critic Jules Janin had carried out on Diderot's famous eighteenth-century novel, *Rameau's Nephew*. The main character in this novel is a cynical, almost nihilistic sponger, and to reduce Diderot's complex portrait to the simple suggestion by Janin that Rameau's 'perversity' flowed from his failure to become a *'gentilhomme'* offended Marx. He much preferred Hegel's characterization of Rameau as the 'self-conscious and self-expressing pessimism of the consciousness' affirming his self through his 'imperious spirit' and his 'scornful laughter at existence'. Marx's interpretation is hardly dogmatic, and in its conception of the alienated self struggling to some form of self-consciousness is clearly looking forward to Lukács on the one hand and backward on the other to the 1844 philosophical manuscripts.* Both here, and in his remarks on Shakespeare and Balzac, admired not as representatives of economic interests but as great artists, Marx is opposing crude sociological analysis. His remarks, of course, are not in any sense a programme for a sociology of literature: the task of formulating a more systematic Marxist literary theory devolved on Engels.

It has already been observed that more than once Engels treats literature as a mirror reflection of social processes. His later writings, containing two important texts for the Marxist theory of literature, tend to vacillate between economic dogmatism and artistic autonomy. In 1877 he wrote against the crude economic views expressed in *The German Ideology*. In what he called the 'higher ideologies', philosophy, theology,

* Marx and Engels, *Literature and Art*, pp. 69–70. G. Lukács, in his *History and Class Consciousness* (1923), was the first Marxist to suggest the radical Hegelian roots of Marx's theories, long before the discovery of the 1844 philosophical manuscripts which support this interpretation. Marx's comments on *Rameau's Nephew* lend further support to this view.

etc., 'the interconnections between the ideas and their material condition of existence become more and more complicated, more and more obscured by intermediate links'.* The content of art, literature, and philosophy, he went on, is far richer and more opaque than the content of political science and economics, which tend to be expressed more directly in purely ideological terms. This does not mean, of course, that social factors have no influence on the form and content of art and literature, only that these are much more independent than economics and political science and that the linkages between them and society are more obscure, more veiled and the content less obviously ideological. In his comments on two rather mediocre novelists, Engels supports these views.

The two writers were Minna Kautsky, the mother of Karl Kautsky, leader of the German social democratic party, and Mary Harkness, an aspiring English socialist. Both women submitted their novels to Engels's critical judgement. Minna Kautsky had fictionalized class conflict in Austria, her novel (*The Old and the New*, 1885) opening with a mountain landslide and the sudden appearance of an economist called Marr whose 'mighty head with the silver white mane flowing about it' clearly indicated its real-life model. Miss Harkness in *A City Girl* (1887) told the somewhat unlikely tale of an innocent working-class girl who, seduced on a weekend trip to Kew, becomes pregnant, gains help from the Salvation Army and then when her child dies is shown the empty cot by none other than her seducer, now the hospital secretary. After these tribulations, her first love, whom she had abandoned, not wishing to disgrace his family, reappears, and love and bourgeois marriage carry the day.†

In his comments on these two novels Engels made two basic points. First, the 'overt political tendency' of the writer should be implicit; political ideology is not the major concern of the artist and the work itself benefits if the author's views remain hidden. While not wholly opposed to strictly tendentious literature, Engels urged that the point of any novel must emerge naturally from the situation and action depicted within it: 'I

* Engels, *Ludwig Feuerbach and the End of Classical German Philosophy* (1877).
† Marx and Engels, *Literature and Art*, pp. 41-6.

believe that there is no compulsion for the writer to put into the reader's hands the future historical resolution of the social conflict which he is depicting.

A socialist-biased novel fully achieves its purpose ... if, by conscientiously describing real mutual relations, breaking down conventional illusions about them, it shatters the optimism of the bourgeois, instils doubt as to the eternal character of the existing order, although the author does not offer any definite solution or does not even line up openly on any particular side.*

For Engels, Balzac is the epitome of this approach, for although a Catholic and political reactionary he was forced, through the dictates of his art, to go against his own political interests and class sympathies: 'He saw the necessity of the downfall of his favourite nobles ... he saw the real men of the future.' The writer, then, can articulate in a quite non-conscious way on ideology which he would consciously repudiate. The so-called 'para Marxists',† characterize those Marxists who adhere to Engels's formulation, and whose aesthetics are diametrically opposed to dogmatic Marxism with its emphasis on an activist and committed literature.‡

Engels's second point is more dogmatic. He argues that any novelist who is striving for realism must aim to create in his works 'representative figures', since the notion of realism 'implies beside truth of detail, the truthful reproduction of typical

* ibid., pp. 39–40. The English Marxist Edward Upward, in his essay, 'Sketch for a Marxist Interpretation of Literature', in C. Day Lewis (ed.), *The Mind in Chains*, London, Frederick Muller, 1937, argued that any writer who 'wishes to produce the best work that he is capable of producing, must first of all become a socialist in his practical life, must go over to the progressive side of the class conflict' (p. 52). This, of course, is fundamentally opposed to Engels's arguments and indicative of the trough into which English Marxism had sunk by the 1930s.

† A term coined by the French critic, Michel Crouzet.

‡ Thus Zhdanov, at the first Soviet Writers' Congress in 1934, proclaimed the wholly tendentious character of socialist literature. 'Our Soviet literature is not afraid of the charge of being tendentious ... for in an epoch of class struggle there is not and cannot be a literature which is not class literature, not tendentious, allegedly non-political.' The source for this clear revision of Engels is often given as Lenin's document, *Party Organization and Party Literature* (1905), in which it is argued that literature must become party literature, 'a part of the general cause of the proletariat ... an integral part of the organized, methodical, and unified labour of the ... Party'. It must be borne in mind, however, that Lenin was not referring to imaginative literature but simply to political and polemical works.

characters under typical circumstances'. The concept of the 'type' in literary analysis was much in vogue during the nineteenth century. Taine had used the notion in his criticism* while the Russian realist school of Chernyshevsky, Dobrolyubov, and Pisarev invoked it as the pivot of their social criticism.† Although the concept can be traced as far back as the Middle Ages, its secular form occurs for the first time during the seventeenth and eighteenth centuries.‡ In Balzac's novels, for example, the representative figure is the dominant concept: his varied human types, the miser Grandet, the scheming Madame Marneffe of *Cousin Bette*, the socially mobile careerist Rastignac, combine the qualities of a number of fairly homogeneous characters: the type in this definition is thus 'many-sided' and invested with great social richness. But there is a problem: who is to judge whether a writer has successfully created a representative figure? What are the canons of proof which will show the writer's 'truthful depiction' of reality and historical necessity? On this latter point especially, Engels seems very close to the tendentious art he had so severely criticized, and certainly he seems to be saying, with Taine, that art mirrors the age, with the dominant tendencies reflected through literature's varied gallery of 'types'.

This is fairly dogmatic. It suggests a direct one-to-one relation between the economic and material base of society and its literary superstructure, the very problem which had first been raised in Marx's ambiguous writings of the 1850s. At the close of his life, in the 1890s, Engels attempted to revise the early economic dogmatism. In a series of letters replying to some well-intentioned criticism of Marxism, Engels moved progressively away from strict economic causality.

The materialist method, he wrote in one of the letters, will

* Taine's most persistent use of the concept of 'type' was as an ideal: the powerful, the elemental heroes of fiction, who 'manifest better than others the important characters, the elementary forces, the deepest layers of human nature'. (For a discussion of Taine's use of the term, see Wellek, op. cit., vol. IV.)
† In Dobrolyubov's essay on Goncharov's *Oblomov*, the main character is seen as a specifically Russian type from whom it is possible to extrapolate social tendencies. See Dobrolyubov, *Selected Philosophical Works*, Moscow, Foreign Languages Publishing House, 1956, pp. 174–218. Cf. Wellek, op. cit., vol. IV, ch. 11.
‡ For a discussion of this, see Demetz, op. cit., pp. 135 ff.

certainly fail if used as a 'prefabricated pattern according to which one adjusts the historical facts'. To another correspondent Engels wrote of the economic factor as the ultimate determining element, but only 'in the long run', and that between all the factors in a given situation, ideological as well as material, there is constant mutual interaction. The absolute sovereignty of economics has been dethroned: the problem becomes the degree of freedom enjoyed by the superstructure. Thus discussing the philosophy of the Enlightenment, Engels suggested that while economic forces influence philosophical tradition it is nevertheless the 'political and moral reflexes which exercise the greatest direct influence'. If economic factors have therefore an indirect influence on philosophy, then it would seem plausible to claim the same for literature. In another letter Engels claims that although political, religious, and literary development hinge on the economic factor, this does not imply monistic determination but 'rather mutual interaction based upon economic necessity that always realizes itself ultimately. The further the area we are investigating is removed from the economic sphere and approaches that of abstract ideology, the more we will find that it shows accidents in its development and the more the curve will run in a zig-zag.' He concludes by reasserting the view that over a long period of time the curve will follow that of the economic structure of society.*

In the writings of both Marx and Engels, then, there is no fashioned theory of literature's relation with society, but merely hints, ambiguity, and some dogma. Their followers, on the other hand, with responsibility to develop the Marxist theory of literature, singularly failed to do so.† They succeeded in raising questions but developed no method – they could claim possibly that their interests lay elsewhere, in the practical transformation of the social world. One writer who did devote a considerable part of his talent to literature was the Russian, George Plekhanov (1857–1918) in whose work one finds both Engels's notion of social mirror and the concept of type.

* Marx and Engels, *Selected Works*, vol. ii, pp. 486–506.
† There have, of course, been many Marxist studies of literature. But most are of absolutely no value at all: they are either tendentious, muddled, or simply banal. For a useful discussion of this, see G. Steiner, 'Marxism and Literature', *Language and Silence*, London, Faber, 1967, especially pp. 335–55, 387–96.

Plekhanov's study of literature emphasized the weaknesses of early Marxist literary sociology. He naturally stated the explicit sociological foundations of art and literature, but in doing so tended to lapse into crude mechanical correlations. He tended, too, to dismiss most literature written after 1850 as a form of bourgeois apologetic.

His approach was remarkably eclectic for a Marxist, borrowing heavily not only from Marx but also from Kant and Taine. From Marx he derived the social function of art. 'Art begins when the human being recalls within himself feelings and ideas that he has had under the influence of the reality surrounding him and gives them a certain figurative expression.'* Art and literature are bound to the means of production and property relations in a largely deterministic nexus.† But Plekhanov is not satisfied with this wholly materialistic interpretation. He goes further than Taine in striving to break out of a too rigid materialist explanation by introducing the notion of an inborn sense of beauty. Man, he argues, has the capacity to judge good from bad, he has an aesthetic sense which Plekhanov derived from the aesthetic writings of Kant.‡ He was fully aware that merely showing the social function of art leaves unanswered the question of value. Kant's idealistic aesthetic, that good can be judged only in a disinterested, and not an involved, emotional state, served as the bridge from the social to the ultimate judgement since although the aesthetic sense is a gift of nature, man is doubly lucky – he has a 'contemplative faculty' which leads him to reject aesthetically all art that is wholly utilitarian, art that arouses only 'considerations of social good'. The aesthetic sense leads man to accept great art and enjoy it for its own sake – a remarkable analysis for a Marxist. To accept Kant's aesthetic cuts right across Plekhanov's conception of the class character of

*Plekhanov, *Art and Social Life* (1912), London, Lawrence & Wishart, 1953, p. 20.
† Another of the themes in Plekhanov was the insistence of work's priority over art, labour over art: 'In the life of society . . . labour is older than play.' Again one sees here the nineteenth-century belief in simple cause and effect: there is no conception that both developed together in unison.
‡ Plekhanov went as far as to suggest that human nature possessed a faculty for recognizing the musical nature of rhythm, and for its appreciation – he added, of course, that the means of production was the major determining factor in its further social development (ibid., p. 4).

art, and it is difficult to reconcile his constant reiteration of art as 'predominantly a reflection of social life' – that art has significance only when it 'depicts or evokes or conveys actions, emotions and events that are of significance to society'* – with his view of a non-social, classless aesthetic instinct. The antithesis is further brought out in his discussion of the ways in which art actually reflects social life.

The concept of reflection, Plekhanov suggests, hinges on grasping the 'mainspring' of social life, that is, the fact of class struggle. Cultural history, he asserts dogmatically, represents no more than a 'reflection of the history of its classes of their struggle, one with the other'.† Thus in his discussion of eighteenth-century French drama, Plekhanov argued that the supremacy of tragedy over farce reflected the cultural and economic dominance of the upper classes, for while farce was eminently lower class, tragedy, the 'creation of the aristocracy', directly expressed the upper classes' social and political views, aspirations and tastes. Plekhanov cites Taine as support for his view that French tragedy under Louis XIV stemmed from the demands of the courtly aristocracy. Its main characters were either kings or those with a high social status, and a dramatist 'whose works lacked the necessary conventional dose of aristocratic superiority would never have won the applause of the audience of his day, however great his talent'. But with the rise of the bourgeois class at the end of the century, a new dramatic model makes its appearance – 'sentimental comedy' – in which the hero is no longer depicted as a 'superior being' but rather as an idealized 'man of the middle estate'.

Thus, according to Plekhanov, fairly straightforward correlations exist between the strong social and political position of the French aristocracy and monarchy and the revival of classical tragedy, and between the middle classes and the decline of classical drama. The theatre is the direct expression of the class struggle. And the class struggle is crucial for grasping the meaning of modern art and literature. The contemporary trend of 'art for art's sake' is seen by Plekhanov as the direct expression of the alienated artist 'in discord with his social environ-

* Plekhanov, op. cit., pp. 60, 108–9.
† Plekhanov, p. 164.

ment'. French novelists such as Flaubert and the Goncourt brothers in consciously rejecting bourgeois society end with an overpowering pessimism which expresses itself in the concept of an autonomous art and artist, for having attacked the middle classes for smugness and narrow-minded philistinism, artists were unable to identify with the new progressive class, the proletariat. The implication is obvious: the bourgeois period after 1848 can produce great literature only if its writers associate themselves *mentally* with the future, that is with socialism.*

This mechanical analysis of the relations between literature and society, which repudiates virtually all post-1848 literature as mere bourgeois apologetics, is the dogmatic cornerstone of the Marxist literary criticism which developed after the Russian Revolution, and especially after the death of Lenin and the growth of bureaucratic socialism. A Marxist literary sociology comes to enshrine Plekhanov's simple truth that all literature is class-bound and great literature is incompatible with bourgeois dominance. Georg Lukács, the most prominent Marxist theoretician of literature after Plekhanov, virtually accepts this dogmatic and negative perspective, and in his writings on modern literature can see only degeneration and despair.†

Lukács accepts Plekhanov's argument that literature reflects the class struggle. 'The historical novel,' he writes, 'in its origin, development, rise, and decline follows inevitably upon the great social transformations of modern times.'‡ Lukács's basic theme, one which runs through all his Marxist writings on literature,§ is the decline of great bourgeois realism, 'critical realism', in the latter half of the nineteenth century, and its

* ibid., pp. 191–2. Plekhanov argues that writers such as Zola, while appearing to attack the middle class, actually support bourgeois society. Zola's naturalism fails to grasp the social determinants of men's actions, desires, habits, etc., explaining man rather in terms of physiology and pathology. Persons are depicted as individuals but not as 'members of a great social unity'. The naturalistic method was incapable of seeing new trends and had to end with a critical acceptance of bourgeois society.
† Especially in his *The Meaning of Contemporary Realism*, London, Merlin Press, 1963.
‡ G. Lukács, *The Historical Novel*, London, Merlin Press, 1962, p. 17.
§ Lukács's writings fall into two distinct phases. The first is mainly the pre-Marxist works of his early years, roughly 1908–19, which will be discussed in the next chapter, and the second, the Marxist writings which followed his entry into the Hungarian Communist Party in 1919. The works referred to in this chapter are as follows: *Studies in European Realism*, New York,

replacement by a specious technical literature. Like Plekhanov, Lukács accepts a mechanical correlation between creative literature and the class structure: after 1848 it is impossible to write novels without rejecting or accepting a socialist perspective; writers who ally themselves with the bourgeoisie will merely reflect that class's historical decline. His attacks on 'modernism' clearly embody a dogmatic orthodoxy which had served Lukács well during the years he spent in Stalin's Russia in the 1930s and later as chief Communist spokesman on cultural matters for the Hungarian socialist bureaucracy.*

All literature, Lukács argues, is written from the point of view of a class, a world view, and thus implies a perspective. His criticism of modern literature is that it denies perspective precisely because it pretends to an 'unbiased', objective view of the world; without perspective there cannot be any distinction between the significant and superficial features of reality, only an unselective reportage which indiscriminately lumps together the trivial and the important. Like Plekhanov, Lukács makes fidelity to socialism the touchstone of artistic creativity – the writer who rejects socialism 'closes his eyes to the future, gives up any chance of assessing the present correctly, and loses the ability to create other than purely static works of art'.† This loss of a socialist humanism leads to a literature which is characterized by an intensely subjectivist outlook in which subjective experience is accepted as reality, and man depicted as alienated, isolated, and essentially morbid, lacking any meaningful relation with the social world.‡ Proust, Musil, Joyce, Samuel Beckett, illustrate for Lukács the collapse of a bourgeois literature which aimed to depict man *as a whole* into a form which portrays man as fragmented and partial. Lukács's great admiration for bourgeois realists such as Balzac and Dickens springs

---

Grosset & Dunlop, 1964, and *The Historical Novel*, London, Merlin Press, 1962 (both written in Russia during the 1930s); *Essays on Thomas Mann*, London, Merlin Press, 1964, and *The Meaning of Contemporary Realism*, London, Merlin Press, 1963 (both largely written after his return to Hungary in 1945).
* For details on Lukács's life and his uneasy relationship with Stalinism, see G. Lichteim, *Lukács*, London, Fontana/Collins, 1970; G. H. R. Parkinson, *Georg Lukács, The Man, His Work and His Ideas*, London, Weidenfeld & Nicolson, 1970, especially ch. 1.
† *The Meaning of Contemporary Realism*, p. 60.
‡ ibid., especially pp. 17–92.

from his conviction that literature is in no sense a passive cultural object, but part of the struggle, which capitalist society itself engenders through socialism, to abolish the distorting, inhuman consequences of an extended social division of labour; socialism strives to retain in its theory a vision of a fully integrated personality, 'the great perspective of the all-sided man'.* Thus contemporary modernists, having no perspective, simply depict reality in a partial, therefore distorting way: the whole man is replaced by the fragmented man; a totality by a subjective, limited impressionism.

The result of this loss of totality is that modernist literature has no 'types'. For Lukács, as for Engels, great writers are those who, in their work, create 'lasting human types', the 'real criterion of literary achievement'.† We have already seen that Engels demanded the creation of 'typical' figures in 'typical' situations as the criteria for genuine realism, and while it may be argued that here Engels was merely making a remark on a specific historical form of literature, bourgeois realism, Lukács extends this general statement into a dogma: *all* literature must be measured by this criterion.

The 'type', argues Lukács, conveys 'the innermost essence of past epochs', and it is only through the creation of 'comprehensive types' that 'the greatest values of the past have remained immortal'.‡ In his essay on Balzac's *Lost Illusions* Lukács argues that the type flows out of the artist's awareness of progressive change, that society is not a fixed, immutable thing, that it constitutes a totality of relations in flux. Thus Balzac's characters, 'complete within themselves, live and act within a concrete, complexly stratified social reality and it is always the totality of the social process that is linked with the totality of character'.§ Balzac could create the 'eternal types of capitalist society', Nucingen and Creval, while Stendhal could not, for unlike Balzac he refused to accept that the 'heroic period' of the bourgeoisie had come to its close, that from the 1830s capitalist society had triumphed and its bourgeoisie was forming a new, repressive and philistine ruling class.¶ The triumph

* Cited in Parkinson, op. cit., p. 155.
† *The Meaning of Contemporary Realism*, pp. 56–7.
‡ *Studies in European Realism*, pp. 115–16.
§ ibid., p. 55.
¶ ibid., pp. 78–84.

of realism was the triumph of the type, of the artist's awareness of progressive social change. Increasingly after 1830, and especially following the 1848 revolutions, writers turned to the average rather than the typical, substituting for their lack of action mere descriptions of milieu, novels without plot and genuine character.

Realism, then, declines because the subjective and objective conditions which made it possible no longer exist. Objectively the bourgeoisie is now a ruling class faced with *potential* revolution, the working class, and socialism; and subjectively, for the writer ceases to participate actively in society, he remains a mere spectator and chronicler of events. The really great novelists, Lukács writes, are 'always true-born sons of Homer' who overcome the 'unpoetic nature of their world, through sharing and experiencing the life and evolution of the society they lived in'.* Thus writers who can no longer share the aspirations of their class, the bourgeoisie, and who feel indifferent towards the working class and socialism, clearly cut themselves off from the 'intense' experience of social life which in itself is the only way to 'uncover the essential social factors that determine the world depicted'.†

Thus Lukács ends with his belief in a new, revitalized realism – socialist realism – which will transcend the old bourgeois humanism‡ and, portraying man in action struggling to achieve a socialist society, will end decisively modernist *angst*. For the bourgeois artist there is simply one choice: between the critical realism of Balzac, Tolstoy, and Mann (the lone survivor of this tradition in the twentieth century), and Kafka:

There is no necessity for a writer to break with his bourgeois pattern of life in making this choice between social sanity and morbidity, in choosing the great and progressive literary tradition of realism in preference to formalistic experimentation.§

* *Studies in European Realism*, pp. 152–3.
† ibid., pp. 147–8.
‡ For Lukács, Tolstoy was able to continue the realist tradition precisely because capitalism had developed more slowly in Russia than in Western Europe and thus 'bourgeois ideology had not as yet been driven to apologetics' (ibid., p. 135). Thomas Mann, on the other hand, portrays 'a totality of the inner problems of contemporary bourgeois life', from the perspective 'that socialism is unavoidable if the human race is not to be swallowed up by barbarism' (*Essays on Thomas Mann*, pp. 105, 162).
§ *The Meaning of Contemporary Realism*, p. 80.

This is Lukács at his dogmatic worst,* incapable of understanding contemporary literature and assessing its aesthetic validity. Doubtless a novel of such pessimism as Céline's *Journey to the End of the Night* (1934) would merely reflect decadence, doubly so for its lack of a universal type – yet Trotsky in his review of Céline's novel could praise its realistic presentation of life in post-war France and America for its *detail*, its naturalism, its fearless honesty, although the author was anti-bourgeois yet not socialist – Lukács would see in it only average figures, decadent and pessimistic, with no *universal types*.†

4

Surveying the development of an explicit social interpretation of literature, from its origins in theories of *physical* determination to positivism and Marxism, it is instructive to note the areas of agreement and divergence. Both positivism and Marxism agree in citing specific external factors as the ultimate determinants of literary creativity and production, in the need to study the growth of literary audiences, reading publics, and publishing as possible conditioning factors on the structure of literature. Disagreement occurs, of course, on the question of social class and ideology.

Socially aware literary critics such as Hoggart and Watt tend to minimize the role of class in the determination of literary creativity, while for Marxists the concept constitutes the socially critical dimensions of analysis. Great literature is an expression of class interests, not the result of individual psychology, group affiliations, or type of audience. The danger here, as we have seen with Lukács, lies in a dogmatic and schematic use of class, in correlating literature with this one segment in an overtly mechanical way; a theory which dismisses most of the literature

* Lukács's slavish adherence to Stalinism can be seen in all his works written after 1923. On the other hand, a statement that Mann's novel *Dr Faustus* constitutes the 'fullest intellectual and artistic confirmation' of the notorious Zhdanov decree against modernist tendencies in art and literature, particularly 'those parts which so brilliantly describe modern music', must be seen partly as Lukács's deep-seated adherence to classical bourgeois culture, so strikingly documented in his pre-Marxist writings.

† *The Basic Writings of Trotsky*, ed. I. Howe, London, Secker & Warburg, 1963, pp. 343–56.

after 1848 as decadent and non-progressive must surely be rejected or substantially revised. Marx himself was not dogmatic; and in his writings the concepts of alienation and reification may constitute a more viable approach to analysing literary works than those employed by Plekhanov and Lukács. There is, too, the concept of dissociation which both Engels and Lukács have developed, that between the author's own ideology and the world he depicts artistically there may exist a contradiction. In Balzac and in Tolstoy the most reactionary ideas coexist with a realistic portrayal of contemporary society, their imagination seemingly correcting ideological illusions. The latent tension between prior intent and truthful portrayal of reality may well provide an important clue to the structure of a literary work.

With this in mind, we can now examine the most recent attempts to go beyond the mechanical, external, and frequently reductionist approach of positivism and Marxism, an approach which above all concentrates on the literary work itself as *literature*.

3 Literature and Structuralism

At the end of the nineteenth century the dominant tendency in literary criticism, shared by bourgeois writers and Marxists like Plekhanov, was positivism. In the work of Taine, Brandes, and Plekhanov, literary analysis worked away from the literary text itself focusing attention on *extrinsic* factors, which were held to determine its mode of existence, and by implication facilitate the *understanding* of the work. Literature was thus a mere epiphenomenon of the social structure, a reflection either of the author's life or his times. Literature was explained away; literary creativity was held to be no more than the end product of an external, determinate causality. Historical and social backgrounds and not the literary text became the focus of interest and point of departure for analysis; literature was effectively dissolved in the face of such determining factors as race, milieu, class forces, and personal biography.*

This crude reductionism produced two important responses: the structural analysis of the Russian Formalists and the Prague Linguistic Circle, and a much more flexible Marxism inspired by the early work of Lukács and most recently by Lucien Goldmann. Structuralism, one of the key terms in social science today, is the common approach of these two different perspectives.

I

Russian Formalism arose as an attempt to reinstate the literary text as the only viable unit of criticism.† The main task of

---

* For a useful discussion of these tendencies, see R. Wellek, *Concepts of Criticism*, New Haven, Yale University Press, 1963, especially the essay 'The Revolt against Positivism in Recent European Scholarship'.

† The Formalist school developed between about 1913 and 1930, when it was officially disbanded by Stalin as a form of 'bourgeois ideology'. The

literary criticism, they argued, lay not so much in studying literature but its 'literariness'. Art was a self-enclosed system and if sociological factors exercised any influence they did so indirectly.* Formalist criticism aimed to establish an independent science of literature in which literature had the status of an autonomous cultural object. The mirror image was wholly rejected, since literature does not passively reflect social life but rather creatively distorts it through the use of specific literary devices. The 'artistic device' became the Formalists' major critical concern. They argued that each device existed within an 'aesthetic system' where it performed specific functions. Devices of plot, narrative, and technique existed independently of external factors, constituting what one Formalist called the 'self-determined use of material'.† Their emphasis was on literature as a system, a literary totality in which all the constituent parts added up to a coherent whole. Style was one of the main elements in the *dynamic* integration of the system, and the duty of the critic lay in determining 'the specific function of the artistic device in each particular case'. Devices thus functioned within a unified whole which was the literary text.‡

---

leading theorists were Shklovsky, Tomashevsky, Eichenbaum, and Roman Jakobson (who left Russia in 1921 and helped found the Prague Linguistic Circle). Some of their essays have been translated by L. T. Lemon and M. J. Reiss in *Russian Formalist Criticism*, Lincoln, University of Nebraska Press, 1965. On the history of the Formalist school, see especially V. Erlich, *Russian Formalism*, The Hague, Mouton, 1955.

* In their early writings, the Formalists argued that art was totally self-enclosed, but they gradually modified this extreme formulation to include some external factors. Tomashevsky argued that a theme can only survive if it carries an external reference, an external appeal (Lemon and Reiss, pp. 61–4).

† This interior approach to literary analysis is summed up by Shklovsky: 'The form of a work of art is defined by its relation to other works of art, to forms existing prior to it . . . The purpose of any new form is not to express new content, but to change an old form which has lost its aesthetic quality' (Lemon and Reiss, op. cit.).

‡ The Formalists were soon under attack from Marxism for their radical non-sociological approach. Lunacharsky suggested that Formalism was a 'cultural survivor' from pre-Revolutionary Russia, 'escapism', 'a decadent ideology'. On the other hand Trotsky agreed with the Formalists that the ultimate judgement of any literary text must be based on its literary qualities, that art has its own laws, and that Marxist sociology cannot pass aesthetic judgement. He disagreed, however, on the question of origins, that the appearance of a particular type of novel could only be explained causally,

The importance of the Formalists' analysis clearly lies in their emphasis on the specific 'aesthetic' qualities of literature, and in grasping literary works as integrated wholes. In their analysis the devices act to create a dynamic unity, 'an unfolding dynamic whole'. There is here a close kinship between the work of the Swiss linguist Saussure and the Formalists, especially with Saussure's concept of system and the Formalists' notion of the functional significance of devices. As one Formalist wrote, anticipating in many ways the Prague Circle's concept of aesthetic structure as a dynamic system of signs, 'the constructive function of each component of the system lies in its relatedness to other components and, *eo ipso*, to the entire system'. In his posthumously published *Course in General Linguistics* (1915), Saussure had drawn an important distinction between language* as it exists at a particular moment ('synchronic') and as it develops through time ('diachronic'). Saussure was mainly concerned in developing what he called the science of semiology – the study of 'the life of signs within society', of which language was one part. Saussure went on to argue that language was a social institution, external to man with its linguistic system (its 'code') pre-existing the individual act of speech, the 'message'. Thus the emphasis on the need to study the system of communication between the 'signified' and the 'signifier', two aspects of a code which everyone uses. Saussure argued strongly for the synchronic study of language, and in the structuralism which has largely developed from Saussure's concepts, the notion of system is all important; but it is a system at a given moment, and in this sense structuralism tends to be ahistorical and non-genetic.†

Structuralism, has, however, many meanings, but in its most general sense it employs the crucial concept of system, whether it is linguistic, literary, or social,‡ in which the element

that is, sociologically. See L. Trotsky, *Literature and Revolution*, New York, Russell & Russell, 1957, ch. 5.

* Saussure distinguished between *la langue* and *la parole*, between the external public language which is used as a code by everyone, and the personal use made of it by individuals.

† Cf. R. Barthes, *Elements of Semiology*, London, Jonathan Cape, 1967.

‡ Thus in C. Lévi-Strauss's analysis of kinship, the law which governs the exchange of women in certain societies in seen as a universal order covering all kinship systems independently of those individuals who constitute it (*Structural Anthropology*, London, Allen Lane The Penguin Press, 1968.)

under analysis forms numerous dynamic relations with other elements, with the other parts of the system, and where every element has a meaning only in relation to the other parts. Fundamentally it is holistic and integrative, implying a fluid relationship between the parts and the whole. But there is an important difference between the proponents of historical and non-historical structuralism. An emphasis on the synchronic aspects of a system frequently leads structuralist studies to minute concentration on details at the expense of the system's *development outside itself.* In his criticisms of the Formalists, Trotsky had drawn attention to their 'excessive one-sidedness' in ignoring the actual sociological environment of the literary work, an environment which is pre-eminently human and therefore historical.* In fact the Formalists modified their extreme position to some extent, Tomashevsky writing that if a 'verbal structure' was to be coherent it must possess a unifying theme which was not self-contained, since the survival of any literary work depends on the choice of themes, whether they are significant or insignificant to man himself. Tomashevsky thus implied a connection between the intrinsic and the extrinsic dimensions of literature – it is only through enlarging the limits of realism that the writer actually reaches 'general human interests' of love and death, for the merely topical does not survive.†

A-historical structuralism, then, must be distinguished from historical structuralism, that is, from a method which conceives the text under analysis as 'historically specific' and explicable both in terms of its inner structure and its external history, the social, political, and economic environment which produced it. From the point of view of the sociology of literature, structuralism pinpoints the literary work as a basic datum of research, seeing it as 'a layered system of meanings' which add up to an integrated whole and which is closely related, but not wholly determined, by external factors. Thus for Goldmann works of literature must be grasped pre-eminently as 'wholes' – what he terms 'significant wholes' – in which the various parts function only as elements of a literary and social totality. His argument is that all great literary and philosophical works have

* Trotsky, op. cit.
† Lemon and Reiss, op. cit., pp. 63–5.

a total coherence and that the structures which make up the texts have a meaning only in so far as they give 'a complete and coherent picture of the overall meaning of the work'.

Let us now briefly examine Goldmann's method.

2

Goldmann's approach to the sociology of literature is highly idiosyncratic, fusing structural analysis with historical and dialectical materialism.* It is important to note that while Goldmann develops a specifically Marxist theory, many of his key concepts and much of his inspiration derive from the early pre-Marxist writings of Lukács.† Under strong pressure from the Communist Party, which demanded rigid orthodoxy in all matters of theory, Lukács was forced to repudiate these early works, especially the collection of essays he published in 1923. In these he claimed Marxism as pre-eminently a method, not a dogmatic set of truths handed down from Marx, and thus subject to continual revision in the light of changing experience, a 'critical' as well as scientific theory of society, employing the concepts of alienation and reification. Lukács demonstrated, long before the actual publication of Marx's early writings, the centrality to Marx's thought of these categories which in the writings of Plekhanov and Engels had been largely forgotten. But his most important concept, one which Goldmann has carried over into his sociology, is that of 'totality', a concept which, like those of alienation and reification, had been ignored by orthodox Marxism.

* Goldmann's most important writings in the sociology of literature are as follows: *The Hidden God* (1956), trans. P. Thody, London, Routledge & Kegan Paul, 1964; *Pour une sociologie du Roman*, Paris, Gallimard, 1965; 'The Sociology of Literature: Status and Problems of Method', *International Social Science Journal*, vol. XIX, no. 4, 1967; 'Criticism and Dogmatism in Literature', in D. Cooper (ed.), *The Dialectics of Liberation*, London, Penguin Books, 1968. For his general sociological method, see *The Human Sciences and Philosophy* (1952), London, Jonathan Cape, 1969; *Recherches Dialectiques*, Paris, Gallimard, 1959.

† Georg Lukács (born 1885) is mainly known for his explicit Marxist writings, which were discussed in the previous chapter. The most important of the early writings are *The Theory of the Novel* (1914-16) and *History and Class Consciousness* (1919-23). For Goldmann's discussion of these texts, see his essay, 'Introduction aux premiers écrits de Georges Lukács', appended to the French translation of the *Theory of the Novel* (*La Théorie du Roman*, Paris, Gonthier, 1968).

63

For Lukács, it was not 'the predominance of economic motives in the interpretation of society which is the decisive difference between Marxism and bourgeois science, but rather the point of view of totality. The . . . domination of the whole over the part is the essence of the method which Marx took over from Hegel and . . . transformed into the basis of an entirely new science.'[*] In his Preface to the *Critique of Political Economy* (1857), Marx had argued that society constituted a totality of *concrete* historical conditions, relations, and values, and that the task of science was to begin with the constituent parts, simple conceptions such as division of work, labour, exchange (abstractions from the whole), and gradually work up to the whole so that 'the abstract definitions lead to the reproduction of the concrete subject (society) in the course of reasoning'.[†] Scientific analysis must always proceed from the abstract to the concrete, from the individual part to the whole, the method being a continual oscillation between abstractions and what Marx called the 'pre-given, living concrete whole'.

Literature, like society, is a totality, each literary work a living whole which can only be understood in terms of its constituent parts. Lukács uses the concept, 'significant dynamic structure' to refer to philosophical and literary works that are totalities of thought and experience. As products of a constantly changing social world they are dynamic rather than static entities and significant for embodying the crucial values and events of their time. Thus two of Lukács's dynamic structures, tragedy and the novel, total complexes of thought about the world and man's position within it, are related concretely by Goldmann in his research to specific social, economic, and political structure. The early work of Lukács had analysed these structures idealistically, as 'atemporal essences' which transcended social structure.[‡]

[*] G. Lukács, *Histoire et Conscience de Classe*, Paris, Editions de Minuit, 1960.
[†] K. Marx, *A Contribution to the Critique of Political Economy*, New York, Charles Kerr, 1904.
[‡] In Lukács's early writing a significant dynamic structure is called a 'form' (novel, tragedy), and, having absorbed the concepts of 'atemporal essence' and 'significance' from the German idealist philosopher, Dilthey (1833–1911), he arrived at his 'significant, atemporal structure'. Lukács, of course, was writing in the wake of that 'revolt against positivism' which characterized

From Lukács, too, Goldmann derives his concept of the world vision (*'vision du monde'*) which, he argues, all great philosophical and literary work embodies, investing them with internal coherence and external 'validity'. A world vision is defined as 'a significant global structure', a total comprehension of the world which attempts to grasp its meaning in all its complexity and wholeness.

What I have called a 'world vision' is a convenient term for the whole complex of ideas, aspirations and feelings which links together the members of a social group (a group which, in most cases, assumes the existence of a social class) and which opposes them to members of other social groups. This is ... a tendency which really exists among the members of a certain social group, who all attain this class consciousness in a more or less coherent manner ... In a few cases – and it is these which interest us – there are exceptional individuals who either actually achieve or who come very near to achieving a completely integrated and coherent view of what they and the social class to which they belong are trying to do. The men who express this vision on an imaginative or conceptual plane are writers and philosophers, and the more closely their work expresses this vision in its complete and integrated form, the more important does it become. They then achieve the maximum possible awareness of the social group whose nature they are expressing.*

In the absence of a fully worked out typology of world visions, Goldmann suggests as examples empiricism, rationalism, and the tragic vision – total complexes of thought in which reality is grasped as a *whole*; moreover, world visions are forms of consciousness closely bound up with social classes – a world vision is always a vision of a social class.

An obvious objection to this conception of world vision is that it is no more than an ideology. However, Goldmann argues, the essence of an ideology lies in its partial, one-sided view of the world, in its falsity, a distorting rather than 'true' picture

---

early twentieth-century literary and philosophical discussions, culminating in Russian Formalism and structuralism. In sociology, the German sociologist Max Weber (1870–1920), who had some influence on Lukács, argued against the positivistic tenet that social science and natural science share an identical methodology, postulating instead the centrality to sociology of the concepts of 'understanding' and 'significance'. See especially M. Weber, *The Methodology of the Social Sciences*, New York, Macmillan, 1949, and more generally, H. S. Hughes, *Consciousness and Society*, New York, Knopf, 1958, chs 2 and 8.

* Goldmann, *The Hidden God*, p. 17.

of reality; Marx and Engels in fact called all ideologies 'false consciousness', implying that 'true consciousness' was possible but only if the world was seen as a whole. This is not to suggest that absolute truth exists, only that at particular historical moments man attempts to understand the world as a whole and this vision, embodied in literature and philosophy, is true for him and his class. Thus Adam Smith in his analysis of commercial capitalism used the method of empiricism to show how the bourgeois society which was then emerging was historically the end of history – he could not understand that *its* negation was the industrial working class, then undeveloped, and that only Marxism would embody this truth later in the next century. For Smith conflict ceased at the threshold of bourgeois society; for Marx class conflict was the basic fact of bourgeois, capitalist society. In other words, empiricism passed into ideology because it failed to account for a world characterized by social conflict and rapid social change.*

A further difficulty arises over the precise nature of a world vision. Goldmann states that it is not 'an immediate empirical fact' but rather a structure of ideas, aspirations, and feelings which serves to unite a social group *vis-à-vis* other social groups. A world vision is therefore an abstraction; it achieves its concrete form in certain literary and philosophical texts. World visions are not 'facts', have no objective existence of their own, but merely exist as theoretical expressions of the real conditions and interests of determinate social strata. Goldmann in fact calls world visions a form of 'collective group consciousness' which function as a kind of cement, binding individuals together as a group, giving them a collective identity. World visions are, moreover, not only the expression of a social group but of social class also. Why class? Because, argues Goldmann, the most important social group to which a writer can belong is a social class, since it is through a class that he is linked with major social and political change.

Up to the present day, it is class, linked together with basic economic needs, which has been of prime importance in influencing the ideo-

* Following Lukács, Goldmann argues that Marxism is truer than bourgeois science simply because in the bourgeois period only the working class have a need to understand the real movement of capitalist society, for they are the only class capable of effecting the transition from capitalism to socialism.

logical life of man, since he has been compelled to devote most of his thought and energy either to finding enough to live on or, if he belonged to a ruling class, to keeping his privileges and administering and increasing his wealth.*

Social and political change is, for the Marxist, the expression of class antagonism and clearly impinges on class consciousness. No articulate member of a social class can be ignorant of, or indifferent to, major social and political change. His class affiliations sharpen his consciousness of the world and drive him to express, however obliquely, the significant social tendencies of his period in a literary or philosophical medium. World visions are thus the theoretical expressions of social classes at particular historical moments, and the writer, philosopher, or artist articulates this consciousness.

Goldmann makes extravagant claims for his concept. A world vision, he writes, will enable the researcher to separate the accidental from the essential features of a work and to focus on the text as a significant whole. This latter point leads him to make the usual distinction between the 'great' and the 'inferior' writers, arguing that only a great writer's work will have an internal coherence constituting a significant whole. This distinction is based on *internal* criteria and not on external factors as in Taine and Plekhanov, for what Goldmann is arguing here is that the internal coherence of a particular literary work depends exclusively on the world vision held by the writer. The concept allows the researcher to grasp fully this inner coherent structure. It should be noted that Goldmann is not claiming sovereignty over traditional literary criticism, for the world vision does not supplant aesthetic judgement of style, imagery, syntax, etc., but merely acts as the main methodological tool in the *understanding* of the *whole text*.†

A world vision, then, determines the internal structure of a text. What Goldmann calls 'valid literary works' are thus characterized by an inner coherence which allows them to express a 'true universe', and a 'rigorous and unified genre'. The question

* Goldmann, op. cit., pp. 17–18.
† This is not at all clear. After all, to explain and to understand the whole text, or even the 95 per cent minimum which Goldmann claims for his method, is surely to dismiss or at least relegate traditional aesthetics to a very minor status – as supportive to a sociological hegemony? On this question, see chapter 4 below.

of what actually constitutes a valid literary work brings Goldmann close to traditional literary criticism and to positivism. For Goldmann, a valid literary work is one which expresses the basic and universal human condition:

A philosophy or work of art can keep its value outside the time and place where it first appeared only if, by expressing a particular human condition, it transposes this on to a plane of the great human problems created by man's relationship with his fellows and with the universe.*

The mediocre writer merely reflects the historical period and his work has only documentary value. But great literature tackles the major problems and it achieves its inner unity because only the 'exceptional individual', the truly great writer, identifies with the fundamental social tendencies of his time in a way which allows him to achieve coherent expression of reality – the average writer, the average member of a group, will also grasp the social tendencies but in a confused and vague manner. What Goldmann seems to be saying is that only good sociological-cum-philosophical literature is worth studying, since it is only within these texts that a world vision is expressed, based on the human condition and an exceptional awareness of major social trends.

These, then, are Goldmann's main terms. It is important to see the manner of application in concrete research. His method, which he calls 'generalized genetic structuralism' (historical structuralism) seeks firstly to identify certain structures within particular texts, and secondly, to relate them to concrete historical and social conditions, to a social group and social class associated with the writer and to the world vision of that class. The emphasis throughout is on the text itself as a whole and on history as a process. Goldmann's approach is to extrapolate from the social group and the text under analysis an abstraction, that is, a world vision, which then becomes a working model. He returns to the texts seeking to explain the whole, that is, their structures, by reference to his model. In essence the method is a continual oscillation between texts, social structure (social groups and classes), and the model, between abstractions and the concrete, Marx's 'pre-given, living, concrete whole'. Thus, in

* Goldmann, op. cit., p. 20.

his analysis of the philosophy of Pascal and the plays of Racine, Goldmann is able to connect the tragic vision which these works express with an extreme religious social group, the Jansenists, and a social class, the *Noblesse de Robe*. 'Outstanding cultural events', he argues, such as Pascal's *Pensées*, are rarely linked with insignificant social changes; he is able to demonstrate how the shifting balance of power in seventeenth-century France between the Court, the Church, the aristocracy, and the Third Estate gave rise both to an extreme form of Jansenism and to a tragic vision of the world.*

Goldmann's concrete research has always been problem-oriented. His study of Pascal set out initially to explore the reasons for Pascal's transition from a philosophically optimistic point of view, in his *Provincial Letters* (1657), to the far greater philosophical speculation in his pessimistic *Pensées* (1662). Similarly, in his study of the French novelist André Malraux, the problem lay in explaining the 'qualitative' change from the early allegorical fantasies (1920–23)† to the great novels of China (1928–33).‡ In both cases the answer is a world vision.

3

In *The Hidden God*, Goldmann shows that the philosophy of Pascal and the theatre of Racine constituted the theoretical expression of a 'marginal' social group, the Jansenists, and a 'marginal' social class, the *Noblesse de Robe*. Both Pascal and Racine express a tragic view of life, what Goldmann calls the 'tragedy of refusal', that is, a rejection of the world coupled with a desire to remain within it and thus not a retreat to some form of other-worldliness, such as mysticism.§ Pascal's *Pensées* are

---

* For Goldmann's concept of world vision, see especially *The Hidden God*, ch. 5.
† *Royaume Farfelu* (1920), *Lunes en Papier* (1921), *La Tention de l'Occident* (1923).
‡ *Les Conquerants* (1928), *La Voie Royale* (1930), *La Condition Humaine* (1933).
§ Goldmann derives his concept of tragedy from Lukács in his *The Soul and the Form* (1908), although, of course, providing it with a socio-economic base. The extreme form of Jansenism with which both Pascal and Racine were involved was that developed by a sect known as 'The Friends of Port-Royal'. See Goldmann, op. cit., especially pp. 142–50.

characterized by this extreme position: the world is no longer in harmony with God and man, for although God is not absent from the world, he is silent, he is hidden; in order for man to live, therefore, he must 'wager', man must gamble on God's existence and thus on his own salvation.

This tragic vision, argues Goldmann, could only have occurred at a particular historical moment. All forms of tragic thought share a common characteristic, for they all 'express a deep crisis in the relationship between man and his social and spiritual world'. The crisis of the social world lay in the inability of the emerging bourgeois groups, the *Noblesse de Robe*, to break royal absolutism and its centralized state bureaucracy and thus develop capitalist society. Goldmann succeeds in showing how the extreme Jansenist creed, 'a refusal both of the world and of any desire to change it historically', was bound up closely with the social discontent of the *Noblesse de Robe*. Originally recruited from the Third Estate and ennobled by the monarch to form part of the administrative structure of the state bureaucracy, the *Noblesse de Robe* constituted a deliberate counterweight to the power of the traditional aristocracy, the *Noblesse de Cour*. But with the consolidation of the Crown and thus the absolutist state, the *Noblesse de Robe*'s power and prestige waned considerably although it remained tied to the Crown economically. Goldmann suggests that this highly ambiguous position, entailing both opposition to and need for the Crown, produced a philosophy and a literature dominated by a tragic outlook: a bourgeoisie which was in opposition to and economically independent of the monarchy would have developed a more *active*, worldly philosophy, rationalism, and empiricism, as indeed occurred in the eighteenth century.*

The concept of the tragic vision, then, enables Goldmann to

* Goldmann makes the interesting observation that while Pascal's texts show an awareness of the dialectical character of the world, its contradictory nature, its oppositions, and its essential flux, his social link with extreme Jansenism, through the politically impotent *Noblesse de Robe*, prevented him from extending his pristine dialectical understanding in favour of a wholly tragic outlook in which change in the world by man himself was impossible. During the next century, Hegel, and in the nineteenth century, Marx, would extend the dialectical understanding to social life and thus provide a *social* solution to what appeared to Pascal as a situation of ineluctable pessimism and tragedy.

explain the shift between the 'moderate' philosophical position occupied by Pascal in his *Provincial Letters* and the tragic extremism of the *Pensées*: it was in no sense a question of individual psychology but rather the development of a particular, historically specific world vision. World visions appear thus as the key to literary history. We would expect, therefore, great novelists to express world visions in their work since without it, on Goldmann's terms, their novels would lack coherence, validity, and so on. But there is a difference between philosophy as expressed by Pascal, written at a high conceptual level, where one might reasonably expect to find world visions, and the novel form which, apart from its concreteness and particularity of detail, incident, and character, has almost overridingly been concerned with the 'private life' of its protagonists. There is, too, the question of audience: novels are written usually for specific markets in which they have to sell. Frequently the writer is a professional author unsupported by religious, political, or court patronage and the history of the novel as a genre parallels the writers' growing emancipation, from a servile and unstable literary fealty, to the status of a 'free-floating intellectual'.* More particularly it raises the question of the writer's social position within a classs or group, as well as his relations with the dominant class. One reason why modern literature is often termed 'problematic' is that the writer no longer expresses the vision or views of a particular social class.

Goldmann's definition of the writer's function as 'one of criticial opposition . . . a form of resistance to the ongoing development of bourgeois society' brings us to the crucial problem: for if the novelist embodies this critical consciousness, then he is most unlikely to express through his work an abhorrent class consciousness. Similarly, he is unlikely to be part of the working class, since most writers originate and remain within a middle-class environment and rarely identify with a social class they hardly *know*.† The utility of the concept of world vision as the master key to world literature is surely

* Many contemporary novelists, for example, find employment in the academic world more congenial than living off their own writing, especially the Americans, for example, Saul Bellow, Bernard Malamud, John Barth.
† Many writers have identified with the working class through the Communist Party but few have created works of enduring literary value.

challenged by the writer's ambiguous class position after the revolutions of 1848, when, with the European bourgeoisie as the dominant class, it became progressively more difficult for the writer to be both critical and enthusiastic for bourgeois values. Flaubert typifies this increasing social alienation in his hatred of both bourgeoisie and proletariat, in his conception of the writer as an impartial spectator withdrawing from active participation in the society he depicts artistically.

In his discussion of the problems of the sociology of the novel,* Goldmann is clearly aware of these difficulties. There is nothing surprising, he argues, about the development of the novel as a literary genre, since it embodies, above all else, a search for values in a world emptied of 'authenticity', a world 'degraded' and dominated not by human but by exchange ('use') values.† Lukács, in his *Theory of the Novel* had argued that the novel (the romanesque form – a significant structure) was characterized essentially by a radical antagonism between the hero and the world. Unlike the hero in Greek epic, he does not enjoy an organic and living relation with his society but is 'set free' to work out his own destiny through his own efforts within a wholly secular world. But as hero he is bound not to the conventional values of the empirical world but rather to 'authentic' values, and thus the novel becomes a quest for authenticity in a world where authentic values remain implicit. The novel is a 'literary form of absence' with the hero searching hopelessly for values which constantly elude him, and it is the problematic character of these values which leads ultimately to the novel form.‡

Goldmann extends Lukács's idealized, wholly internal interpretation to the socio-economic sphere: the novel form develops as a result of class development and he proposes a 'rigorous homology' between economic and literary structures. The novel is fundamentally to do with man's alienation from the social world; it is the artistic expression of a society in which money takes precedence over man, and where man is degraded to the

* Goldmann, *Pour une Sociologie du Roman*, pp. 19–58.
† Goldmann employs the categories of the young Marx, for whom the increase in economic values was paralleled by a constant devaluation of human life.
‡ Lukács, *Théorie du Roman*, part 1. See also P. Mann, 'Lukács' Theory of the Novel', *Modern Language Notes*, December 1966; Demetz, op. cit., ch. 8.

status of an 'object' in that his labour, his essence, is defined as a commodity to be bought on the market by the highest available bidder. But this definition leads to a problem: for if great art is wholly the expression of the world vision of a social class, then the novel must constitute, in its origins and development, the vision of the bourgeoisie against whom the hero must be in opposition. In other words, the 'problematic hero' must draw his inspiration from his opposition to the 'collective consciousness' of the bourgeoisie.* Goldmann's answer is to argue that since no social group can 'effectively defend' capitalist 'exploitation', or at least can do so only through ideology, through the distortion of truth, then great literature ceases to be bound up exclusively with the fate of social classes. Capitalism, he suggests, has succeeded not merely in 'degrading' the world but in transposing directly its economic activity into mental life: 'In market geared societies the collective consciousness progressively loses all sense of active reality and tends to become a simple reflection of economic life.'† It is not, however, an automatic, mechanical adjustment: Marx developed his theory of alienation in the 1840s but it was not until the middle of the twentieth century that it became part of imaginative literature. In the novels of Robbe-Grillet especially, Goldmann claims to find the reified consciousness of modern man.

Thus Goldmann suggests that a direct causal link exists between the forms of the modern novel and *society as a whole*. Indeed, he goes further, arguing for a similarly direct relation between the novel and particular phases of capitalist development. He describes three broad historical periods, beginning in 1880, and ending with the present time. The first period, corresponding to the growth of cartels and monopolies and colonial expansion (1880–1914), is reflected in the decline of the hero within the novel; between 1918 and 1939, the period of 'crisis capitalism', the hero more or less disappears from the novel, a process which 'consumer capitalism', 1945 onwards, completes. Goldmann, then, is suggesting that social class as the focal point of genuine literary creativity becomes relatively unimportant, and that society as a whole, especially its economic

* Cf. E. Knight, *A Theory of the Classical Novel*, London, Routledge & Kegan Paul, 1969, pp. 55–6.
† Goldmann, *Pour une Sociologie du Roman*.

structure, is the determining factor. And, if he is to be wholly consistent with his stated method, there is the further problem that on his own terms the only genuine world vision which can find expression in an advanced capitalist society must be that of Marxism, given the world vision's oppositional character – all else must surely be mere ideology, sheer perspective.* How does Goldmann deal with these problems in his study of the novels of André Malraux?

Malraux's fiction falls into three distinct phases, beginning with the three allegorical fantasies written in the early twenties, and ending with the philosophically pessimistic *Walnut Trees of Altenburg* (1943). In between lies the great creative period embracing the novels of the Chinese and Spanish civil wars, *Man's Estate* and *Days of Hope*.† Goldmann argues that it is in this second stage that Malrux creates a genuine novel form ('*une structure proprement romanesque*'). His early fiction had been written as satirical allegory, expressive of a pessimistic philosophy shared by many European intellectuals after the First World War, feelings which attest to the crisis of individualistic values in an increasingly collectivist society. These early stories indicate a remarkable talent, but no more. They do not explain Malraux's sudden transition to the truly great novels of his middle period; if it was merely a question of increasing technical competence then his development would have been more gradual. The sudden 'qualitative' change is explicable only in terms of the values which govern the novels' fictional universe. Malraux, argues Goldmann, embraced 'universal values' although of a 'problematic character'. For Goldmann, then, following Lukács's argument that the novel is a structure held together aesthetically by 'problematic values', it is Malraux's acceptance of the world vision of communism which provides the authentic values necessary for the creation of a 'rigorous and unified genre' – the novel form.‡ Goldmann's

* Goldmann has in fact stated that the Marxist analysis is no longer applicable to advanced, consumer capitalism, in which the working class has been assimilated and is thus no longer a revolutionary class. He appears to believe in a form of evolution rather than revolution, involving technical workers rather than the proletariat as the main agencies of change as understood in classical Marxist theory.

† *La Condition Humaine*, 1933; *L'Espoir*, 1937.

‡ The suggestion of Knight, op. cit., that Goldmann's theory only applies to the picaresque novel form, is wholly inadmissible – the quest for values is

74

method is to work through the novels and show how the waxing and waning of the authentic values parallels the emergence and the decline of a genuine novel.*

In *Man's Estate*, usually regarded as Malraux's greatest work, the orientation is 'towards the replacement of individual heroes by the collective personality'. In this novel Malraux portrays the conflict which developed between a group of Chinese communists situated in Shanghai, dedicated to proletarian revolution, and the representatives of the Russian Communist Party who advocated joint action with the national bourgeoisie led by Chiang Kai-shek. The novel sketches the relation between the 'problematic community' of revolutionary communists, problematic because their values and actions were challenging capitalist society, and the Stalinist policies of the Chinese Communist Party which eventually doomed the revolutionaries to defeat and death. As long as Malraux was critical of the policies followed by the official communist leadership he could create a novel of 'authentic values', although one in which the hero has been replaced by the community. In the later *Days of Hope*, when Malraux had come to accept uncritically the policies of international communism it was impossible for him to depict any kind of 'authenticity'.

Goldmann's argument is that a coherent structure is dependent on the 'global vision' expressed in a novel and its resultant values. Thus in *Man's Estate* the world vision of communism enables Malraux to depict love between men and women only where the characters are organically connected with a community; in *Days of Hope*, a novel which has neither problematic hero nor problematic community, love, eroticism, family life, are portrayed as *obstacles* to the disciplined direction and success of the Communist Party. Structure and value are closely bound: the values of the revolutionary community in *Man's Estate* are compared with the value of discipline in *Days of Hope* in a way which suggests that human values, love, and the human community are possible only if a *problematic* dimension of some kind is present. In *Days of Hope* there is none, only the Communist

---

not identical with a roving hero but is implied in the very act of human participation within society.

* Cf. H. Levin, 'Toward a Sociology of the Novel', in *Refractions*, New York, Oxford University Press, 1966.

Party, disciplined and dogmatic, with its 'correct political line' opposed to any spontaneous revolutionary action.* In *Man's Estate*, Malraux had not yet wholly identified with the Communist Party, and thus the 'fundamental values which structured the universe' of the novel were different from those of the Party. Thus the fluctuations of 'authentic' and 'non-authentic' values within Malraux's fiction flowed directly from his awareness of the world vision of communism, pre-Stalinist and post-Stalinist. His final novel, *The Walnut Trees of Altenburg*, completes Malraux's journey, from pessimistic satire through Marxism to Stalinism and finally to this series of dialogues which propose as a solution to the world's problems an efficient and trained élite which would be both privileged and cultivated. This wholly conceptual structure with no heroes or community clearly points the way for Malraux's years with de Gaulle in post-war France.

It should be clear from this brief discussion of Goldmann's analysis of Malraux's fiction that the link between the novels, social groups, social class, and world vision seems the simple one of critical fraternity with communism producing 'authentic values', while a dogmatic relation yields only a non-problematic and 'non-authentic' fictional universe. But what precisely was Malraux's relationship with communism and therefore with the working class whose vision he expresses? Goldmann is unclear: were Malraux's communist affiliations between 1926 and 1937 an individual phenomenon, or an expression of a more general commitment by certain groups of French intellectuals towards the Russian Revolution and thus to Marxism and the working class? There is, too, the question of ideology. If the world vision of Marxism provides the inner unity of *Man's Estate*, what of the vision expressed in the Stalinist *Days of Hope*, for here the Spanish Civil War is depicted in purely technical and military terms, not as a problem of policy and values. The absence of any kind of problematic element implies not a world vision but rather an ideology – in this case, Stalinism. Thus it seems that a world vision becomes an ideology in a writer's own time.

Many of these problems remain unanswered in Goldmann's brief discussion of the *Nouveau Roman*.* The novels of Robbe-Grillet and Nathalie Sarraute fit perfectly into his schema of the modern novel; as realistic novels their literary structures are

* Goldmann, *Pour une sociologie du Roman*, pp. 156–60, 220–22.

in every way analogous to the social reality of consumer capitalism. The hero and the human community have been eclipsed totally by a world of objects, and external things that now dominate man. Objects in the classical novel existed merely in terms of their relations with individual characters; but in the new novel, with its origins in Joyce, Kafka, Musil, they take on the appearance of autonomy, having their own structure and laws but at the same time expressing 'in a certain measure human reality'. Thus, in Robbe-Grillet's *Le Voyeur*, man is depicted as essentially passive, a spectator living in a world of other 'indifferent onlookers', thus reflecting 'one of the fundamental facts of contemporary industrial societies', man's complete lack of initiative.* Man is an object, dominated by economic and social self-regulation; the world is a hostile, alien place, where individuals have neither the wish to intervene, to act positively, nor to transform life qualitatively. These writings, argues Goldmann, carry 'a realistic, critical, and perfectly coherent vision of contemporary society' and constitute 'valid and authentic literary works'.‡

This seems a strange conclusion: world visions by definition strive towards totality, to grasp the whole: the trend of contemporary fiction (and this applies with force to Robbe-Grillet and the practitioners of the new novel) is away from literary totalities towards a wholly private, individual, subjective world – a *partial* rather than total view. But Goldmann raises more questions about the sociological study of literature than he provides solutions. In the next chapter we shall examine more critically Goldmann's major concepts and general theory, and attempt to relate them to the problem of method in cultural analysis.

* ibid., pp. 279–334.
† Goldmann, *Criticism and Dogmatism in Literature*, p. 147.
‡ ibid.

4 Problems of Method

In the preceding chapters we have tried to sketch the main tendencies in the sociological study of literature, noting some of their similarities and differences. A somewhat schematic differentiation was suggested between the tendency to see literature as largely a reflection of the socio-economic process, as in positivism, and the more critical, internal perspective of structuralism. Both perspectives conform with Taine's comment that books do not drop from the sky like meteorites* but have their basis in a specific social context which can be analysed sociologically. The positivistic method, however, leads to a relative lack of concern with literary texts ('reductionism') while structuralism makes the text the centre of research. We have, then, two fairly distinct lines of sociological inquiry: first, a sociology of literature which begins with milieu and works outwards, seeking to relate literature to purely external factors through their reflection or refraction in the text – its method is to elucidate the social correlates of literature at a certain moment in its production (Taine, Plekhanov); secondly, a literary sociology with its basis in the literary text, which relates structures to genre and society.

There is here a difference both in terms of method and general emphasis. Goldmann's work, for example, is painstaking in its search for the social conditions underpinning literary creativity, but his starting point is the literary text itself. His method does not 'dissolve' literature into its surrounding environment or make it a simple function of class consciousness. Yet within Goldmann's work there are positivistic tendencies and a conception of the novel, for example, as a *reflection* of society, especially in his analysis of Robbe-Grillet and in his homology of structures in which literature *reflects* the dominant elements

* Quoted in Levin, *The Gates of Horn*, p. 9.

of capitalism (its three phases). The emphasis in this approach clearly undermines the possibility both of an autonomous literary sector as Engels suggested, as well as seeming to ignore the importance of literary tradition in shaping an artist's consciousness. Every writer works within a tradition, an inherited literary culture, and his own work will show in various ways the influence of this background; writers are influenced too by the other cultural traditions, especially philosophy and politics. The important point is not the tracing of 'influences' in an abstract manner but studying the ways in which a particular writer absorbs a tradition and from it develops his own authentic voice, his ideas, his view of man, for what he creates from preceding influences will be one of the most significant clues to a complete understanding of his work: the elements of antecedent tradition which are accepted or rejected, developed, modified, or simply left unchanged will reflect in some measure the changes which have occurred in the social structure.* The Russian Formalist, Shklovsky posed this question idealistically when he wrote that 'the form of a work of art is defined by its relation to other works of art, to forms existing prior to it . . . The purpose of any new form is not to express new content, but to change an old form which has lost its aesthetic quality.'†

In this formulation Shklovsky is close to the nineteenth-century French critic Ferdinand Brunetière, who argued for an autonomous evolution of genres in which, of all the influences on literature, the most important was that of literature itself, 'work on work'. The number of causes, he argued, should not be increased on the assumption that literature expressed society, nor should the history of literature be confused with the history of 'morals and manners'.‡ But since literature is about man living within a specific social context it can hardly be discussed independently of society: Zola's social reportage type of novel was

---

* For example, in Flaubert's historical novel, *Salammbo*, the characters are invested with a nineteenth-century psychology – Salammbo herself is another Madame Bovary sharing her hysterical longings and torments. In Scott's novels, on the other hand, the psychological presentation of character is on the same level of historical development as the period depicted. Lukács links this change, and others such as the excessive attention to brutality in Flaubert's novel, to the development of a fully bourgeois capitalism (*The Historical Novel*, pp. 188–99).

† Lemon and Reiss, op. cit.

‡ See R. Wellek, *History of Modern Criticism*, vol. 4, pp. 58–71.

written from a realistic perspective and in this sense he follows the tradition of Balzac, but his concept of the author as observer, as someone who is not involved in the process he is describing, can only be understood in terms of the changes which had occurred in French society between 1830 and 1880 – the writer as spectator is explicable as a function of increasing marginality and the uncertainty of intellectuals who could no longer easily identify their basic assumptions with the dominant class.

The influence of literature on literature must be considered and integrated into the method of the sociology of literature. It raises the question of how conscious the writer himself is of writing both within a specific literary tradition and in a specific type of society. Fielding was clearly aware of his debt to the seventeenth-century picaresque tradition, as his introductions to each part of *Tom Jones* illustrate; similarly, Robbe-Grillet is self-conscious of his *rejection* of the nineteenth-century realist tradition, and of his attempt to be scientifically objective in his distinction between the world of things, of objects, and the world of man. But neither writer can be so aware of the *social conditioning* process which affects all cultural creation: Robbe-Grillet, in seeking a new form, actually creates an alienated and reified structure in which man is merely a passive object living outside human relations. This is not Robbe-Grillet's intention, and a critical distinction must always be kept in mind between intention and achievement. Imaginative literature is a reconstruction of the world seen from a particular point of view, and while the writer may be aware of literary tradition, it is the non-conscious reworking of experience, fused with his values, which produces the fictional universe with which the sociology of literature is concerned. Goldmann emphasizes values, although not literary tradition, arguing that it is the writer's values which in the end yield an aesthetic structure. Structuralism in literary analysis departs radically from this formulation; it agrees with Goldmann's precept that literature can only be approached as literature, but argues that it must be wholly internal. 'The object of structural analysis of literature,' writes one structuralist critic, 'is literature, its literariness,' not its relation with other things.* The importance of Goldmann's approach, as we have seen, lies in his stress on the internal unity of a literary text as

* T. Todorov, 'Structural Analysis of Narrative', *Novel*, Fall, 1969.

the result of an external world vision held by a certain social group and class; the values which hold a particular work of literature together aesthetically are the direct expression of this world vision, and a coherent text is possible only in this way. It is important to stress this, since Goldmann's perspective on the sociology of literature is not a sociology of an occupational group – writers, their life styles, norms, social background, career patterns – but an attempt to link the text of particular authors in a meaningful way with particular historical conditions. The overall meaning of the text is its aim, and not the positivistic delineation of an occupational category.

We have seen that Goldmann's argument employs the functional necessity of a world vision for the existence of 'a unified and rigorous genre'. But can there be world visions today? At one point Goldmann remarks that great literature is created at moments of exceptional crisis in man's relation with others and the world:

... all forms of consciousness express a provisional and mobile balance between the individual and his social environment; when this balance can be fairly easily established and is relatively stable, or when it can pass fairly easily from one form to another, men tend not to think about the problems raised by their relationship to the external world. On the social as well as on an individual plane, it is the sick organ which creates awareness, and it is in periods of social and political crisis that men are most aware of the enigma of their presence in the world.*

Obvious examples suggest themselves: the relation between the development of the picaresque novel – *Don Quixote* for example – and the decline of the feudal world; the political and social upheavals engendered by the French Revolution which inform the work of Goethe, Beethoven, Hegel; and in this century, the protracted crisis of central Europe played against the background of the Russian Revolution and the rise of fascism, producing the *angst*-ridden writers, Musil, Kafka, Hesse, Céline.

But what of the great English realistic tradition? Was there a protracted crisis in nineteenth-century England spanning the years of Thackeray's novels to those of Gissing at the close of the century? There was certainly a social and economic crisis

* Goldmann, *The Hidden God*, p. 49.

during the 1930s, but it would be the most naïve of critics who would argue that in this period English literature was especially 'great'. The concept of crisis is a tenuous one and unlikely to help in the sociological analysis of literature: capitalism, as Marx remarked, is in a perpetual state of crisis in any case. But Goldmann links his notion of a world vision directly with crisis: in seventeenth-century France in a situation involving an historically impotent middle class, and a resultant tragic vision; and the modern crisis of collective versus individualistic values, communism and its antagonist, capitalism, in the work of Malraux. The significant element in both of Goldmann's analyses lies in his discussion of values. Thus for him, Pascal, Racine, and Kant, for example, developed a tragic view of life because social conditions obstructed the empirical working out of their fundamentally optimistic and progressive values. Kant emphasized reason in a world which seemed dominated by unreason, superstition, and custom; Pascal noted the dialectical character of the world, that everything tends towards flux and thus to change, but he could not extend this to the social sphere and thus go beyond his tragic vision of man as essentially in-active, as fundamentally passive. Malraux's *Man's Estate* expresses the progressive values of non-dogmatic, non-bureau-cratized communism, while *Days of Hope* is built around the theme of party discipline, Stalinist policies and a war which is depicted almost entirely from a military angle: Malraux's vision was now a rigid orthodox ideology incapable of generating progressive values.* Goldmann seems to be suggesting here that a world vision is not merely a totality of social relations conceived at any one moment but also an awareness of the future; great writers are related to the present through their group and class affiliations, and to the future through the world vision. He is close to Engels's formulation on Balzac, who, although a Catholic and political legitimist, grasped the 'necessity' for the down-

* Progressive values are not necessarily those of the Communist Party, but are meant to imply a *human* as opposed to a market content. For example, it would be impossible to write a novel embodying the medieval values of blind obedience to State, religion, and family except as a work of pure propaganda. It is no accident that fascism has produced no writers of great creative ability, while Russian communism has produced as great literature only strong anti-communist and highly critical novels, such as *Doctor Zhivago* and Solzhenitsyn's *The First Circle* and *Cancer Ward*.

fall of his favourite nobles and success for the bourgeoisie. The distinction between ideology and world vision is important: ideology is a false consciousness of the world, a partial, one-sided distortion of the real relations between men and their society, a perspective rather than totality. It would seem impossible, given this definition, for world visions to exist today unless they are Marxist, and since the vision creates the values which determine the aesthetic unity of the literary text, it would follow that modern literature is wholly ideological and partial. The unity of the text, after all, does not depend on its literary qualities but purely on *social* values; and without these values, there cannot be a unified genre, a genuine novel, an aesthetic totality.

Is it possible, for example, that a novelist who holds non-progressive values, a conservative reactionary or even neo-Fascist, could create a genuine literature? D. H. Lawrence, for example, is usually regarded as a major novelist, yet he was strongly anti-democratic,* while his conception of some kind of mystical blood bond existing between men and women and men and men is the antithesis of reason and might conceivably suggest a fascist mentality.† Lawrence wrote frankly on sexual and emotional relationships; his novels are rarely political or even social in the sense that milieu is concretely realized, and in his important works, *Sons and Lovers*, *The Rainbow*, *Women in Love*, he writes almost to the exclusion of extrapersonalized themes. The theme of woman asserting her independence from man is a subject which many novelists had explored before Lawrence: Clarissa Harlowe refusing to marry for the sake of family property; George Eliot's Gwendolen Harleth (*Daniel Deronda*), Henry James's Isabel Archer (*The Portrait of a Lady*), and the heroines of the novels of Doris Lessing, are portraits of

* Writing on relations between men and women, Lawrence observed that the next relation 'has got to be a relationship of men towards men in a spirit of unfathomable trust and responsibility, service and leadership, obedience and pure authority. Men have got to choose their leaders, and obey them to the death. And it must be a system of culminating aristocracy, society tapering like a pyramid to the supreme leader' (D. H. Lawrence, *Fantasia of the Unconscious*, New York, Viking Press, 1960).
† Raymond Williams, in his chapter on Lawrence in *Culture and Society*, dismisses the claim that Lawrence was in any sense fascist but he cannot explain why undoubted fascist sentiments continually recur in Lawrence's philosophical and fictional writings.

women who endure unhappiness precisely because they refuse to compromise with the role which bourgeois society has allocated them. The sociological studies of widely different cultures have demonstrated that the differential treatment of men and women is more the result of cultural conditioning than of inherent abilities. Women are socialized to accept the feminine role, while men are defined through a tough masculine role, and society supports these definitions through institutionalized inequality of work and pay.* Conformity to prescribed roles constitutes at once a key component in bourgeois ideology.

Lawrence's treatment of the male/female, and male/male relations flows from his acceptance of the prescribed definitions accorded to men and women by his society. Women are by nature instinctive, they are not reasonable in the same sense as a man; intellectual women are frequently unhappy in their relations with men and it is better for the relation to be one of dominance by the man and passivity in the woman. Men and women *are* different inherently; the differences in socialization between the sexes is clearly an irrelevant detail for Lawrence, with the result that this *value*, this perspective on human relations, determines the asocial treatment of sexual relationships within his novels. In *Lady Chatterley's Lover* the relationship between the sexually frustrated Constance Chatterley and the gamekeeper, Mellors, is depicted as essentially a physical attraction mellowing into a deeper range of feelings in which the intellectual Constance submits to the 'pure' fire of the man. During their first sexual experience she fails to achieve orgasm but it lifts a 'great cloud' from her mind although 'her tormented modern woman's brain still had no rest'. Complete contentment is possible only in virtual submission to her purely feminine role: Lawrence indeed has a simple message, for as women are by nature different from men they will strive towards intellectual equality at the risk of losing their essential being,

* For useful discussion and references, see J. Mitchell, 'Women, The Longest Revolution', *New Left Review*, 40. This conservative ideology is nowhere better expressed than in television commercials, especially those concerned with wholly domestic products: the wife cleans the shirts of her two men and, waving goodbye to both in the mornings, one to school, the other to work, the commercial suggests she goes with the whiteness too, is part of it – the wife and the soap powder are one.

their femininity.* Thus in *Lady Chatterley's Lover* the real
point is not Lawrence's apparent sexual iconoclasm, his attack
on bourgeois hypocrisy and the deadening effects which industrial civilization has on human relationships, but the development of the Constance/Mellors relation from one of pure
physical passion towards a social and human connection. But
Lawrence succeeds only in isolating the erotic element in love
and rarely grasps the social determinations of human emotions;
he does not structure relationships *socially*, for he sees the
basic relation, men and women, as asocial, as belonging to the
realms of 'pure' blood and longing. Numerous passages could
be cited showing this asocial approach: in *Women in Love*, Birkin,
who is in love with Ursula, lies sick in bed and muses on sex
and love:

In the old age, before sex was, we were mixed, each one a mixture.
The process of singling into individuality resulted into the great
polarization of sex. The womanly drew to one side, the manly to the
other. But the separation was imperfection even then. And so our
world cycle passes . . . The man is pure man, the woman pure woman,
they are perfectly polarized. But there is no longer any of the horrible
merging, mingling self-abnegation of love. There is only the pure
duality of polarization, each one free from any contamination of the
other. In each, the individual is primal, sex is subordinate, but perfectly polarized. Each has a single, separate being, with its own laws.
The man has his pure freedom, the woman hers. Each acknowledges
the perfection of the polarized sex-circuit. Each admits the different
nature in the other.†

What Birkin is pondering is roles, and roles are social and not
inherent; each of us performs certain roles every day, we follow
rules, custom, and habit. As individuals we have been defined by
others, by the roles others expect us to perform. What Lawrence
is saying is perfectly clear: it is that human relationships, that
is social relationships, are pre-eminently the result of non-

* The sexes must be kept pure, 'pure maleness in a man, pure femaleness in
a woman. Woman is really polarized downwards, towards the centre of the
earth. Her deep positivity is in the downward flow, the moon-pull. And man
is polarized upwards, towards the sun and the day's activity. Women and
men are dynamically different, in everything. Even in the mind, where we
seem to meet, we are really utter strangers . . . The apparent mutual under-
understanding, in companionship between a man and a woman is always an
illusion, and always breaks down in the end' (Lawrence, op. cit., p. 215).
† D. H. Lawrence, *Women in Love*, London, Penguin Books, 1960, p. 225.

social factors, especially, one might almost say, solely, the 'dark brooding of the blood'. Thus between Gudrun and Gerald, two other lovers in this novel, 'a diabolical freemasonry subsisted between them',* a relationship which ends despairingly in the Alps and in death.

Lawrence is a reactionary thinker; he has a distinct ideology which results in depicting love relations, that is, social relationships in non-social terms. There is no totality within his novels: the foreground is wholly taken up with the basic problem of the blood and sexual polarity; human relationships develop within this field – thus in *Lady Chatterley's Lover*, the conversations between Constance and Mellors are exclusively discussions of sex, of man and woman, and the self in love: 'But I tell you, the old rampers have beaks between their legs and they tear at you with it till you're quite sick. Self, self, self.'† Human relations are defined in terms of sexuality; and a sexuality which is sociologically absurd, for men and women live within a society which defines their range of interests as well as their sexuality; a genuine human relation is one of equals, and this Lawrence never depicts.

Lawrence's values, therefore, can be seen as the structuring principle behind his novels. Perhaps this is an obvious point, the fact that he could hold non-progressive values on an area which is crucial for any proper grasp of man in society, human sex relations, and that his attitude here defined his *overall novelistic universe*. But this could be seen as one approach to analysing his fiction sociologically, as well as fruitfully suggesting his limitations as a great novelist.

But all this is tentative, and is merely introduced to illustrate the problem of a unified text written from a non-progressive value position. The same points would apply to the contemporary French novelist Henri de Montherlant in his tetralogy of novels which depict the love life of a writer, Costals.‡ Everything is seen from his position: women are scheming for a marriage. He prefers simple, physical types, not the intellectual, and the

* ibid., p. 137.
† D. H. Lawrence, *Lady Chatterley's Lover*, London, Penguin Books, 1961, p. 210.
‡ H. de Montherlant, *Les Jeunes Filles*, *Pitie pour les Femmes*, *Le Demon du Bien*, *Les Lepreuses*, Paris, 1936–9.

descriptions of his relations are couched in the language of conflict and opposition:

He thought she might be armed, and was going to kill him, or at least slap his face, and in order to be able to ward off the blow, he moved still closer to her, as modern bullfighters stick close to the bull's flank in order to be 'inside' a blow from its horns.[*]

Montherlant, like Lawrence, isolates the erotic component in love, defines women's proper position as different from men in that the intellect obstructs femininity and emotional satisfaction.[†] Montherlant is a conservative ideologist, his values are non-progressive, and like Lawrence, his definitions flow from an acceptance of the definitions which society has accorded its members. His novels are never totalities; they depict men and women in isolation from society in that their relation has no organic connection with it – they develop from mere passion, continue from habit, and are characterized by conflict because of the basic differences in temperament, intellect, etc., which Montherlant clearly believes differentiate the sexes.

These, then, are some of the problems in the methodology of the sociology of literature. The values which a writer holds may be on the decisive clue to his status as a great writer – but this would imply that a writer does not go against his values through his art, as does Balzac for example. But Balzac's realistic method corrected his reactionary values; it may be more difficult for contemporary authors to transcend conservative theory, given the novel's development from realism to its subjectivist state today. This is, however, a problem and we have merely hinted at it.

In conclusion we may say that the sociology of literature can develop only through its grip on texts, not in reducing literature to the status of a reflection of society. Not only do writers articulate social values within their work, and these will surely have certain ramifications for the work's unity and possible

[*] *Les Jeunes Filles*, trans. T. Kilmartin, as *The Girls*, London, Weidenfeld & Nicolson, 1969.
[†] Thus in conversation with his mistress, Costals remarks, 'Everyone knows that a woman's body, when it's no longer young, tends to become a ridiculous and often repulsive object, a joy for cartoonists, whereas a man's body as old age draws near, keeps in much better shape' (ibid., p. 221). Such is the curious language of love, if indeed Montherlant depicts this.

literary qualities, but writers are part of the world they describe, frequently struggling with the question of values, and this *potential* activism must not be discounted in the analysis of their work.

Part Two:
The Writer and Society
by Diana Laurenson

Introduction

As has been outlined in Part One of this book, there is a growing body of theory in the study of literary works which suggests that works of literature do not arise autonomously. While not causally determined by the extraneous situation, they are connected with a number of social factors which help us to understand their genesis, form, and content. The type and economic level of society in which the writer is working; the social classes and groups to which he belongs or with which he relates directly or indirectly; the character of his audience, sponsorship, and patronage; the literary tradition in which he works; his own psychology – these are some of the variables which must be considered in any comprehensive sociology of literature. The strength of any of these, the total equation, will vary according to the period in which the author is writing, and according to the pulls and pressures, sanctions and opportunities, which are operating, moulding the way in which he structures his world, affecting the presentation of his material. Goldmann and others have suggested that in the present century there has been a twofold process of fragmentation of coherent world views in Western society, a questioning of values and norms of behaviour, together with pecuniary pressures which drive many writers to find second jobs within a formalized social pattern, such as the mass media, the universities, and other professional occupations. The equation varies according to subject matter and readership: whether the author is writing works of information, entertainment, or aiming at creating serious literature in the form of novels, plays, short stories, essays, criticism, or poetry. With the enormous increase of published works, with the growth of distinct reading publics and specialized authorship, the sociological study of literature in the modern age becomes a formidable undertaking; although first-hand information can be obtained as to biographical data, we lack advantages resulting from temporal distance. We do not know for certain which works will be accepted as 'great art' (if any – and why); our own closeness and predilections distort and confuse. None the less much work can be done, if only to provide material for a future theory of twentieth-century literature to be formulated in a meaningful way. In the first two of the following three chapters, the changing market situation of the author in England is examined in relation to growing professionalization in the nineteenth century. In the third, a look is taken at the situation of the modern writer. A connection is evident between economic and social structure, the author's perspective, his self-image, and the character of his work.

5 Origins of Authorship and Patronage

It is generally assumed that the oral and written arts arose out of the magical formulae and rituals of paleolithic times, closely associated with the visual and plastic arts.* This must have been preceded by a period of linguistic experimentation, of 'sensory grasping', as language itself developed.† As structured and communicating groups became established, the use of signs, whether written, oral, or of gesture, developed into stylistic techniques. These techniques of communication had various functions for the community.

Besides the obvious function of imparting information, records could be kept and transmitted, thus providing the group with a history. Meaning was bestowed to remembered experiences and exploits, rendering them more or less permanent. The group was provided with a historical dimension denied to structured groups of animals. The elements of case law and a reference for comparison now existed. This reservoir of history enhanced the sense of conscious identity of the group and its reduplication acted as a medium for memories, fantasies, hopes, and fears. The ceremonial presentation of these records gave scope for elaboration and decoration, for differential styles of display according to the situation and the talents of the communicator.

Another important function was manipulation of the unknown. Oral and written techniques provided a medium for incantation, ritual and ceremonial, together with pictorial representation, dancing and mime. The arts became a type of property which could be commanded and used as status symbols by tribal kings and power groups. A class of people emerged whose role was the

* Arnold Hauser, *The Social History of Art*, London, Routledge & Kegan Paul, 1962, vol. 1, ch. 1.
† Ernst Fischer, *The Necessity of Art*, London, Penguin Books, 1963, ch. 2.

specialized provision of this commodity, at first closely associated with magic and the priesthood,* and related to some rewarding and protective figure, to a 'patron'. The early bards reproduced and composed songs and sagas and as such were the first authors. Early literary productions manifested the principles of imitating or mirroring reality, information, and decoration, their function being largely one of providing emotional release and a transcending of individuality. Myths developed, embodying human needs and goals, becoming vehicles for symbolic figures and common predicaments, handed on from generation to generation.

The talents and training of the earliest literary craftsmen and artists, together with their priestly associations, contributed to the image of the writer as a blind seer, filled with 'inner light', able to foretell the future yet unfit for the noble occupation of war. From early times, we find awe and respect mingled with a certain contempt and an awareness of 'difference' towards the artist; these attitudes are still evident today. But the early writers were much more integrated into the social group than the estranged, free-floating writers of this century, whose work is frequently characterized by subjectivity and withdrawal. In Greece the epic writer Homer was closely involved with the values, fears, aims, and goals of his people, expressing their world view. With the breakdown of such organic social solidarity we find writers moving away from their integrated position and new genres and specialisms developing.

This process is accelerated by the development of division of labour and capitalist modes of production, which provide a perspective in which the artist is no longer a key and central figure in the social group. Capitalism evolves an ideology in which the artist does not have a vital and integral function to perform; he feels therefore edged to the periphery of society, encouraged to produce diversions for leisure hours, literature of entertainment, escape, or naturalistic social reporting that does not constitute a fundamental challenge. The developing class structure and inequalities in the provisions for education and leisure tend to restrict readership to the upper and middle classes, and to gear literary content to the views and tastes of these classes. Hence – with a few exceptions – the loss

* For an account of magical invective, see Mathew Hodgart, *Satire*, London, Weidenfeld & Nicolson, World University Library, 1963, pp. 18–21.

of totality and universality in literary works. Contact between the social classes diminishes, and structural separatism is reflected in the literature of the day. Great writers alone can withstand these pressures. They have the talents and acumen necessary to express a wide experience of life on all social levels, and the integrity to offer a critique of bourgeois values and ideology. They can transcend their own position and resist pressures to conformity and restriction, being conscious of society as a structured social system with inherent contradictions and conflicts. Finally they develop insights into focal points of change. Shakespeare can foreshadow modern despair and nihilism while retaining a realistic and comprehensive awareness of the dynamics of his own world. Goethe and Tolstoy are other obvious examples. Totality of vision is more difficult to achieve as capitalism develops, although social criticism may be facilitated by the decline of personal patronage and of severe censorship penalties. The hegemony of bourgeois values itself breaks down in the latter half of the nineteenth century, and the conflicting values which remain contribute to the fragmentation and obscurities of much of modern literature.* In England there were forces promoting relative integration of the writer until the 1880s, when his economic and social position deteriorated.

Throughout history, social factors affected the evolution of literary genres such as the ritualistic epic, lyric poetry, the essay, drama (comic and tragic), the mime, the courtly romance or picaresque tale, and finally the novel. While the development of systems of ancient feudalism was closely connected with institutions of fealty or loyalty of vassals to their protecting lords – these duties overriding personal loyalty – classical tragedy was often concerned with conflict between these loyalties: a conflict in which the author himself might be involved. Fresh genres evolved with changing economic and social conditions: as wars increased in scale, ritualistic forms of literature gave way to war sagas, becoming epic, fluctuating with or returning to lyric forms for the celebration of other community or personal experiences such as peace, birth, love, or joy in nature. The feudal hierarchy gave the bard or court poet a recognized and relatively stable position, enabling an institutionalized role and self-image to develop. At the same time wandering players

* See Ernst Fischer, op. cit., p. 52.

and singers were also welcome for their novelty in a world of severely circumscribed communications.

Aspects of authorship still evident today are therefore discernible from early times – in this case two types of author: the established, institutionalized, and the marginal, nomadic. In an organic society, however, this did not necessarily result in differential fragmentation in the works themselves. Within the community the transmuted saga in its epic form gave way finally to the tragedy of tension, authors gradually differentiating themselves from reciters or workshops of players. In some instances, however, works continued to be performed by their group authors: examples here are the mime and the morality play written, embellished, acted, and produced by church and guild members. There was a continuous development of both folk and professional literature in feudal society, the latter mainly connected with the Court. At times these merged: the Nibelunglied, for instance, originated at Court, then was taken among the people by the wandering poets and minstrels, passing through a folk poetry stage, finally returning to courtly patronage and a courtly form again. The important thing to note from the point of view of the sociology of literature is that early authors were in close touch with their audience, whether Court or people. They shared their world view, and consequently achieved totality in their work, avoiding fragmentation.

As societies increased in complexity, as commerce and division of labour developed, and as capitalistic modes of production were adopted, totality was more and more difficult to achieve. Writers lost their social integration and their texts became more esoteric and partial.* They lost their position of centrality and were forced increasingly to rely on some powerful personal patron or sponsor. This relationship became common, and lasted until the widening market situation of the nineteenth century made a return to a different form of professionalism possible, bringing important changes in literary works.

*This was accentuated in the present century. In England the circulating libraries and middle-class magazine clientèle enabled novelists to remain in relatively close touch with their readers until the 1880s. But their works did not reach the bulk of society, the working classes being in the main excluded.

The central aspect of patronage relevant to the sociology of literature is that it constitutes an exchange relationship between a pair of persons of unequal status; one of these, the patron, giving the other, the author, certain material or protective benefits which enable the literary work to be produced and distributed in an uncertain or even hostile environment. One obvious benefit is the necessary leisure for the gestation and creation of books; there is also insulation from censorship or prosecution, and spokesmanship by the patron in return for a eulogistic dedication. The writer offers or pledges his patron various rewards such as loyalty or fame. There is a wide range of types of allegiance and protection, merging into coercion and servitude; patronage can be long or short term. There is also a range of techniques for avoiding the full impact of domination by a patron and of manipulation by the writer. Naturally, social conditions, institutions such as censorship, types of class and power structures, differential economic opportunity, and chances of regional and social mobility affect these techniques.

Since the artist, as a manipulator of visual or linguistic symbols, had a recognized role in the social group, he could fulfil a meaningful function. He offered a variety of services including entertainment and emotional catharsis, depending for his existence on the support of king or élite group power-structure. In a small cohesive society his relationship with both sponsors and audience was close and intimate. He knew the needs, fears, goals, and world views of his environment, and these he expressed in his work, which became a mode of group expression, whether or not it was written by one person. The poetic epics of Homer are obvious examples. But this happy situation could not last; societies grew and engulfed other groups, positions in the social hierarchy increased and became more sharply defined. This brought a gradual loosening of close social bonds between some layers of society and the artist. The artist's role itself became specialised as division of labour developed: poets, dramatists, singers, musicians, sculptors, painters, differentiated and aimed at perfecting a preferred mode of artistic expression.* A money

* This process was gradual. During the Renaissance it was still common for artists to be proficient in various branches of art.

economy with its accompanying commercial activity offered new prizes and goals; the position of the artist became hazardous and marginal. It became a major task for him to find and please a patron of means who would sustain, protect, and favour him rather than his rivals. These were increasing in number as society expanded, and were becoming both allies and threats; writers could band together in coteries but they competed for fame and recognition.

One feature of artistic creativity which marks it off from many other occupations is that a period of gestation, contemplation, and planning usually precedes the end product. A period of initiation or training may also be essential. The role of the patron before the days of the bureaucratization of the literary profession was complex: like the early capitalist he had to invest in a risk. Often he had to support his client for many years, help him in his training, protect him from rivals, always with the possibility that the results might not be to his tastes and predilections – although the artist obviously felt constraints to please his patron. This affected the character of the work; in an environment where alternative openings were few, the writer was particularly coerced.

In the cohesive group, ideology was shared and so the bargaining situation was relatively simple. For the graphic artist ideology might be irrelevant or unimportant. But the writer uses words upon which subtle constructions can be placed: his message may be ambiguous and contain threats to the social hierarchy at the apex of which his patron stands. When ideology was not shared, in a society where factions were becoming vocal and conflicting world views were developing, the writer might be dangerous and censorship was necessary. The Tsar of Russia's relationship with the poet Pushkin is informative on this type of patronage. The relationship of Chaucer with the English monarchy is an example of a smoother patronage, where ideology was shared, yet contact with total society was not yet lost.

An example of coercive patronage of an extreme nature can be examined if we look at the relationship between the Tsar Nicholas I and Pushkin. This association stands out as shaped to a great extent by forces outside the immediate control of both participants: on the one hand a tradition of rigid repression by a dynasty claiming magical sanctions for its autocracy, on the other hand a period of repressed unrest, of feudalism changing from within. This state of affairs was reflected in a literature using symbolic cryptic literary messages – 'Aesopic language' – of a revolutionary nature, as well as by acts of violence committed directly or indirectly by members of the intellectual class. The role of the Russian Tsar was even more hazardous than that of the Russian writer: three of the last six Tsars met violent deaths, regicide plots were numerous and suffered barbarous retaliation. Censorship control was highly centralized and terroristic; it was mainly negative since it was concerned to obliterate all ideas which appeared iconoclastic or advocating change; this attitude produced suspicion of works of popular education and information for wider audiences. During the mid nineteenth century there seemed to be a culmination of censorial absurdity. Phrases such as 'forces of nature' and 'free currents of air' were banned, Roman emperors could not be 'killed' but must 'perish', and penalties included suppression or mutilation of works, and the exile of authors and publishers.* *158918*

Yet over these years a flourishing literary realist movement developed, and the nineteenth century produced a display of Russian writers of genius: Tolstoy, Dostoevsky, Chekhov, Turgenev, Gogol, Gorki, Pushkin, and many others. This was during a time when the number of officials engaged in censorship exceeded the number of books published in a year; a committee to censor the censors was set up; while the number of bodies concerned with scrutinizing the written word included the Church, the military, the universities, the ministries of education and transport, the police, and even the administration of state horse-breeding. Censors were so anxious not to be penalized for inactivity that they would object to innocuous material: on one occasion, calling a woman's smile 'heavenly' was deemed blasphemous or immoral. Some conservative writers such as Goncharov actually became censors themselves. Periodicals were often suppressed. To give but two examples of literary mutilation: Tolstoy's *Resurrection* received five hundred alterations, and Dostoevsky's *Notes From The Underground* (1864) was 'ruined by those swine of censors' who 'banned the section where I deduced the need for a belief in Christ'.† The

* Ronald Hingley, *Russian Writers and Society*, London, Weidenfeld & Nicolson, 1967.
† Quoted by Ronald Hingley, op. cit., p. 230.

unpredictability of the process (or the stupidity of the censors) is manifested by the appearance of *Capital*, uncensored, in 1872, Russia being the first country to publish a translation. Writers responded by evolving secret codes, privately circulating manuscripts and publishing abroad. Clearly the social conditions propitious for the generation of literary genius are complex.

As a young man, Pushkin was involved in the 1825 Decembrist Revolt, the five leaders of which, including a poet, were hung; Pushkin himself, whose secretly circulated *Ode to Liberty* had fallen into the hands of the police, was lucky only to receive banishment to a minor clerkship in the south of Russia. Later, Nicholas I summoned him and announced 'Send me your writings: from now on, it is I who shall be your censor.' It is alleged that he added, pointing at the leaving poet 'From now on he is mine.' In exchange for a humiliating position at Court and some security for his wife and children, Pushkin found that he was closely watched by the notorious Count Benckendorf, Chief of Police. He was sent criticism and advice, asked to change the content of his work by the Tsar, and also subjected to the official censorship. The publication of *Boris Godunov*, for example, was delayed for five years because the author read it privately to a literary circle without first submitting it to the Tsar, who later sent advice through Benckendorf that it should be changed from a dramatic poem to a 'historical tale or novel similar to Scott's' (1826). To this Pushkin replied, 'I am sorry that it is beyond my power to recast what I have written'; the eventual publication was only allowed as a special favour to help with the expenses of his marriage. The Tsar took a social interest in the poet's wife, refusing him leave to travel or to retire to the country to work, subjecting him to intolerable supervision, and forcing him to attend Court functions. Pushkin died, aged thirty-eight, as the result of a duel with his wife's suspected lover; as he was dying, word was sent that the Tsar would settle his debts and look after his wife and children, thus concluding the questionable benefits of a patronage that was enforced as an Imperial favour, but which was motivated mainly by political fear, resulting in stultifying and even fatal effects on its recipient.

This is an extreme example of one pole of the patronage

continuum: not all Court patronage, of course, was of this bizarre and possessive nature. What did the patron gain from the relationship? Clearly from the crudest point of view both works of art of all kinds and their creators could be regarded as status symbols to impress other élite figures. In a cohesive society, as we have seen, rulers needed not only the information, historical records, and adjuncts to magic and ceremonial provided by literature but also a medium for entertaining and distracting the people, which provided a rationale of events and policies, offering emotional release. From early on, the political value – and dangers – of authors were obvious; pressure on them to provide propaganda overtly or obliquely in return for protection was recurrent. Patrons themselves had the wealth and leisure for taste and discrimination. Many became connoisseurs of a high level, although others were notoriously insensitive and greedy. In a mainly illiterate world, a writer at Court possessed useful expertise: some patrons formed circles of scholars and artists whose fame and impact was widespread.

In ancient Rome a situation developed which was particularly conducive to dyadic patronage. Before the rise of capitalism the artist performed a twofold task: the expression of the needs of his social group, and the ordering and structuring of his own experience of social reality. In the ancient world these aims could be harmoniously intertwined. In Rome, however, the severe factional conflict which culminated in the murder of Caesar was followed by the reign of Augustus, who was anxious to reconcile the factions and to promote peace and consolidation at home and in the Empire. With the aid of Maecenas he deliberately cultivated and used writers such as Virgil, Horace, and Livy to present a favourable image of his person and to promote a return to the harmony of the old Republic. Naturally he feared the fate of his predecessors; a general policy of encouragement of the arts was accompanied by patronage of specific writers to promote his goals and safeguard his person. Maecenas became an archetypal and legendary figure; his name was a synonym for the literary patron. A similar deliberate cultivation of writers by patrons for their own ends occurred during the eighteenth century in England, in a different sociological setting. This is one reason why the literary world of the time was called the Augustan age; another reason is the similarity between the two compact, intimate, and flourishing cities, Rome and London. The writers of the second upheld the values promoted by Augustus in the first: order, balance, elegance, and retrenchment, the values of the so-called 'classical temper'.

The break up of the Roman Empire, with the ensuing barbaric invasions, disrupted these values. Cultural activity withdrew into the Christian monasteries: writers and scholars could here find a haven and patronage so long as they did not infringe Catholic susceptibilities. The west coast of Ireland was one such retreat. Ecclesiastical patronage of writers continued into the feudal age and beyond; it occurred when affluent ecclesiastical figures or groups valued the arts and scholarship for their own sake, when records needed to be produced and preserved, and when policies or doctrines had to be promoted. Latin was a language which superseded national boundaries and facilitated communication and unity in the Catholic world: it was the language which articulated the Catholic world view. Before the age of printing, ecclesiastical manuscripts in Latin were valued for their visual as well as their literary merit – they were embellished by illuminators and craftsmen. Their scarcity value and intrinsic aesthetic appeal meant that even after the invention of printing much literature continued to appear in manuscript form. This was limited in quantity and circulated only within Court and ecclesiastical élite groups. Vernacular literature was mostly oral folk poetry and tales for an illiterate audience. Much has been lost, although some has been retrieved by scholars.

During the twelfth and thirteenth centuries a movement of secular vernacular poets and writers developed, bridging the gap between Court and folk literature, combining the advantages of feudal literary patronage and contact with popular literary audiences. The troubadours and trouvères in France and Spain, and the Minnesingers in Germany wrote love lyrics conforming to the feudal tradition of courtly love and romances for a wider audience. The work of Chrétien de Troyes was a starting point for the Grail romances: he developed many of the Arthurian legends which appear to have originated in old Welsh bardic sources. Secular literature in praise of nature, drinking, lovemaking, and other 'natural' phenomena appeared, was transcribed, and was circulated alongside sacred works, old legends, and tales of heroic deeds. Some of these illustrate interesting changes in values. The *Roman de la Rose* (1240), for example, by Guillaume de Lorris, started as an allegorical romance on the art of love, and was finished forty years later by Jean de Meung with a refutation, in the rationalist vein of the thirteenth century, of the doctrine of courtly love. This stressed naturalism and a cynical view of the relations between the sexes; fragments exist of a translation by Chaucer. The famous vernacular *Chanson de Roland* of the twelfth century is a version of an earlier work written in Latin. Writers would often record and embellish existing myths and legends.

The spread of literature in vernacular English, French and German promoted specific national literature written for a popular audience. Some of this was by itinerant scholars, who wandered from one medieval university to another, but much was by Court or church writers sustained by affluent ecclesiastical or aristocratic patrons, or by the monarchy itself. In England, Chaucer and Gower are always cited as writers who benefited from a cross-fertilization between Court and people. Chaucer was the son of a vintner; he became a Court page and married a lady-in-waiting. After being captured as a member of Edward III's army in France he was ransomed, and thereafter had a regular Court position, his duties ranging from making the King's bed to entertaining the court with songs, poems, and romances. He came into contact with the works of Dante, Boccaccio, and Petrarch while on diplomatic missions to Italy; later he held Court positions of some responsibility, such as Controller of Customs in London and Clerk of the King's Works. Royal patronage brought him a life pension relatively early, together with various marks of the king's favour such as a daily pitcher of wine, enabling him to satisfy his 'wit to make books, songs, and ditties in rime', to give time to 'sitting at a book as dumb as a stone', living when he wished 'as a hermit, though unlike a hermit his abstinence was little'. Chaucer, then, is an example of one who benefited from regal patronage without losing contact with the social realities of his society or the freedom to portray them, warts and all.

It is impossible to assess the losses to literature which must have resulted from hazards blocking potential writers. Some could not obtain even a rudimentary education from monastery, grammar school, or private sources. Others were locked by feudal custom into arduous occupations, or conscripted into armies. Some died at an early age from diseases which are curable today. Others were imprisoned for sedition and prevented from writing, or merely failed to find patronage. As towns developed, and with them commerce and the guild system, writing skills became more generally in demand and a more varied patronage structure developed. The encouraging and constrictive factors affecting literary creativity are thus intimately associated with the growth and development of social institutions.

The princedoms and city-states of Renaissance Italy occupied a peculiar position in the development of patronage. Although factional rivalries, despotism, and inter-city conflict were common, a tradition of benevolent patronage emerged, which was emulated by European aristocracies and men of means. The early development in northern Italy of banking and commerce, under the Medici family and others, brought affluence which enabled the finest artists to be employed and protected by the ruling bourgeoisie. An outstanding example is Lorenzo the Magnificent, who was invited by the citizens of Florence to rule the city in 1469. He was himself deeply interested in the arts; he invited artists, musicians, scholars, and writers, who made Florence the cultural capital of Europe – at a time when England was embroiled in the Wars of the Roses, when France and Spain had hardly emerged as national states, and when Germany was split into three hundred principalities, some of them run by robber barons. The example of Florence became a legend that encouraged European rulers, and later the wealthy bourgeoisie, to become literate and to patronize the arts. Travellers and diplomats brought home news of Italian patronage; men of taste and letters were protected not merely as court or family entertainers; patrons themselves learned from them and fostered scholarship and taste. This encouraged widespread familiarity with the culture of ancient Greece and Rome, which in turn influenced the emerging humanism which challenged the dogmatism of the Roman Church. On the economic level, Italian institutions of banking and commerce facilitated the breakdown of feudalism and the rise of capitalism in countries ready to profit from interaction with them.*

In England, then, interaction with Renaissance Italy had

* The Name of Lombard Street in London is a reminder of this interaction.

many repercussions. In the field of literary patronage it reinforced the tradition of honouring scholars and men of genius which had been handed down from the days of Alfred, but which had lapsed during times of strife and foreign wars. The self-cultivation of the Tudor monarchs owes much to Italian example. Like Lorenzo the Magnificent, Henry VIII and Elizabeth wrote poetry and studied the arts; an additional role for the writer and musician – that of court mentor – was renewed. This was particularly important in England, where cultural sophistication lagged behind that of many parts of Europe. Special economic conditions obtained here which were conducive to the early development of capitalism; commercial activity hastened the transition to so-called bourgeois art, with 'expression taking the place of decoration as a prominent stylistic device*.' This promoted the extension of a patronage which was not circumscribed to a few potentates within the city-state boundary, as it was in Italy. Sustained, nurturing patronage, like the feudal concept of order and the Catholic hostility towards usury, was in conflict with a large-scale society moving from an agricultural economy with a rigidly closed social structure.† During the fourteenth and fifteenth centuries English patronage was confined mainly to the centralized monarch and his family, and to the greater ecclesiastical dignitaries: during the sixteenth century it spread to a circle of cultivated aristocrats and became less permanent, more commercialized.

By 1600 the clarity of what has been called the 'old patronage system', where protection and fealty were dominant in most areas, where most writers sought court appointments or lived permanently in an aristocratic home, was breaking down in England. Writers were looking to wider audiences than simply to the select aristocratic clique, with its private jokes and favoured stylistic devices. Some of the ramifications of the rigid class system were becoming fluid and unpredictable. This change affected the classes and groups from which writers themselves

---

* Phoebe Sheavyn, *The Literary Profession in the Elizabethan Age*, Manchester, Manchester University Press, 1967.
† E. H. Miller, *The Professional Writers in Elizabethan England. A Study of Nondramatic Literature*, Cambridge, Harvard University Press, 1959, p. 94.

were drawn, and was reflected in the work of major writers who were sensitive to social change. We have a foretaste of fragmented perspectives and individualism in the work of Shakespeare and John Donne. Anxiety connected with discontinuities and insecurity are expressed, together with a fear that the crumbling of the Catholic world view and the medieval belief in an ordered social hierarchy (corresponding to the angelic ranks about the deity) might 'cause the heavenly bodies to start madly from their spheres', with a final reversal to primeval chaos. Shakespeare expresses this fear:

> Take but degree away, untune that string
> And hark what discord follows. Each thing meets
> In mere oppugnancy: the bounded waters
> Should lift their bosoms higher than the shores
> And make a sop of all this solid globe:
> Strength should be lord of imbecility
> And the rude son should strike the father dead.*

The themes of madness and chaos are constantly present in the texts of Shakespeare: 'But I do love thee – and when I love thee not, Chaos is come again,' cries Othello. Timon of Athens, the deranged Lear, and Feste, the fool mock the 'corruption' of the age; Timon especially attacks its commercial prop, gold.

Likewise Donne:

> The sun is lost, and th'earth, and no man's wit
> Can well direct him where to look for it:
> And freely men confess that this world's spent,
> When in the planets and the firmament
> They seek so many new; they see that this
> Is crumbled out against his anatomies:
> T'is all in pieces, all coherence gone,
> All just supply and all relation . . .†

The style of life of an Elizabethan actor and dramatist and the fact that his audiences were more representative of total society – unlike those of the later Restoration drama – facilitated a comprehensive grasp of social pressures. Shakespeare remained in

* William Shakespeare, *Troilus and Cressida*. These themes intertwine, of course, with others. Shakespeare also presents heroes who epitomize optimism, vitality, and humour: Harry Hotspur, Falstaff, Trinculo, the Nurse in *Romeo and Juliet*.
† John Donne, *An Anatomy of the World*.

contact with all social levels, with both town and rural society.* While the patronage situation of the writer had become insecure by this time, certain advantages were available, especially to the dramatists who were not confined to the artificialities of the court.

By the time of Elizabeth, poets were demanding dedication fees: the usual price for the dedication of a drama was forty shillings, although at times the sums exchanged were as low as two shillings and sixpence. The cash nexus had entered the patronage situation, and literary works were assuming the aspect of commodities to be offered to the highest bidder. In this era of 'late patronage', continuous personal bonds had become loosened and barriers increased between writer and patron, the latter being offered extravagant eulogies as baits for sponsorship. This accelerated the turnover of patrons: Robert Green had sixteen patrons for seventeen books. Political insecurity, censorship, and the often unpredictable whims of the monarch increased the caution and uneasiness felt by patrons: a pool of unsponsored authors took refuge in the Elizabethan Grub Street.† Here fawning, starving, and feckless hacks were said to drink away their gains in the ale-house, a prey to political schemers.

Some notable patrons, of course, were evident: Philip Sidney, himself a poet, sponsored Spenser and many others. Together with his sister, Mary Herbert, he was renowned for discrimination and generosity. Others employed writers as tutors, secretaries, and private diplomats. Most of the non-amateur writers between 1520 and 1650 came from 'humble origins' and by the time of their death many had become courtiers and members of the top fifth of the social hierarchy.‡ Literature became a means of social mobility when aligned to favourable sponsorship; a deep gulf emerged – and has remained – between the successful and the unrecognized.

This close identification of the writer with his patron, which

---

* A further point here is that no barrier of language separated the social classes; popular idiom mingled with the language of the court. (See L. C. Knights, *Drama and Society in the Age of Jonson*, London, Peregrine Books, 1962, pp. 20–21.)

† An actual street in Shoreditch, later renamed Milton Street.

‡ J. W. Saunders, *The Profession of English Letters*, London, Routledge & Kegan Paul, 1964, p. 35.

was characteristic of 'old patronage', was becoming dislocated by 1600 and had deteriorated long before the eighteenth century, which is generally assumed to be the age of the decay of patronage.* As we have seen, this affected the social perspectives of writers, and the character of their texts. While the feudal poet had an established position in the great household, sharing the basic assumptions of his benefactors and often considering his vocation as writer secondary to fealty to his lord in peace and war, few Elizabethan writers remained in close association under the roof of their protectors. One cannot even trust dedications as evidence of patronage. Some were attached to works without the knowledge of the hoped-for benefactors; many euphemisms are ridiculous. An increasing number turned on the system with disgust, Spenser in *The Shepherd's Calendar* citing Maecenas as 'yclad in claye', and Nashe punning 'Maecenasses'.

Fragmentation of patronage in England was accelerated by the early development of the mercantile temper. This encouraged a demand for publications of 'utility' such as trade manuals; literary figures and their works were considered 'foppish' or 'fantastic' by many practical men. The character of the English class structure is another important factor. The fortunes of the English nobility fluctuated in the fourteenth and fifteenth centuries; new aristocratic power figures were continually being created: this created a climate of favour-seeking, and dislocated the continuity of affluent noblemen, destroying the contemplative leisure necessary for a discriminating patronage of the arts. Until the end of Elizabeth's reign the nobility sought preferment by concentration on official policies of political consolidation and peace; government pamphleteers were protected and sponsored rather than literary writers. Translators and producers of utilitarian booklets supporting the government's policies were particularly encouraged: in the 1560s a group of translators was given continuous patronage by the Privy Council; their obvious usefulness was enhanced by the unity of their social background.† Patrons and translators alike came from the 'gentry' class, sharing education at university and Inns of Court; many were linked by family ties and held similar humanistic beliefs and opinions. They were clearly considered 'safer' than

* E. H. Miller, op. cit., ch. 4.
† Such as Golding and Turberville (see E. H. Miller, op. cit., p. 103).

authors from a different social class – Spenser, for example, was the son of a journeyman clothmaker, Drayton of a tanner or butcher, Marlowe of a cobbler, Kyd of a scrivener, Webster of a merchant taylor, Green of a saddler, and Herrick of a goldsmith. Unlike these figures, the gentlemen translators mostly possessed a private income and did not need continuous pecuniary support; this was useful when their patrons were themselves suffering from the growing aggrandizement of the merchant class. Hence they were chosen in preference to the self-made intellectuals of greater creative ability; the latter usually reached the university (with the exception of Shakespeare, Jonson, and Drayton), but not the security of sustained patronage.

The situation of the Elizabethan writer was therefore complex. One myth to be dispelled has been called the 'Gloriana fallacy'. 'The reputation of Elizabeth as a patron of letters and learning has been derived, not from her deeds, but largely from legends based on the many adulatory dedications to her. No such reputation was probably more cheaply bought.'* A survey of English poetry in 1589 cites the 'scorn and ordinarie disgrace offered unto poets in these days'† and the neglect of literature by the Court. Other writers bear witness to the Queen's manipulating and dallying habits resulting from her own personal and monetary insecurity. Neale called her court and the nobility 'the illustrious order of Mendicants'.‡ But there was one area where she did perform a service to literature. She encouraged the drama, effectively thwarting magistrates who sought to close the theatres. This action safeguarded the position of the actor-author Shakespeare: 'if this central sun had been extinguished the whole galaxy (the minor lights of the Elizabethan drama) would have remained in comparative obscurity'.§ The Court's interest in the theatre, which permitted performances before varied audiences, was patronage of an indirect but vital type.

* B. B. Gamzue, 'Elizabeth and Literary Patronage', *Proceedings of the Modern Language Association*, New York, XLIX, 1934.
† George Puttenham, *The Art of English Poesie*, ed. G. D. Willcock and A. Walker, Cambridge, Cambridge University Press, 1936, ch. VIII, pp. 16–23.
‡ J. E. Neale, *Elizabeth I and Her Parliaments 1559–1581*, London, Jonathan Cape, 1953.
§ Leslie Stephen, *English Literature and Society in the 18th Century*, p. 9.

Drama as a genre had important advantages for a prospective writer without a private income or continuous patron. It was relatively immune from censorship, and an actor-author could increase his income (approximately £6 10s. a play) by buying shares in a company, thus sharing in the costs and profits. Although actors were notoriously poor and of low status, those who could collect the funds and become 'sheavers' could improve their position considerably. Shakespeare was probably given £1,000 by the Earl of Southampton to buy four shares at the Globe in Burbage's company, and two at Blackfriars; he could retire in relative comfort. Yet even in his case there was not complete freedom of expression; the deposition scene in Richard II was omitted in early performances and editions, and in Sonnet 66 he complains of 'art made tongue-tied by authority'.

The four main institutions of censorship were the Court of Star Chamber, the Court of High Commission, the Corporation of the City of London, and the Stationers' Company. These kept a close watch on all writing printed or circulated. Printing was limited mainly to London, and authors and bookseller-publishers ran formidable risks if they disseminated opinions considered to be prejudicial to official political and religious policy.* The unprotected writer's position was precarious. Pirating was rife; severe penalties awaited the producers of treasonable or blasphemous literature. Kyd was tortured for an unorthodox paper found on him and attributed to Marlowe; a fellow undergraduate of the latter was burned to death for his opinions. On Raleigh's advice, Spenser laid *The Faery Queen* before Elizabeth; his subject, a legend of the age of King Arthur, was chosen as 'furthest from the danger of envy and suspicion of the present time . . . for avoiding of jealous opinions and misconstructions'. The moral censors have been accused of discrediting the whole profession of literature, of making writing suspect, destroying liberty and creating a climate of spying and provocation; despite this a literature of outstanding vitality and sensitivity developed.† Notwithstanding contempt and hostility,

* For further information on censorship, see Richard Findlater, *Theatrical Censorship in Britain*, London, Panther, 1967, and Donald Thomas, *A Long Time Burning* (A History of Literary Censorship in England), London, Routledge & Kegan Paul, 1969.
† Phoebe Sheavyn, op. cit.

writers emerged from all classes, offering works characteristic of the age: at times sordid and brutal but containing a critical questioning of values, a gusto, a lyrical power of remarkable quality. Adverse patronage conditions, in an age of economic and social expansion, cannot repress curiosity and a reassessment of values conducive to literary creativity. In England a flourishing drama, together with some educational opportunity, encouraged writers to develop in a climate of change and growth. Society was still sufficiently cohesive for them to achieve a totality in their work by expressing the hopes, fears, and world views of the various social classes and groups with whom they were in touch.

2

The Civil Wars brought a serious dislocation to aristocratic patronage. Milton (called by some the first professional writer) and other puritan authors survived. The Restoration brought an initial return but at the end of the century we find professional writers such as Johnson dispensing with private patronage and turning to widening reading publics mediated by a developing market situation. This included innovatory schemes, such as subscription publishing, for selling books. Lending libraries were developing and a new journalism helped out the freelance writer. The Copyright Law of 1710 enabled authors to own bargainable property, suppressing piracy. The eighteenth century represented a fundamental shift in sponsorship for authors, in the direction of publishers catering for a growing reading public.*

Between 1688 and 1721 a peculiar type of patronage, which placed writers in a favourable position, became prevalent. Ministers of State, in particular Harley and Bolingbroke for the Tories, Dorset and Montague for the Whigs, paid authors well to write polemics, to celebrate or denigrate suitable events and personages. The House of Commons was now a powerful institution, with Ministers in a dominating position employing authors and rewarding them with regular salaries and pensions,

* A. S. Collins, *Authorship in the Days of Johnson Being a Study of the Relation between Author, Patron, Publisher and Public, 1726–1780* London, R. Holden and Co., 1927, ch. 4.

lucrative posts, and protection. Writers were given a new role and could command a price; Halifax saw the 'Trimmer' as performing a useful social function 'to preserve a Mean between Barbarous extremes . . . directed to Principles in reference to the public . . . [who] will neither be Bawled, Threatened, Laught or Drunk out of them'.* The writer's position, it was alleged, had returned to that prevalent in Augustan Rome; he was seen as 'one who keeps even the ship of state', rather than trimming between opposing parties according to his own interests.

Time-serving and impoverished hacks continued to exist, but some writers followed their own interests with integrity. With the development of the party system conflict on certain issues and interests varied. The interests of the Court Party and the Country Party often cut across the Whig and Tory dichotomy: Whigs and Tories were in both groups. The Crown and its ministers tried to enlist support by sharing administration over roughly a hundred M.P.s who formed the Court Party. The landed gentry, the Country Party, were not necessarily in opposition to the Court Party, but they would oppose certain policies, particularly taxation on their estates.† Their political allegiances might vary: the Jacobite Tory Squire Western vows he'd be 'anything than a courtier, and a presbyterian and a Hanoverian too', while Tom Jones swears that 'the cause of King George is the cause of liberty and true religion'. Both would be for the Country Party's interests. Fielding himself had the attitudes of 'a good old-fashioned Whig, with an intense aversion to papists and foreigners, and a slightly superstitious veneration for trial by jury and Habeas Corpus'.‡ The religious spectrum further complicated matters. Swift switched from writing for the Whigs to the Tories, on account of the Whigs' alliance with dissent; Defoe's support of the Dissenters, Dryden's and Pope's of the Catholics, affected their political considerations.

There was, therefore, a whole complex of bargaining arrangements; writers' choice of patrons varied more with interest or judgement than with party alignments. A pamphleteer like

* George Savile, Marquis of Halifax, *The Character of a Trimmer*, London, James Duncan, 1833.
† A. R. Humphries, *The Augustan World*, London, Methuen University Paperbacks, 1961, p. 104.
‡ Leslie Stephen, quoted in A. R. Humphries, op. cit., p. 112.

Defoe was not necessarily corrupt or inconsistent in writing first for one side and then another; political patrons turned to writers for particular issues, finding skilled satire and lampoonery useful. In a society still relatively small – London only numbered 500,000 inhabitants in 1700 – private jokes and skits were easily decoded by the intimate reading and theatre public. But unscrupulous or needy writers would write for the highest bidder.

After the Restoration of the monarchy in 1688, two theatres reopened; these flourished, catering for a small court audience, until the Licensing Act was passed following a controversy over the unbridled character of Restoration drama. Unlike the Elizabethan theatre the audiences were not representative: their public, insufficient to fill both theatres together, consisted of courtiers and their satellites, noblemen, fops, beaux, wits and would-be wits, courtesans, and masked prostitutes. The Theatre Royal was ultra-monarchist while the Duke's Theatre tended more to Protestant sympathies, patronized by the Duke of York; for both the King's approval was essential, the theatre being the toy of the Court. Dramatists reacted from puritanism and turned instead to contemporary Spanish drama and to Roman and French classics. Elegance of dialogue embraced personal satire in the 'comedy of manners'; private court jokes were expressed in bawdy and colourful settings. In the midst of these productions the audience talked, quarrelled, drank, and groomed themselves. As the eighteenth century progressed this intimacy was dispersed; more theatres were opened for middle-class audiences. Unbridled burlesques gave way to masques, opera, domestic and sentimental drama. Heavy censorship was introduced after 1737.

A further opening for writers, alleviating the need for sustained patronage, was the development of journalism: newspapers, magazines, and reviews were published and circulated among the clientele of the growing number of coffee-houses and clubs, and to private families in town and country. The *Tatler* and the *Spectator* were produced as often as three times a week; these were read aloud in the coffee-houses, of which there were over 3,000 in London in 1708. The exclusive preserves of men (unlike the French *salons*), they were centres of gossip and news. Here writers met with political patrons, or read their work to admirers. Journalism developed within their orbit, providing a new type of sponsorship for authors.

Political satire needs a measure of freedom, adequate sponsorship, the background of large cities, and some sophistication in an audience which is closely-knit enough to understand the disguised shafts and nuances. Dryden's *Absalom and Achitophel* supported the government and attacked Shaftesbury and Monmouth in allegorical language understood by its readers. This style was far more effective than a direct panegyric of Charles II, whose private life was only too well known both to friend and enemy. Divine right of kings was no longer assumed; political change had become accepted; there was much floating discontent and some freedom of speech; the reading public was widening; and intense political rivalry existed between the political parties. All the conditions essential to political satire were present, and a large volume of such literature resulted, directly involved with public affairs and ranging from heroic narratives to scurrilous broadsheet ballads.* After Queen Anne's death in 1714,† and with the election of Addison in 1721, political patronage of writers declined; the new Prime Minister refused to use this weapon. Writers were turning to a new type of literature which was in demand by the rising middle-classes, many of whom were dissenters. Leisured women were an important ingredient of this new market: they favoured novels rather than political satire.‡ Augustan satire was increasingly supplemented by domestic literature; however, a brief revival of political satire took place in the 1760s and 1770s with Wilkes's periodical, the *North Briton*, and with Hogarth's caricatures. Hogarth was the friend of Fielding and the character of their social comment is closely connected. There is no doubt that the rise in social status of writers up to 1721 was connected with their value to politicians, which brought their affluence; thereafter some deflation was felt, particularly at the end of the century.

The situation in 1730 was described in Fielding's play *The*

---

* Mathew Hodgart, *op. cit.*, ch. 5, Forms of Satire.
† George II could neither speak nor read English.
‡ Alexandre Beljame, *Men of Letters and the English Public in the Eighteenth Century, 1660–1774*, ed. with an introduction by Bonamy Dobrée, London, Kegan Paul, 1948, Introduction, pp. xviii–xix.

Author's Farce. A poet joining a bookseller in Hell is asked, 'What news bring you from the other world?' The poet replies, 'Why, author's affairs go much in the same road there as when you were alive, Authors starve and Booksellers grow fat, Grub Street harbours as many pirates as ever Algiers did – they have more theatres than are at Paris, and just as much wit as there is at Amsterdam, they have ransacked all Italy for singers, and all France for Dancers.' Bookseller: 'I find things go swimmingly.' The new sponsor is now seen as the greedy bookseller; there is no mention of other patronage; the change in the drama and the rivalry of Grub Street are all noted.* The renewed economic uncertainty worsened the position of the minor writers until a more steady market situation developed. This enabled some writers to achieve professional status without private patronage.

The depressed situation of the hack writers – who had proliferated during the fruitful years of political patronage – made successful writers ashamed of their calling. Byron described them, 'with pens peeping from behind the ear, and thumbs a little inky'; writers as late as Byron and Scott insisted on considering themselves as gentlemen rather than authors, although it was the success of the latter which did much to re-establish the literary image. Dr Johnson was an important innovator in this process: after experiencing the vicissitudes of the literary struggle eked out by journalism, he sought patronage from Lord Chesterfield for his *Dictionary*. He addressed the plan of the work to him but did not receive the hoped-for monetary aid. After its publication in 1755 Chesterfield wrote two favourable reviews in the *World*: thereupon Johnson wrote 'the famous letter' in which he castigated the institution of late patronage:

Seven years, My Lord, have now passed since I waited in your outward room or was repulsed from your door, during which time I have been pushing my work, through difficulties of which it is useless to complain, and have brought it at last to the verge of publication without one act of assistance, one word of encouragement, or one smile of favour. Such treatment I did not expect for I never had a patron before ... Is not a patron, My Lord, one who looks with unconcern on a man struggling for life in the waters and when he has reached the ground encumbers him with help ... The regard now shewn me by

* Pope's *Dunciad* (1728) and *New Dunciad* (1742) are further attacks on the book market.

your Lordship, had it been early had been kind. But now it has been delayed till I am indifferent and cannot enjoy it, till I am solitary and cannot impart it, till I am known and do not want it . . . Having carried thus my work so far with so little help from any favourer of learning I shall not be surprised though I should conclude it, if less be possible, with less: for I have been long awakened from that dream of hope in which I once subscribed myself with so much exaltation. My Lord, Your Lordship's most humble servant, Samuel Johnson.*

This letter nicely represents the growing disillusion with private literary patronage. It was now possible for a writer to manage without seeking favours from the higher echelons of society, to negotiate directly with publishers who catered for a widening middle-class audience.† Literary works were becoming commodities to be sold on an open market, affected by demand and cost curves, as were other commodities in the capitalist world. The publisher emerged as the dominant risk-taker in this transaction and the writer's role as salesman took on a new character. The rise of the novel with its extended appeal is an important factor in this change.‡

* See also Johnson's 'On the mischiefs of following a patron', *The Rambler*, No. 163.
† Interim schemes such as subscription publishing were introduced. Johnson published *Lives of Poets* by this method.
‡ Muted forms of patronage continued together with the widening of the market. Johnson himself received a pension from Lord Bute of £300 a year in 1762.

6 The Professionalization of the Writer

I

The relationship of patronage was one of the set of crucial social
factors which affected the complex situation of the writer and
the character of his work: its genre, scope, content, and at times
its subtleties and ambiguities. The permutations of these factors
varied with the type and differential impact of this relationship.
In a society where there was a concentration of wealth and of
interest in the arts in a single figure or aristocratic class, where
there was no sizeable literate middle class and no alternate
system of distribution, sustained personal patronage was necessary.* As wealth and education became more dispersed, as the
middle class developed to serve extending commerce and industry, alternative institutions for sponsoring and distributing
literature grew up, increasingly free from censorship and insecurity. The theatre was an early alternative to personal patronage, although frequently depending itself on some figure of
affluence for protection; journalism was another alternative, and
direct negotiation with a publisher the final outlet. The eighteenth century was an age of expanding population, a swelling
new middle class, and growth in printing and publishing. These
changes altered the groups to which authors looked as sources of
social norms and arbiters of taste,† and shifted the sources of
remuneration. Circulating libraries emerged to mediate the demands of the growing reading audience; improvements in
transport and communications enabled a network of these to
penetrate remote rural areas and to reach industrial towns
beyond London.

* R. Escarpit, *Sociologie de La Littérature*, Paris, 1958.
† Their 'reference groups'.

The writer was consequently able to develop a more prestigious self-image and to dispense with subservience to the idiosyncrasies or policies of an aristocratic patron – yet he still had to consider the tastes of a power figure in the person of his publisher or the owner of the circulating library, and he also looked to a wider audience whose demands and conventions might determine the sales of his work. Increasingly there was a choice of publishers to whom he could apply, and a variety of reading publics as specialisms in literature proliferated. Moreover, the range of alternate and alternative occupations which the writer could pursue to supplement his income was widening. Patronage in the form of personal spokesmanship still remained, and continues today in a supplementary form, but its essence had changed.

There were, therefore, pressures towards independence, but also to relative isolation: the writer became more autonomous but more alone: no longer was he integrated into an aristocratic family or given an indispensable role in a closely-knit social group. This position fluctuated: the short periods of political patronage reversed the process; and the relatively compact middle-class world of the novel and domestic journalism kept him in touch to some extent with his readers. The forces promoting his insecurity increased at the end of the nineteenth century, when the circulating libraries lost their hold, when cheap one-volume novels flooded the market, and when average literary remuneration declined. The writer was, then, more unprotected and open to the dictates of a competitive market while his public had widened and expanded to the extent of fragmentation. We see some of these changes reflected in the texts: in the twentieth century we find the personalized, subjective novel written in the 'stream of consciousness' style, concentrating on psychological depth, on microscopic areas of experience at the expense of 'totality'.

The nineteenth century was a favourable era for the author: particularly for the novel writer.* Some aimed their work directly at the popular reading public, their ambition being to write a best or better seller. Others employed more internalized

* Conrad Tanzy, unpublished Ph.D. thesis, *Publishing the Victorian Novel: A Study of the Economic Relationships of Novelists and Publishers in England, 1830–80,* Ohio State University.

standards and scorned the salesman's role. Both types benefited from increasing professional status, improved rates of remuneration, and from the efforts of specific figures such as Walter Besant who founded the Society of Authors in 1888. It was possible for the image of the writer to be reconciled with the Victorian ethos of self-help, 'respectability', and pecuniary stability. The writer could become upper middle-class by his efforts, and upper middle-class writers need no longer be ashamed of their calling. The hack writer 'ready for a guinea to write satires, epigrams, anything for or against either side or anybody', gave way to the self-made, self-respecting craftsman rising via journalism to regular lucrative activity.* Not all, however, subscribed to an establishment ideology. An interesting sub-group with atypical social origins – Scots, Irish, Jews, nonconformists, working-class writers – existed, frequently critical of conformism to a conventional middle-class professional image.† Withdrawal from societal norms characterized an increasing number of artists, from William Blake to Katherine Mansfield. These artists tended to feelings of isolation and subjectivity; their texts are inward-turning and not geared to maximum popular sales. Their reference groups are a select coterie or certain private canons of taste.

The last half of the eighteenth century saw important changes which accelerated during the next hundred and fifty years. The demand situation was revolutionized: reading figures soared as more literate consumers of books came into being.‡ At the same time technical improvements and innovations in the production and distribution of books were developing, with the publisher distinct from the bookseller and the printer, and emerging as the dominant middleman who negotiated with the writer to satisfy the tastes of the new public.§ Until the 1880s the lending libraries – Mr Mudie's in particular – employed the writer on contract to produce three-decker novels to be rented to families

* Walter Besant, *The Pen and the Book* (advice to authors), London, Thomas Burleigh, 1899, Introduction, 'The Life of Letters'.
† Raymond Williams, *The Long Revolution*, p. 240. These writers from 'new social groups' were responsible for much of the 'most original social thinking' during the nineteenth century, according to Williams.
‡ Q. Leavis, *Fiction and the Reading Public*, London, Chatto & Windus, 1932.
§ S. H. Steinberg, *Five Hundred Years of Printing*, London, Penguin Books, 1961, pp. 214–30.

with leisure on their hands. Book production became a capitalist business, as did many other specialisms, with a consequent decline of traditionalistic and personalized procedures. However, an element of the personal relationship of patronage remained in the at times fruitful and sustained contact between the writer and the better publisher. In the peak period of the 1880s vast fortunes could be earned by novel-writing. Dickens's estate was valued at £93,000 after his death; Anthony Trollope's mother educated a family on the proceeds of her novels.

2

The rise of the novel was one of the most spectacular events in the history of literary genres. It began in the early years of the eighteenth century with the writings of Daniel Defoe, Samuel Richardson, and Henry Fielding. These writers no longer looked to the aristocratic echelons of society for sponsorship and readership; in a society of developing capitalism and a new middle class, they wrote for the families of the new commercial magnates as well as for those of gentry and farmers. They either negotiated directly with publishers or used the subscription system: collecting sums of money from friends or friendly booksellers who were in touch with the public taste.

Tales and dramas of adventure and romance had always been popular with the public at large, as were religious allegories in story form. *Everyman*, a fifteenth-century morality play of Dutch origin, was performed in various versions in many countries; John Bunyan's *Pilgrim's Progress* was a European best seller. The first edition of the latter, 1678, numbered 2,000 copies; by the time of Bunyan's death in 1688, ten editions by the original publisher, each numbering 4,000 copies, had been struck; while in the absence of copyright legislation many other pirated versions were in existence. This is an astonishing demand for a religious dream allegory by a Puritan tinker, written for an non-aristocratic audience without aristocratic patronage; it is rivalled only by the Bible. In Europe a secular literature was also spreading: in Spain Cervantes wrote *Don Quixote* in the picaresque tradition as a burlesque of the old romances of chivalry. His story developed into a critique of the values of contemporary society, with the character of the hero deepening and intensifying. It was translated into English as early as 1712; pirated versions had a wide circulation and impact. Other less serious romances from Italy, France, and Spain were also distributed; an example is *Gil Blas*, another series of adventures of a rogue-hero in the picaresque style.

There was an increasing demand for non-religious entertainment and for allegories of quest and excitement containing some assessment of current norms and values, familiarizing readers with unknown layers of society and types of character. But book prices remained high, there was no adequate copyright protection, and censorship was punitive. In mid seventeenth-century England the book-buying public numbered only tens of thousands; small indeed when we consider the swelling sales of the nineteenth century. Less than one in twenty read a newspaper.*
By 1801 the population was 10½ million, multiplying itself three and a half times by 1901 to become 37 million. The average annual publication of new books, excluding pamphlets, grew nearly fourfold between 1666 and 1802. From 1666 to 1756 it averaged less than 100 a year; from 1792 to 1802, it averaged 372. Illiteracy and semi-illiteracy, caused by inadequacies of education, poverty, lack of leisure, and the high price of books, delayed the growth in demand until the second half of the eighteenth century. The surveys of both Gregory King (1696) and Defoe (1702) indicate that the majority of the population were living in extreme poverty, unable to afford schooling, newspapers, and books. The original price of *Robinson Crusoe* (1719) was 5s. a copy; working-class income averaged between £6 and £20 a year, that of the roughly 2 million small freeholders and farmers, shopkeepers, tradesmen, and artisans was £38 to £60 a year. Consequently the price of novels, even when sold by the sheet, was beyond the means of the bulk of the population. *Tom Jones* cost more than a labourer's weekly wage: this contrasts sharply with the price of a ticket for the Globe theatre in the time of Shakespeare, which was one penny, the cost of a quart of ale.

An undergrowth of literature existed for the poor and semi-educated; this encouraged reading skills. From feudal times

* Marjorie Plant, *The English Book Trade, An Economic History of the Making and Sale of Books*, London, Allen & Unwin, 1939, ch. 12.

pedlars and travelling chapmen had dispersed a scattering of cheap pamphlets, receipt books, practical manuals, accounts of murders, ballad sheets, pirated romances, and religious or political polemics, either openly or secretly for a few pence to villagers and homesteads. As towns and markets developed these were available on stalls or in shops. By 1744 bookshops were increasing: in that year John Newberry opened a shop in St Paul's Churchyard, stocking only children's books: reading instructors, tales of entertainment, and homilies. A demand for specialist literature was fostered by puritanism and commerce; particularly among the lower middle classes and 'earnest artisans'. Books of information about science and travel, together with scurrilous broadsheets and Mademoiselle de Scudéry's translations of French romances, were embellished by new techniques of illustration, such as woodcuts.

The development of the newspapers was another incentive to literacy. Periodical pamphlets or 'Corantos' ('currents of news') first appeared in the seventeenth century. These were followed by newsbooks and newsletters sent periodically to subscribers. Gazettes, magazines, and newspapers increased in number after 1695 when Parliament declined to renew the 1662 Licensing Act which limited the master printers to twenty. Thrice-weekly mail posts made the establishment of some daily and provincial newspapers and periodicals possible between 1695 and 1730. But government fears of sedition were expressed by the oppressive Stamp Duty, the advertisement tax, and paper duties, which kept up prices and restricted circulation. To overcome expense, readers were employed in coffee-houses: for a penny, foreign or domestic news, romances, novels, and satiric poems could be relayed. Hence book and newspaper sales give but little indication of the size of readership at this time.

The rise of capitalism produced a structural shift in society. Division of labour increased and the 'new' middle classes emerged alongside the 'old' occupations of the Church, the Army, and the Law. Entrepreneurs, merchants, and shop-keepers increased in number, and new professions were born: doctors, dentists, accountants, specialized businessmen, book-keepers, clerks, master builders, engineers, factory managers; many were nonconformist in religion and outlook. Individualistic, frugal, careful, and ambitious, gaining affluence by their own efforts, they set up homes in which wives, daughters, and servants had leisure on their hands in a world where leisure pursuits were circumscribed. Here was a potential audience for the new novel: increasingly interested in the changing social world around them and curious about travel, crime, and even sex.

This new reading public responded instantly to the publication of *Robinson Crusoe*. Defoe was a merchant and a dissenter;* all his heroes pursue money, which he calls the 'general denominating principle in the world'. At this date (1719) there is no stress on romantic love; sex is subordinate to business. Self-help and industry are the chief concerns of the hero who has been called an embodiment of economic individualism.† Even God is depersonalized, becoming 'Providence' which brings blessings or retribution according to deserts. Marx noted the secondary quality of Crusoe's devotions: 'Of his prayers we take no account, since they are a source of pleasure to him, and he looks on them as so much recreation.‡ The novel portrays an isolation reminiscent of the self-reliant new middle-class entrepreneur in an increasingly secular and individualistic world of pecuniary struggle and manipulation.

Other novels followed, satisfying the public in other dimensions: notably domestic settings and adventures connected with worldly life and sexuality. *Moll Flanders* (1722) combines the contemporary interest in criminality with that of self-seeking and monetary aggrandizement – themes which would have been considered vulgar by an aristocratic audience. Swift had suggested to John Gay that 'a Newgate pastoral might make an odd, pretty sort of thing',§ and Defoe extended this theme. Moll, a thief and a prostitute, finally marries her seducer, a former highwayman, pooling their spoils. She spends her declining years in penitence and prosperity; thus squaring the puritan conscience, although in this case vice appears to escape its deserts. A reflection here of the developing capitalist values of self-help and strategic manipulation is evident.

Richardson, son of a joiner, himself a scantily educated

* He started work as a hosiery merchant.
† Ian Watt, *The Rise of the Novel*, ch. 3.
‡ Cited by Ian Watt, ibid., p. 84.
§ Gay responded with *The Beggar's Opera*.

printer, came on the literary scene almost by accident, tapping another vital interest of this new reading public, the position of women as regards the marriage market. Asked by two other printers to prepare a 'little volume of letters in the common style on such subjects as might be of use to country readers who are unable to indite for themselves', he had produced four volumes of *Pamela* by 1743. Aimed at the new semiliterate public of servant girls and apprentices, it also attracted the families of rising businessmen, merchants, and farmers seeking gentility and entertainment. Pamela, a young serving girl whose mistress has just died, is pursued by the son of the house. She shows considerable ingenuity in avoiding seduction, finally manipulat-a marriage with him. Later she suffers with dignity the fate of a profligate husband. Fielding lampooned this novel in *Joseph Andrews*; although the obvious butt of readers from the gentry, it had considerable influence. Vividly portraying the difficulties of an unmarried girl of poor background in a changing society, its popularity among women readers is not surprising. More-over, Richardson stood for moral reform: the book is a critique of the standards of the previous Restoration age and of the still existing rakish squirearchy. But Pamela's foresight was named hypocrisy and scheming by the 'anti-Pamelaists'; and Richard-son was criticized for his frank treatment of sex in an age becoming progressively squeamish as the influence of non-conformist Christianity became more pervasive.

The epistolary novel provided an intimate, 'key-hole' per-spective in contrast to the formalities of some Augustan prose: the technique was repeated in *Clarissa Harlowe*, and by Smol-lett in *Humphrey Clinker*. Colloquial language which was familiar to its readers could be used; even Diderot describes his surprising empathy with Richardson's characters. Dr Johnson considered *Clarissa Harlowe* 'the first book in the world for the knowledge it displays of the human heart',[*] and Rousseau wrote, 'no one, in any language, has ever written a book that equals or even approaches Clarissa'. Richardson's readership extended beyond his own class; his work had considerable social and literary repercussions.

The first circulating library was established in London in

[*] Johnson also called Richardson 'the greatest genius that had shed its lustre on the path of literature'.

1740. For a subscription of half a guinea to a guinea a year, books could be borrowed at the rate of a penny a volume, threepence for the usual three-volume novel. The success of this scheme was an incentive to novelists. Families could share out the volumes or read them aloud in the household. Literary prudery was insisted on by publishers with this market in view. The necessity of spinning out the novel to three volumes contributed to the leisurely pace of early novels; 'padding' is noticeable in the inferior works that were circulated alongside those of acknowledged masters – these became increasingly common as the nineteenth century progressed. The 'Queens of the Circulating Libraries'* grew affluent on the proceeds of what George Eliot called 'Silly novels by Lady Novelists'.† But a feature of the times was the popularity of good writers, of Jane Austen, George Eliot, Scott, Dickens, and Thackeray, who had a wide readership and were responsive to its interests. Their concern for the tastes of their public did not as yet necessarily result in a lowering of quality.

Religious works were still the largest category of books published in the eighteenth century. But the ratio of religious publications per head was falling, although they were still dominant in 1851.‡ Novels gained a numerical dominance of the market at the end of the nineteenth century. A taste for them was fostered by the family magazines – the *Tatler* (1709) and the *Spectator* (1711), which appeared thrice weekly and daily respectively. These catered for the middle-class domestic audience who were potential novel readers. Articles, stories, skits, and poems were provided: the series based on the activities of Sir Roger de Coverley is similar to the anecdotal novel of character, appearing in parts, which was developing at the time. Other literary journals included the *Rambler* (1749–52), mostly written by Johnson himself. Johnson's *Rasselas* (1759) was a didactic allegorical romance written in a week to pay for his mother's funeral: it achieved considerable success.

* Alan Walbank, *Queens of the Circulating Libraries:* selections from Victorian Lady Novelists 1800–1900, London, Evans, 1950.
† George Eliot, 'Silly Novels by Lady Novelists', *Westminster Review*, London, 1856.
‡ R. D. Altick, 'The Sociology of Authorship', *New York Public Library Bulletin*, 1962; D. F. Laurenson, 'A Sociological Study of Authorship', *British Journal of Sociology*, September 1969.

In contra-distinction to this tendency to offer entertaining leisure reading for increasingly commercial and worldly tastes, providing realistic detail, characters, and plot, there was also a movement away from reality, stemming from the Romantic movement and shewing a revulsion for the values of capitalism such as self-help, thrift, 'common sense', pecuniary profit-making. This expressed itself in the vogue for 'Gothic' novels in the 1790s. We have forewarnings in the lengthy dwelling on death and funerality in *Clarissa Harlowe*. Horace Walpole's *Castle of Otranto* (1764), the novels of Mrs Radcliffe, and Mary Shelley's *Frankenstein* (1818) catered for this taste, which was shared both by the aristocracy and serving girls. This was a literature of escape: for those bored with drudgery as well as those fearful of encroachment by the new commerce. Romanticism had repercussions in both conservative and radical ideologies; the romantic writers such as Byron and Shelley developed a self-image of a fighter for popular freedom against clogging conventionality and established authority; others tended to heroic élitism with anti-popular connotations. Later, Romanticism came to be connected with a tendency to extremism, the image of a search or journey, and with a struggle to achieve personal or national identity. These themes had an influence on both realist and escapist novels, the latter being media in which repressed elements could find expression, elements denied in the new society.

Important influences in the new novels of the eighteenth and nineteenth centuries were, therefore, tendencies both to realism and to romantic escapism, reflecting economic and commercial changes in society. Often these are intertwined in the same novel: in Stendhal's *Le Rouge et le noir*, and Goethe's *Wilhelm Meister*, for example. Extreme escapist novels were often ludicrous and were satirized by Jane Austen in *Northanger Abbey*. The works of the poets Shelley, Keats, and the early Wordsworth was of a different order, stressing imagination in an increasingly mercantile world. Elements of romanticism are strong in the novels of Scott, Dickens, Charlotte and Emily Brontë, Disraeli; they intensify in George Eliot's *Daniel Deronda*, and appear, debased, in the 'silver-fork' novels of 'high life' in the nineteenth century, by such writers as Bulwer Lytton. Romanticism is also a strong element of the writings of the aesthetes:

Oscar Wilde, Swinburne, and others. There are obvious links between these manifold tendencies and the changing character of society; revulsion against capitalism led to literary flights into fantasy, irrationality, or imagination.

A greater volume of reading material was accompanied, then, by a diversification of subject matter; but increasingly the nineteenth century became the era of the novel, the majority of novelists being women. Research shows that of all writers, the female ratio varied from about a fifth to a quarter between 1800 and 1935. Writing was a congenial occupation for women circumscribed by domesticity or by the absence of other opportunities. The fact that – unlike men – women did not have much formal education until the turn of the century indicates that feminine qualifications for authorship are complex. Domestic help, the absence of other outlets, and the growing prospect of gratifying monetary reward are obvious motives. In addition there appears to have been a peculiar combination of precipitating factors such as Protestantism, constricted and emotionally cool upbringing. Women were able to use their own subjective domestic situation as raw material, turning their constrictions to advantage. In the present century more women took alternative jobs in teaching and journalism. But writing remains a favourite occupation: support by a husband taking the place of the small private income stressed by Virginia Woolf as an essential prerequisite.* The dominant numerical position of women in the reading population as a whole contributed to the popularity of the novel during the nineteenth century. A stream of novels – some on a high level, others of interest now only to the social historian – were written, published, and read in the era before other leisure activities became available and popular.

The extension of the middle class was accompanied by some improvements in education. This increased the total number of literate people in the lower middle and upper working classes. Notwithstanding the delays here resulting from religious dissension, there was a gradual trend to increased reading, influenced by free library provision and cheaper newspapers. John Wesley's dictum, 'reading Christians will be knowing Christians', was taken seriously by his followers and even the Tories realized the necessity to 'educate our masters'. State education was

* Virginia Woolf, *A Room of One's Own*, London, Hogarth Press, 1913.

slowly introduced: Anglican and nonconformist schools supplemented the Grammar schools and private schools. As writing became increasingly a profession, more male authors were drawn from the 'public'-school sector (which itself was growing).* Statistics of literacy are suspect because of inadequate criteria; information such as that 69 per cent of males and 55 per cent of females were literate in the 1851 Census tell us little about the quality of reading ability.† It is reasonable to suppose that the majority could read by the 1870s despite the poor quality of education which was neither universal nor free until that decade. The expansion of higher education is also reflected in authors' educational history; it contributed also to increased demand for certain types of reading matter. Writing skills over the population as a whole were improved by the introduction of the penny post in 1840, together with better communication and postal services.

3

Demand for and supply of books were therefore in a state of constant interstimulation throughout the century. But the book trade has always been cautious and technical improvements were introduced slowly. Caution had been necessary because of censorship and dangers of penalties for bookseller-publishers, printers, and writers. Defoe, for example, had been pilloried and his ears slit for his satirical pamphlet *The Shortest Way with Dissenters*. The monopoly by the Stationers' Company and the virtual limitation of printing to London, Oxford, and Cambridge, with twelve 'licensers' to censor books produced, had delayed developments. Cromwell had heavily censored new books and newsletters – well after Milton had produced his famous plea for freedom, the *Areopagitica*. The Restoration Licensing Act lasted until 1694: it was chiefly concerned with

* D. F. Laurenson, op. cit.
† R. K. Webb, *The Victorian Reading Public*, Pelican Guide to English Literature, ed. Boris Ford, vol. 6, *From Dickens to Hardy*, London, Penguin Books, 1960. See also R. K. Webb, *The British Working Class Reader 1790–1848*: literary and social tension, London, Allen & Unwin, 1955; R. D. Altick, *The English Common Reader, A social history of the Mass Reading Public 1880–1900*, Cambridge; Cambridge University Press, 1957; and Raymond Williams, op. cit.

religious sedition and blasphemy, but it also controlled the book trade. Parliament refused to renew it, following the objections of John Locke, yet the government continued to prosecute under common law, using informers. As late as 1713 a man was hanged for asserting in a pamphlet that James III was the rightful king. Journals such as the *Freeholders Journal* and the *True Briton* were suppressed by seizure of papers and type and arrest of printers.

Wilkes in 1766 challenged this practice, obtaining a favourable verdict; he also attacked the directing of juries by judges, which was finally abolished by Fox's Libel Act of 1792. Another impeding law was the Stamp Act of 1712, which forced up the price of newspapers; some working-class papers, such as the *Black Dwarf*, circulated clandestinely to avoid this. In general, interference with the press began to diminish over the eighteenth century; although in 1791 Thomas Paine had to escape to America to avoid prosecution for his *The Rights of Man*, and in 1810 Cobbett received a sentence of two years' imprisonment and a fine of £1,000 for denouncing army flogging. The Copyright Act (1709) gave authors property rights over their products; subsequent acts reinforced this, International Copyright being achieved by the Berne Convention in 1885. In this year the Stamp Duty also ended. Censorship of 'immoral' literature continued: libraries would take no book which infringed a strict code. An unexpurgated British edition of Zola's *Germinal* would have been unthinkable. Standards gradually relaxed over the present century, and books became increasingly similar to other commodities bought and sold in a competitive market.

Innovation in the book trade could not be delayed indefinitely. Refinements in printing type, binding, and paper were introduced with paper-covered binding boards instead of the flimsy paper covers which needed replacing by the private binding of the buyer. In 1814 the first newspaper was produced by steam; in the 1860s the web press was introduced, printing on a continuous roll of paper. In the 1870s practical type-setting machines appeared; at the same time more paper was produced, new processes such as chemical pulp processes overcoming the rag shortage. By 1900 domestic paper production had risen to over 650,000 tons, from 11,000 tons in 1800. Prices dropped from 1s. 6d. a pound to three farthings after the removal of paper duties on exports; a change which was reflected in the price of books. Books became both cheaper and mass-produced; this had a crucial effect on the social situation of the writer. The circulating libraries lost their hold and the writer became freer – but more vulnerable: his remuneration both fell on average, and became less secure. Meanwhile books became more attractive to the mass market: new methods of illustration were introduced, such as lithography, engraving, and finally, photography. The realistic woodcuts in the 'blue books' – Royal Commission Reports – of the 1840s did much to increase their impact; and even the working-class *Penny Magazine* was illustrated. Middle-class magazines such as *Punch* employed well-known writers and illustrators. Dickens was first commissioned to write a text for Seymour's cockney portraits: the role of illustrators such as Leech and 'Phiz' had at times equal importance with that of writers, and the interaction between the two influenced the character of the final work.

The economic and social situation of book production, then, received a boost from a number of factors connected with the Industrial Revolution. New roads opened up remote country districts, fast mail-coaches carried newspapers, journals, and books to new shops in local towns; by 1850 the railways were becoming established. Printing, bookselling, and publishing became differentiated concerns with their own trade associations and organizations. The prolonged controversy between free trade and protectionist booksellers during the nineteenth century (the 'war of the booksellers') was ultimately resolved in favour of fixed prices – resulting in the Net Book Agreement (1899) whereby a book could not be sold at a price lower than that determined by the publisher. This prevented underselling and facilitated amalgamations between publishers, with larger networks bringing cost economies.

During the nineteenth century, if authors kept to the convention of 'titillation without sex' and avoided disturbing religious or political controversy, they could enjoy rewards on a scale never before reached. The publisher was emerging as the most powerful figure in the trade, employing authors and printers and organizing his business on bureaucratic and contractual lines. He had regular contracts with booksellers and libraries; books were advertised and received press notices; the roles of agents and critics were being developed. The *Edinburgh Review* (1802) initiated a new era in literary criticism – and a lucrative second employment opportunity for writers. The distinction between magazine and review was more apparent: reviews such as the *Quarterly* and later the *Westminster Review* taking a serious intellectual and often a political perspective, while magazines such as *Blackwood's Magazine* and the *London Magazine* were miscellanies aiming at entertainment. Serial fiction appeared in the magazines: Dickens's novels appeared in his *Household Words* and *All the Year Round*; Thackeray edited the *Cornhill*. Other more specialized journals appeared, contributing to the diversification and fragmentation of publics apparent at the end of the century.* The nineteenth century represents an age when the web of intellectual activity was greatly extended; books and periodicals came to be reckoned in terms of millions rather than of thousands, and writers became suppliers of popular commercial products.

Defoe had already described writing as a 'very considerable branch of English commerce'. During the nineteenth century this description became progressively more appropriate. Popular consumers formed a market for a final product whose production had occupied a range of specialized workers – hence the flow of mediocre works which reached a public deprived of alternative comparable leisure commodities. This monopoly widened the audience for high quality novels: George Eliot, Dickens, and Scott provided an awareness of serious issues and some comment on the values of their time. But there were also openings for the meretricious and sentimental, which brought their authors rewards on a far higher scale than is possible to the same extent today. So whereas proportionately more readers read serious literature, trivial writers could make proportionately higher profits.

Until the 1880s, publishers usually used the system of outright purchase of copyright for three-volume novels suitable for the circulating libraries. This system particularly favoured the mediocre novelist who might lose on royalty payments; he could, by regular production, make a steady income and achieve some security. His position became comparable to that of a salary earner, the publisher acting as the entrepreneur and claiming

* Gross, J., *The Rise and Fall of the Man of Letters*, London, 1969, chs 1–3.

profit as his due for risk-taking. Many women favoured this method for its safety, although a best seller might have fared more lucratively on the royalty system. Sometimes profit-sharing or bonuses were granted on the second printing. The royalty system took over in the last decade of the century. Marie Corelli's *Vendetta* brought her £50 on publication, £25 when sales reached 2,000, and a shilling royalty on each subsequent copy sold. Less well-known writers might have to publish on commission, being responsible for promotion and cost of production; the publisher claimed a fixed share, usually 10 per cent of the gross receipt. Mrs Henry Wood's *East Lynne* was published in this way; it proved a best seller although rejected by George Meredith, the reader for Chapman & Hall. The outright sale of the three-volume novel was mourned by many after it had disappeared; although Gissing portrays the system as a form of coercion. The writer had to provide three hundred pages a volume with twenty lines to a page, the total list price was 33*s*. 6*d*., and no offence to the taste and predilections of Mr Mudie and his colleagues was allowed.*

Some authors could avoid this system if they had alternative income or great success, persuading publishers to back one-volume novels, or editors to publish in monthly parts or in magazines. But great novels were written within its confines; George Eliot's *Adam Bede* (1858) was written as a three-decker, earning £800 for the copyright for four years. Mudie later increased his supply from 500 to 1,000 copies when success was assured. Three thousand copies of *The Mill on the Floss* were ordered by Mudie. By 1871, Lewes was writing to Blackwoods, 'Mrs Lewes finds that she will require four volumes for her story not three.' Blackwoods then accepted a royalty agreement of 2*s*. for each copy sold of *Middlemarch*, recognizing its quality and the necessity for the author to get 'out of Mudie's clutches'. Mudie threatened to burke the novel; however, its success, selling at 5*s*. a part, was such that he finally ordered 1,500 copies of the four-volume edition. After 1876, George Eliot gained control of her earlier novels which she had 'leased' to Black-wood's for ten years; she obtained royalty agreements on them

* George Gissing, *New Grub Street*, London, Penguin Books, 1968. This is praised by Q.D. Leavis as 'a major contribution to the English novel', in *Scrutiny*, June 1938.

all. The 'Cabinet' edition of her work brought her £4,330 in royalties alone.* Hence a successful writer might benefit from the three-decker system initially, gaining popularity and renown by means of which he might finally escape from it. Many widows, however, valued its advantages, since it provided a steady income, useful for rearing and educating a family.

But at the end of the century came an important change which resulted in a fundamental shift in the authors' position. During the 1890s publishers began to issue a cheap one-volume edition of a three-decker novel at 6s. This badly undermined the position of the libraries, who in retaliation broke the system: in 1894, 184 three-volumes novels appeared, in 1897 only four.† Cheap reading matter provided on railway stations also challenged the monopoly of the private lending libraries – these were being increasingly threatened by the free libraries. The public was becoming interested in a freer type of literature: George Moore's *A Modern Lover*, in which a girl poses in the nude for the artist-hero, was followed by *A Mummer's Wife*, published by Vizetelly for 6s. in a single volume. Shorter, cheaper novels were now popular, religious sanctions were losing ground, and a new approach to reading was evident: an audience was developing which was to appreciate Hardy and D. H. Lawrence. The new perspective had important repercussions on the length of novels – they were no longer lengthy family sagas. Since royalties could no longer be assessed in advance, these changes brought insecurity to the author and the gap widened between writer and public with the disappearance of the private lending libraries.

4

Throughout history many writers have held second jobs either initially or continuously. Dr Johnson has been called the first professional man of letters, Milton the first professional poet, and Defoe the first professional novelist: these writers were able to dispense with patronage by means of supplementing their

* Gordon Haight, *George Eliot, A Biography*, Oxford, Clarendon Press, 1968, ch. 13. This sum is worth three times its value today.
† Bernard Bergonzi, introduction to George Gissing, op. cit.

income by journalism. Others started in or continued alternative professions: Sterne began his career as a parson, Smollett as a doctor. By the nineteenth century it was easier for writers to live by their pen alone: Scott was able to recoup his fortunes by writing twenty-five historical novels in eighteen years. But few writers were entirely dependent on writing: some were priests or ministers, such as Charles Kingsley, Newman, Sidney Smith, Keble, G. M. Hopkins, William Barnes, and George Macdonald; others were academics like Ruskin, Mark Pattison, Walter Pater, Lewis Carroll, and Charles Reade. Public servants included Arthur Clough, Matthew Arnold, Macaulay, Lytton, Trollope, J. S. Mill, and Thomas Love Peacock. Among the barristers were Francis Jeffrey, Bentham, and Wilkie Collins. Walter Bagehot was a banker, Harrison Ainsworth a publisher.* Women usually had alternative means of support from family or husband. Many Victorian writers had private means: Grub Street had not disappeared for the unsupported although the quasi-patronage of the circulating library was available for those willing to conform to its prescriptions.

The improvement in the general status of the author compared with the previous age is stressed by Walter Besant.† Describing the struggling writer in the early eighteenth century, where 'every profession and trade had its uniform guaranteeing recognition and respect' he describes Grub Street:

... Only the writer was to be seen all day long; he haunted the coffee houses, the eating houses, the taverns of Fleet Street and its neighbourhood. Alone among men he had no uniform, yet he could be recognized by his rags. Every body knew the company of wits in the tavern; they were notoriously, horribly poor. Notoriously they had neither principles, nor honour, nor dignity: ... the world saw very plainly that they had no independence but they were the servants of the miserably paid – and the hacks of the booksellers.

Besant claims that by the end of the nineteenth century a striking change had taken place. He asserts that a struggling writer such as Chatterton would no longer be faced with starvation. As a 'bookish' boy he would read at home borrowing books from friends or libraries. He would attend school, where he

* J. W. Saunders, op. cit., pp. 175–6.
† Walter Besant, op. cit. This attitude did not last. By 1850 Carlyle was calling literature 'a morbid substitute for reality'.

could learn shorthand. He might then be put into a newspaper office, where he would be asked to report on meetings, lectures, and police cases – he would learn to 'pick up news and shape paragraphs'. He would write reviews and articles for magazines in his leisure. He might rise further through journalism, becoming an editor; outside journalism an honourable income could also be earned by an author who honoured his obligations and worked hard. The 'feeling that literature should not even be remotely connected with money ... that it is beneath the dignity of an author to speak of money' is strongly condemned. Authorship had become a profession with the Society of Authors its professional organization. There were pulls and ties integrating the writer into bourgeois middle-class life which lasted until the end of the century: this provided him with an ethos resembling that of the Victorian entrepreneur and limited the scope of social criticism for all but those with exceptional independence and insight. For some, then, the ties of patronage had given way to a bondage demanding a renewed subservience.

Public respect for the man of letters was considerable. Carlyle's acclamation of him as a hero – 'our most important person' – citing the oddly assorted trio of Dr Johnson, Rousseau, and Robert Burns was not thought extravagant. The man of letters wrote articles and reviews to support himself rather than relying on cheap journalistic success and the three-decker strait-jacket. Browning, Dickens, the Brontë sisters even, were lionized when in London. There were pressures to despise philistinism, which was equated with the working class and radical agitation. Matthew Arnold quoted his father in the first edition of *Culture and Anarchy*: 'As for rioting, the old Roman way of dealing with that is always the right one: flog the rank and file and fling the ring leaders from the Tarpeian rock.' He added, 'and this opinion we can never forsake'; however, he cut the passage out of subsequent editions. The network of academic and literary families which spread after the expansion and reform of Oxford and Cambridge were firmly attached to ideals of education, civilization, amelioristic reform, freedom of the universities, and a public service open to talent. But they themselves were now entrenched within the hierarchic establishment, anxious to help the nearly literate in a paternalistic way – to save them from drink, cheap excitement and dangerous ideologies.*

The minority group of atypical social origins sought to avoid this subservience, expressing criticism of middle-class establishment values.† But these deviants were not revolutionary. George Gissing, for example, wrote movingly on the evils of capitalism and poverty – yet in *Demos* (1886) he made a violent onslaught on the socialist movement. Samuel Butler, like others, attacked the hypocrisy of the established Church; but he was hardly an extreme radical. George Eliot undertook a stern sifting of middle-class values and norms; yet her *Felix Holt* was disapproving of working-class revolution.‡ Social problem novels by Dickens and Mrs Gaskell deplored many of the evils of industrialism but refrained from a contemplation of radical measures which might transform actual social structure. Victorian social novels retained an element of moralistic protestant paternalism towards the poor which is absent in the novels of Balzac and in Russian literature. The later socialism of William Morris and Shaw was Fabian middle-class reformism – the same limitations are evident in the works of Arnold Bennett and H. G. Wells. Other dissidents such as the aesthetes withdrew from society into subjectivism and fantasy.

Sociological studies of authorship provide some information of relevance: such as that by the nineteenth century most writers were born into the professional middle class. Writers from the upper class became fewer, and those from commercial or business homes were in the minority.§ It is important for studies to be based on adequate source lists: often working-class authors are omitted, unidentifiable through the use of pseudonyms or the occupation of their fathers obscured by phrases such as 'of humble parentage' or 'unknown'. Much of the 'Salisbury Square' fiction was written by authors who cannot be substantiated.¶ The spate of minor novels designed for the 'slop shops of literature' in the early nineteenth century were written by authors many of whom have disappeared into

---

* Noel Annan, 'The Intellectual Aristocracy', in *Studies in Social History*, ed. J. H. Plumb, London, Longmans, Green, 1955.

† Raymond Williams, op. cit.

‡ Ian Milner, *The Structure of Values in George Eliot*, Prague, Karlova University Monograph, 1968, ch. 5.

§ R. D. Altick, The Sociology of Authorship.

¶ Published by Thomas Prest in Salisbury Square, London.

oblivion.* Paid by the sheet, with booksellers' prices as low as half a guinea for a manuscript novel, the writers of these shockers and novelettes were a reminder that, notwithstanding the general rise in status, an undergrowth of popular hack writers remained. Those with ambition and contacts graduated to a higher level of remuneration; more research is needed on those who did not. Some of these were women aiming for a part-time income. Novel-writing became an accepted role for women, an alternative to that of the governess, the dressmaker and the social worker. Many remained on the level of the cheap novelette; others who came from a background of education and awareness achieved more.

Social class and education are two important variables in the situation of the nineteenth-century professional writer: that is, the writer whose majority income came from writing. Increasingly they came from professional backgrounds and decreasingly from the country and merchant classes: this seems to have contributed to the loss of gusto and the growth of 'delicacy' notable in the developing novel. Up to Elizabethan times most writers came from the gentry class, their homogeneity strengthened by ties with Oxford and Cambridge. The period 1530–80 contained an increase of writers coming from families of merchants, tradesmen, and craftsmen; the link with the university continued. Most Elizabethan dramatists came from new classes not related to the old gentry; they benefited from grammar school education and wrote for more heterogeneous audiences, although the influence of the Court was strong. By the time of the Restoration there had been a swing back to writers from families in the nobility and gentry. From 1680 to 1730 these again declined, and more writers came from middle-class professional backgrounds, with an increase of Irish and Scottish writers. The period 1730–80 shows more representatives from tradesmen, farmers, and craftsmen, with a decline of those educated at university; there is also some peasant representation (Blake, Burns, Cobbett, and Paine). From 1780 to 1830 we see a swing back to

* Louis James, *Fiction for the Working Man, 1830–50*, Oxford, Oxford University Press, 1963. J. M. S. Tompkins, *The Popular Novel in England 1770–1800*, London, Methuen University Paperback, 1969, and Margaret Dalziels, *Popular Fiction 100 Years Ago* – An unexplored tract of literary history, London, Cohen & West, 1957.

professional class dominance, the emergence of the woman writer, but an important minority remaining of tradesmen, craftsmen, poor farmers, and labourers.* The nineteenth century has been studied in more detail: studies agree that literary London of the coffee-houses and magazines created a climate favourable to the novel and more organized journalism. Middle-class professional families provided the bulk of writers, most of whom had university education and second jobs if they were men. This age shows maximum homogeneity of social origins; after the 1930s research is less adequate but there is reason to suppose that the social origins of writers have become more varied.

The fall in remuneration and security of the present century is reflected in the recorded social class of the writer. Up to 1961 the Registrar General's classification placed them in Social Class I; after that date they were demoted to Social Class 2, on a par with actors and musicians. In the nineteenth century a writer could write works of a high quality for a popular audience; in this century readership has fragmented into élite versus low culture, with a varied array of specialist reading publics. Writers work for films, radio, television, education, even advertising; these media command a popular audience who may not be consistent readers.† The division between artist and salesman has therefore become more marked; although few have the private means necessary for financial independence: second jobs are still important. The self-image of the writer has varied considerably; from romantic hero (Byron), to country gentleman (Scott), to market-oriented tradesman (Arnold Bennett), to the observing stranger (Henry James), to ivory tower recluse (Virginia Woolf) – these are but a few of the options. At present we see a movement to reintegrate the writer into society by means of State aid, Guggenheim scholarships, Arts Council grants, even sponsorship from industry.‡ The future of the literary role is enigmatic; the extent to which a writer can express a world view of some class or group with which he feels involved

* Raymond Williams, op. cit.
† Malcolm Bradbury, 'The Writer's Profession Today', *New Society*, April 1965, stresses the modern increase of the 'technocrat writer' and the decline of literary bohemianism and the aesthetic approach.
‡ See Malcolm Bradbury, op. cit.

depends to a large extent on structural factors in society. These also affect the orientation of the writer: in an integrated society the dichotomy between popular salesman and esoteric artist need not exist. The function of the novel as a medium for expressing a critique of society and of the social relationships within it remains assured, although qualitative assessment by contemporaries is problematic.

7 The Writer in the Present Century

I

A striking factor in the authorship situation of the present century is the total increase in book production. Paradoxically this has been accompanied by a fall in the status of the writer or man of letters. It is the purpose of this chapter to explore some of these changes.

Problems of definition and indices complicate comparison over time and space. The General Conference of UNESCO 1964, defined a *book* as a non-periodical printed publication of at least 49 pages, exclusive of coverpages. According to this definition novels printed in magazine serial form, such as those of Dickens, are not books until the parts have been collected and printed together. This can be conceded, but when we come to the modern definition of poetry or 'literature', boundaries are hazy. Figures given on different categories of book production therefore provide information of somewhat rough precision which give only an approximate indication of production changes.*

We learn from Escarpit† that world book production as a whole increased by some 40 per cent between 1952 and 1962. The U.K. increased its book production by 35 per cent, and was among the six 'publishing giants', together with the U.S.S.R., China, West Germany, Japan, and the U.S.A., producing over 20,000 titles a year. The U.S.A. is gradually taking over from Britain the place at the head of the English language group, largely because of its mass publication of paperbacks. In 1960

* Sources: *UNESCO Statistical Yearbook*, 1968; *Whitaker's Almanack*; *Bookseller*, London, 4 January 1969.
† R. Escarpit, *The Book Revolution: Books and the World Today*, London, Harrap, 1966, part 2, ch. 1, 'World Production'.

it was estimated that 1,000,000 paperbacks were sold each day in the United States. A paperback revolution has also occurred in Britain, which has broken the virtual monopoly of Penguins.

These figures are of books in general, considered as consumer goods. Further breakdown is less reliable; the inadequacies of

Table 1: Estimated World Book Production, 1955–67 *

Continent	1955	1960	1965	1966
	Book Production by Number of Titles			
World total	258,000	364,000	450,000	460,000
Africa	3,000	5,000	7,000	7,000
America, North	16,000	22,000	64,000	68,000
America, South	9,000	13,000	13,000	13,000
Asia	70,000	83,000	85,000	95,000
Europe	131,000	163,000	200,000	200,000
Oceania	1,000	2,000	5,000	4,000
U.S.S.R.	55,000	76,000	76,000	73,000
	Number of Titles per Million Inhabitants			
World total	106	124	137	137
Africa	13	19	23	22
America, North	66	82	219	227
America, South	72	90	79	76
Asia	47	49	47	51
Europe	320	383	450	445
Oceania	68	121	286	223
U.S.S.R.	279	355	329	313
	Percentage Distribution of Book Production			
World total	100·0	100·0	100·0	100·0
Africa	1·0	1·4	1·6	1·5
America, North	5·6	6·0	14·2	14·8
America, South	3·2	3·6	2·9	2·8
Asia	24·6	22·8	18·9	20·7
Europe	46·0	44·8	44·4	43·4
Oceania	0·3	0·5	1·1	0·9
U.S.S.R.	19·3	20·9	16·9	15·9
	Percentage Distribution of Population			
World total	100·0	100·0	100·0	100·0
Africa	8·3	8·5	9·4	9·5
America, North	9·0	8·9	8·9	8·9
America, South	4·6	4·8	5·0	5·1
Asia	55·0	55·9	55·6	55·7
Europe	15·2	14·2	13·5	13·4
Oceania	0·5	0·5	0·5	0·5
U.S.S.R.	7·4	7·1	7·0	6·9

* Source: *UNESCO Statistical Year Book 1968.*

Class 8 of the Dewey book classification are well known. However, if we assume, with Escarpit, that errors here cancel each other out, we find that there has not been a corresponding proportional increase of books in the 'literature' category in this country, nor in the U.S.A. There has been stability here in the U.S.S.R., China, and West Germany; while in Japan and France there has been a decline. In France the decline was 36 per cent to 33 per cent of the total, 1952–62. It is tempting to associate these figures with the alleged decline of the novel, but further breakdown of this category is necessary. Many other factors are also relevant, such as political policy and censorship, level of education, technological demands, leisure, social stratification, etc. Only a few countries distinguish novels from other forms of literature: of those who do, we find the U.K. heading the list with 4,000–4,500 a year, followed by West Germany – 3,000–3,500; then U.S.A. – 2,500–3,000 (upward trend); France – 2,500–3,000; Spain – 1,500–2,000; and Italy – 1,000–1,500 novels a year. The great majority of books published today are what Escarpit calls 'functional books', and therefore are not the concern of the sociology of literature. These are books mainly in the Dewey classes of Social Sciences, Language, Pure Science, and Technology. Seventy-five per cent of titles published annually, and about the same percentage of the total number of copies, are 'functional books', in particular textbooks. In countries where technology is developing and where the school-leaving age is rising, the reasons for this are obvious. The author of an accepted textbook is in a favourable position in a world where literary rewards are dwindling. Paperback publication is to his advantage when sales are considerable.

Within the total increases, fiction, ever unpredictable, showed a decline in 1964, an increase in 1966, 1967, and 1968, and a smaller increase in 1969. There was a steady decline of religion and theology and an increase of sociology and political science.

The growth of the paperback industry has been called a revolution. Since Allen Lane published the first ten Penguins in 1935 the figures have been spectacular: from 800,000 books in 1935 to nearly twenty times that number today. In the U.S.A. Robert de Graff bought the rights of ten titles in 1937 to form Pocket Books Inc. During the war a cheap novel of the size of a uniform pocket found a ready sale; by the 1950s there was a mass market for Signet, Ace, Pyramid, Popular, Bantam books, and others in the U.S.A.; and Pan, Panther, Fontana, Corgi, and others in Britain. A minor slump in the mid 1950s was followed by further growth; Panther paid £3,000 for Mailer's

Table 2: Great Britain: Number of Booktitles *

	1963	1964	1965	1967	1968	1969
Fiction	4,249	3,957	3,877	4,163	4,315	4,405
Biography	548	714	707	841	902	850
Children's books	2,599	2,469	2,484	2,352	2,189	2,156
School textbooks		1,868	1,869	1,857	1,889	1,821
History	672	922	1,073	1,466	1,647	1,555
Medical Science	1,158	1,174	1,227	1,231	1,256	1,241
Sociology		488	525	541	580	584
Political Science	1,059	1,501		1,986	1,990	2,441
Religion and Theology	1,470	1,435	1,227	1,376	1,336	1,164
Total number of Titles	26,023	26,154	26,358	26,619	31,420	32,393

* Source: *Bookseller*, London, January 1963–9.

The Naked and the Dead in 1958; Corgi gave £15,000 for *Lolita*. New selling techniques such as retail display units were introduced and although competition from television was growing, most lines survived.* The decision in favour of Penguins in the *Lady Chatterley's Lover* case was influential; the James Bond novels produced phenomenal sales.† While Corgi paid £25,000 for Frank Harris's *My Life and Loves*, Penguin developed many non-fictional lines with success; today other paperbacks are beginning to explore the non-fiction market. Titles are now around 35,000 British paperbacks in print, total annual sales (home and export) are approximately 150,000 copies, the total in the English language per annum is in the area of half a billion. Titles which sold over a million include *Lady Chatterley's Lover* (around 4 million), *Dr Zhivago*, *The Kama Sutra*, *The Carpetbaggers*, Homer's *Odyssey*, Kitto's *The Greeks*, and *Aircraft Recognition*. Agatha Christie is a multi-million selling author – having been one of Lane's original ten in 1935.‡

* Although Ace disappeared, while Corgi and Four Square nearly succumbed.
† Pan announced that 20 per cent of their turnover was in Bond books.
‡ See Frederick W. Nolan, 'Paperbacks: A Small Format History', unpublished article, 1970.

Within the total increase of book production, both hardback and paperbacks, fiction figures are now falling.

The emphasis of this book is mainly on 'literature', and on writers of 'literature', particularly on novels, and on the writers

Table 3: Paperback Publishing in the U.S.A.*

	1961	1962	1968	1969
Total production of books in the U.S.A.	18,060	21,904	29,579	30,387
Total production of novels	2,630	2,942	2,811	2,717
Total production of paperback novels	1,044	1,239	1,432	1,277
Ratio of paperback novels to hardback novels	14%	31%	50%	47%

* Source: *Publishers' Weekly*, 1963 and 1970, New York.

of novels. A study of authorship in the nineteenth century would find the majority of authors – 70 per cent at least – classified as novelists: this does not prevail today.

When we consider the position of the modern novelist compared with that of the last century, one striking difference is his fall in average earning capacity. Other changes stand out, such as his loss of contact with the mainstream of his readers. Dickens, Trollope, and other nineteenth-century writers were in constant touch with their public; writing in serial form, they were able to consider audience involvement with their novels; Trollope killed off Mrs Proudie 'on demand' (overhearing a clerical conversation in the Athenaeum Club); Dickens constantly received hundreds of letters from readers, and even felt constrained to justify his separation from his wife to his public in *Household Words*, 1858. The circulating libraries, too, knew their clients' tastes, which they communicated to the writers in no uncertain terms; the code of the bourgeois middle class was not to be infringed. But as the century progressed, the market became less homogeneous; the libraries lost their monopolistic influence, which had been prolonged by the high price of books. The introduction of cheap one-volume novels opened the market, rigorous moral censorship declined, and heterogeneity resulted. Mass production and mass literacy meant that it was increasingly difficult to write 'literature' as a best seller. Kathleen Tillotson notes the change, pointing out that in the Victorian age practically all 'great' novels were best sellers; this situation has altered in the present century.* The mass circulation of newspapers, reaching the never-equalled figure of 600 copies per 1,000 inhabitants, has drawn away novel-readers, and so have the other forms of mass communication: magazines, films, radio, and after 1955, television.

Table 4: Classification of Sample Writers *

Men		Women	
Novelists	56	Novelists	33
Novelists and other	24	Novelists and other	6
	80 (63%)		39 (89%)
Dramatists	8	Dramatist	1
Critics	8		
Specialists or scholars	17	Specialist or scholar	1
Humorists	4	Short story writer	1
Essayists or satirists	5	Writer of children's books	1
Biographers and journalists	2		
Diarist	1		
Sporting writer	1		
Travel writer	1		
Writer of children's books	1		
	128		43

* Source: 1 in 5 sample, 170 writers born or died 1860–1910 (D. Laurenson, *British Journal of Sociology*, 1969).

By 1900, novelettes and poems could be bought for a penny, with hardback novels available for five or six shillings. The spread of railway travel had produced a demand for light reading, and there was further diversification of types of reading matter and of reading publics as the twentieth century progressed. From penny-dreadfuls to stream of consciousness novels, the spectrum covered shockers, adolescent adventure stories, romantic middle-brow novels, the developing detective fiction, short stories, regional literature such as the novels of Arnold Bennett, Thomas Hardy, and the early works of D. H. Lawrence, and psychological novels for an élitist public, for example, the works of Henry James, Joseph Conrad, and Virginia Woolf. There was an increasingly sharp division between what the latter considered as 'high', élitist culture, popular

* K. Tillotson, *Novels of the Eighteen-Forties*, Oxford Paperbacks, 1961, pp. 20–21.

'middle', and 'low' culture, between writers who considered themselves as artists and those who unashamedly looked on themselves as salesmen. Middle-brow culture tended to reflect increasingly the values of late capitalism,* while subjectivity and an atmosphere of critical isolation became characteristics of works which might be considered as 'high' culture. The division was threefold; working-class reading matter, beyond practical manuals and pamphlets, still consisted mainly of 'shockers' and romances, a little-researched 'undergrowth' of literature. D. H. Lawrence, coming from the working class, tried to break these barriers, not altogether successfully.

The comparative affluence and prestige of the Victorian writer had disappeared. After the Second World War the contrast was remarkable. Richard Findlater made two studies for the Society of Authors; the most recent is a summary of a Research Services' survey under Mark Abrams (1965).† He notes the current booming conditions in the book industry: around 300 million volumes published annually in the U.K., thousands more translated and published abroad, the total exported – at present £50,000,000 worth, constantly rising, 100 million paperbacks sold every year. Moreover, millions of hardbacks are bought by local authorities for schools or public libraries, the latter now holding over 80 million copies, borrowed without charge nearly 500 million times a year.‡ 'Yet although the book industry is booming, book writing is not.' Only a sixth of all writers earned more than £20 a week in 1965, a tenth earned between £10 and £20, and almost two-thirds earned less than £6 a week. Almost half had other jobs; of those who earned their entire living by writing, 44 per cent earned less than £500 a year. Virginia Woolf's stipulation of private means and a room for a professional writer is still appropriate: the continuing high proportion of women writers may be partly explained by the fact that many are living on their husbands' earnings. It is true that a

* Some outstanding values of early capitalism, and many deriving from nonconformism, were thrift, self-help, frugality, protestant earnestness, and dislike of ostentation. At the end of the nineteenth century the new generation of entrepreneurs were enjoying affluence, conspicuous consumption, hedonism, and frivolity in their leisure.
† R. Findlater, *What Are Writers Worth?*, London, Society of Authors, 1963; and *The Bookwriters, Who Are They?*, London, Society of Authors, 1965.
‡ Over 70 per cent of books borrowed are fiction.

nucleus of book authors, not necessarily the best, can build up small fortunes in ways denied to the popular novelists of the past, selling their work to the cinema, the theatre, the sound radio, and above all to television, but 'hundreds more, and these by no means the flops and failures, squeeze only a small dole for their work'. Grub Street, it seems, is still with us.

Table 5: Earnings of the Sixth of all Writers Earning over £1,050 per annum*

1964	Total book income	Royalties on U.K. and U.S.A. sales	Subsidiary rights
	£	£	£
Romantic novelist	3,160	2,582	578
Thriller writer (old)	2,487	1,484	1,003
Thriller writer (young)	12,528	987	11,541
Historian-novelist	3,106	1,180	1,926
Literary novelist	2,574	1,786	580
General author	2,292	695	1,597

* Source: R. Findlater, *What are Writers Worth*, 1965.

Table 6: Earnings of Writers from All Literary Activities*

	Over £500 a year	Under £500 a year
Primaries (dependent on writing)	56%	44%
Secondaries (not solely dependent on writing)	26%	74%

* Source: R. Findlater, *What are Writers Worth*, 1965.

The reasons for this position are many and complex. One writer attributes the decline to 'the whole classical system of English publishing since the 1880s of bringing out cheap books and paying the author royalties', which is against the financial interests of all but the most popular writers.* Jane Austen, who in 1811 sold fewer than 1,000 copies of *Sense and Sensibility* at her own risk, made £140 (£1,400 today). Disraeli, writing at the beginning of his career, made £1,000 (£10,000 today) from *Sybil*, and the same on *Coningsby*, selling 3,000 copies of each. On an edition of 3,000 today a writer could expect £375, assuming his novel to be priced at £1·25 and his royalty to be 10 per cent. Findlater notes that, whereas British publishers have

* T. Coleman, 'The Bookmakers', *Guardian*, London, March 1969. Coleman advocates higher book prices for larger returns to authors.

doubled the value of their turnover in the last decade, 60 per cent is from educational and technical books, and much of the expansion has gone overseas, bringing the authors smaller returns. The domestic market is shrinking and inflationary with 'too many books chasing too little space'.

The public libraries system is another factor which penalizes the writer. Nearly a third of the population are now registered readers; the old subscription libraries which brought stable remuneration for many writers have gone. The public libraries make 500 million issues of books each year; yet authors get no more than their royalties on the initial sale. Various ideas for remedying this have been promoted: the 'Brophy penny' scheme suggested that a penny should be charged on each book borrowed, to go mostly to its author.* This was discarded because it infringed the basic principle of the public library: free borrowing of books. Alternative schemes have been outlined by the Society of Authors and others.†

Findlater also blames the perpetual undervaluation and distrust of both books and writers in this country. Authors are forced to follow Byron's advice: 'Never trust entirely to literature.' He writes: '. . . the tiny handful of the top can keep rather more of their literary earnings from the taxman if they can catch the eye of a City group who will buy their copyrights – (as Bookers have done with the James Bond estate and with Agatha Christie Ltd), paying them an annual wage plus welfare benefits'.‡ But other writers must turn elsewhere. There are more opportunities for jobs in academic life and the mass media than in the last century; and there are signs of a new form of patronage in the form of government grants and scholarships.§

The position is bleak for the aspiring writer without means: some have predicted a return to a predominantly oral and visual culture. The conclusion that the novel is 'dying' today cannot be affirmed – novels of quality continue to appear.

---

* R. Findlater, 'The writer considered as a wage-earner', *The Times Literary Supplement*, London, July, 1969. John Brophy's suggestion is frequently revived in schemes advocated by A. P. Herbert, the Arts Council, etc.
† The Public Lending Right is under discussion as we go to press.
‡ R. Findlater, op. cit.
§ M. Bradbury, 'What Are Authors Worth?', *New Society*, April 1965.

2

The changed situation of the writer has occurred over a period of developing capitalism, and over a period of increasing loss of basic assumptions taken for granted by most people, such as national superiority, an acceptance of Christian doctrine and a belief in an ordered scientific progress. There has been growing uncertainty on two levels: on the national and political level, and on the level of personal faith. Political events since 1914 have brought doubts about the possibility of society's moral amelioration; these doubts are reinforced by psychoanalytic findings that man is not wholly a rational being, but is swayed and motivated by forces of which he is not aware. The writer is particularly vulnerable to this cumulative loss of confidence. He is interested in the values of his society as expressed in life and books; his ambivalence towards his role is increased with economic and social insecurity. Many of the novels of this century are concerned with the predicament of the uncertain writer in a hostile world over which he has no control. The subjective novel has taken over from the outward-looking literature of the last century.

We have seen that the 1880s were particularly favourable for writers in this country, although some, like Gissing, seemed to slip through the net of security. For many, integration into a bourgeois role was possible. The writer's life could conform to the Protestant ethic: by hard work he could win security and respectability. Writers such as Dickens, Trollope, and Thackeray did not feel themselves to be at the margin of social life, or resolutely opposed to the philistinism and structural absurdity of their society. They advocated reform and articulated certain social evils and hypocrisies – but they dined and fared well in a Victorian world which accepted and acclaimed them.*

The confident ebullience projected by many such writers reflected the confidence of the age, and the prosperity of the new middle classes in a time of growing industrial and commercial affluence. But in the 1870s – and Dickens died in 1870 – economic depression spread, lasting, with some temporary alleviation, from 1873 until 1896. England was losing her position of economic predominance and was facing rivalry from Europe and

---

* Marvin Rosen, 'Authors and Publishers, 1750–1830', in *Science and Society*, U.S.A., Spring 1968, discusses this situation.

America. Deflation in the heavy industrial sector was accompanied by general depression in agriculture. England turned to the Empire for new markets, and a new Imperialism developed – Victoria was proclaimed Empress of India in 1877. This gave capitalism in Britain a boost; foreign investment continued, together with a somewhat naïve jingoism that was rejected by many intellectuals. The aesthete movement, for example, stood against the hearty involvement and philistinism of commerce and imperialism; it included a number of Irish exiles who did not share British patriotic sentiments. The aesthetic writers, greatly under French influence, were opposed to social realism; inward-turning, they insisted on the superiority of art to nature. The movement represented a radical challenge to the ideas of the bourgeoisie, which it loathed, yet it did not seek political remedies. A cultivation of sensation and intensity – Pater's 'gem-like flame' – was reinforced by the influence of Baudelaire, Huysmans, and Gautier; a move to amorality produced a climate that had many ramifications in academic, literary and even religious circles. The trial of Oscar Wilde in 1895 proved the nemesis of this movement in England: the sentence imposed by an outraged bourgeoisie constituted a further blow to the image and prestige of the writer.

One obvious result of the depression in agriculture was the decline of the rural way of life. England changed from a predominantly agrarian society to an urban or suburban nation: by 1911 roughly 80 per cent of the population was living in urban districts. This swing is reflected in the content of novels and poetry; the changing way of life has been lamented by writers including Hardy, George 'Bourne', and Richard Jefferies.* Cities proliferated and grew: many novels portray the predicament of the author, at the onset of his career, struggling with feelings of anonymity and precarious identity that are fostered by urban life. On the other hand, new inward-turning writers such as Joyce and Virginia Woolf valued the anonymity of the city for bringing a tolerance to individuality, escape, and scope to live uninvolved with the bourgeois society they despised. Writers were increasingly seeing themselves as at odds with

* Ambivalence towards town life and values was expressed by Fielding and Dickens. But the modern city offers anonymity on a scale never before experienced.

society, the cosmopolitanism of city life facilitating emancipation from conventions and outworn traditions. Thomas Mann in *Tonio Kröger* (1903) stressed that being an artist precluded the enjoyment of ordinary human feelings:

Literature is not a calling, it is a curse; believe me ... It begins by your feeling yourself set apart, in a curious sort of opposition to the nice, regular people; there is a gulf of ironic sensibility of knowledge, scepticism, disagreement between you and the others; it grows deeper and deeper, you realize that you are alone; and from then on any rapprochement is simply hopeless.

This separatist image of the writer, rooted as we have seen in his ancient role, was fostered by Romanticism, but had become somewhat diluted in England by the economic success of the Victorian novelists. More writers now turned to it from choice or from necessity. Separatism brought a prestige and a means of bearing their precarious and isolated situation, although the opposition between art and life was not a universal assumption among English writers. However, writers such as H. G. Wells, Arnold Bennett, and Shaw cannot be seen as part of this movement.

National confidence, which received an artificial boost during the First World War, dwindled further during the post-war years. Britain emerged from this war theoretically as a victor; in fact all the disrupting factors that had disturbed her prosperity and eminence among the European powers were magnified: foreign competition, loss of overseas markets and investment, tariff barriers, and an abandonment of balance between industry and agriculture. From 1920 onwards, rising unemployment and general economic depression formed a spiral culminating in the mass unemployment and slump of 1929. Heavy industry suffered most; there was a movement of labour to the light industries of the south. D. H. Lawrence's *Sons and Lovers* gives some idea of changing conditions but in a context of his hatred of industrialism, which he saw as destructive to human feeling, spontaneity, and life. Lawrence disliked the Flaubertian concept of art cut off from ordinary living, but paradoxically, his cult of irrationalism and 'the dark gods' tended to a similar polarity. G. S. Fraser quotes a passage from a short story of Lawrence:

At a certain time the men who are really living will come beseeching to put their lives into the hands of the greater men among them, beseeching the greater men to take the sacred responsibility of power ... At last the masses will come to such men and say, 'You are greater than we. Be our lords. Take our life and death in your hands and dispose of us according to your will. Because we see a light in your face and a burning in your mouth ...' Ah, but my chosen aristocrat would say to those who chose him: 'If you choose me you give up for ever your right to judge me. If you have truly chosen to follow me, you have thereby rejected all your right to criticize me. You can no longer either approve or disapprove of me. You have performed the sacred act of choice. Henceforth you can only obey.'*

Although these were not Lawrence's own explicit sentiments, he advocated a loosening of cerebral control and a surrender to feeling; we feel tendencies, in his work and ideas, towards the fascism which sprang from the economic chaos of the 1920s.

The failure of confidence in progress and enlightenment through science and reason was reinforced by the spread of psychoanalytic ideas. The material structure – economic prosperity, industrial affluence, and the old agrarian way of life – was shaken; so also was the faith in man's conscious powers and reason. There were forewarnings of this before Freud: in the writings of Nietszche and Schopenhauer, in Dostoevsky's *Letter from the Underground*, and even from Enlightenment France in Diderot's *Rameau's Nephew*. The psychoanalytic stress on unconscious influences, on behaviour reflecting introjected childhood experiences and family dynamics, with its emphasis on dream symbols, had an important literary impact; it also reinforced a popular crude determinism and despair which ignored the positive aspects of psychoanalysis as a struggle for insight and integration. This contributed to the feelings of impotence and of menacing chaos discernible in the years between the wars, and may have strengthened the experienced need for salvation through power which is expressed by Lawrence and which found expression in the fascism between the wars.†
More benevolent influences reinforced by psychoanalysis include

* G. S. Fraser, *The Modern Writer and His World*, London, Penguin Books, 1964, ch. 2, p. 90.
† Freud of course did not encourage the cult of irrationality himself. He writes: 'The voice of intellect is a soft one, but it does not rest until it has gained a hearing ... This is one of the few points in which one may be optimistic about the future of mankind ...' (S. Freud, *The Future of an Illusion*, London, Hogarth Press, 1930).

an added depth to character and relationships in literature, an awareness of the complexities of motivation, and an attempt to add psychological realism to the broad social orientation of Dickens, Balzac, and Tolstoy. The influence of psychoanalysis pervades many writers who did not acknowledge it explicitly, for example, James Joyce, Henry James, Virginia Woolf, Joseph Conrad, Aldous Huxley, D. H. Lawrence, and T. S. Eliot. Likewise, psychoanalytic ideas today are part of the equipment of all writers, even if they question their validity.

John Gross writes:

... that writers should have been politically conscious in the 1930s was inevitable; the only puzzle is why they should have been quite as apolitical as they were in the 1920s ... During the years when communism was becoming a central issue for French or European intellectuals, when it was attracting leading European writers from Barbusse to Brecht, the English avant-garde simply ignored it ... Whatever the reasons for this placid state of affairs, it made the sudden swing leftwards at the beginning of the 1930s seem all the more of an invigorating shock to those who took part in it. The literature of the 1920s had been peopled by largely passive figures: Tiresias, Mrs Dalloway, a succession of sensitive introverts, amused observers, melancholy pierrots. Now was the time to act; and if there was one thing which excited writers in the 1930s it was the idea of themselves as men of action. *We're Not Going to Do Nothing* was the title of a characteristic tract of the period (by Cecil Day Lewis) ...*

Although the war literature of poets and writers such as Wilfred Owen, Robert Graves, and Siegfried Sassoon had revealed the realities of modern warfare this was followed by an apparent recoil from social reality. In contrast, the chief characteristic of the literature of the 1920s was an interest in the mainsprings of individual personality, in the enlargement of consciousness and in the sharpening of sensitivity. This shaped a new reading for an intellectual élite. A spate of little magazines – many shortlived – were launched to help this new literature. T. S. Eliot was assistant editor of the *Egoist*, Herbert Read editor of *Arts and Letters*, Middleton Murry of the *Athenaeum*. There was constant friction between the latter and J. C. Squire's *London Mercury*, which represented the 'hearty' literary movement of the era, beer-drinking and cricket on the 'Chester-Belloc' model. Orage (who had edited the *New Age* before the

* J. Gross, op. cit., p. 257.

war) returned to London at the end of the 1920s to start the *New English Weekly*, which launched many new writers.* Murry had founded the *Adelphi* in 1923 largely to establish D. H. Lawrence – who in turn attacked the magazine as 'weak, apologetic and knock-kneed'. The essence of the decade is given to us in Aldous Huxley's *Point Counter Point* (1928). This illustrates the changed character and tempo of society: the frenzied search for lost security and meaning in a post-war world where pre-war assumptions and sexual sanctions had lost their hold. Many of the intellectual figures of the twenties appear: D. H. Lawrence as Rampion, Huxley himself as Philip Quarles, Middleton Murry as Burlap, Oswald Mosley as Webley.

The 1920s saw the development of the 'new' Bloomsbury group: Virginia Woolf and Vanessa Bell and their husbands; Lytton Strachey, Duncan Grant, Roger Fry, Keynes, and Saxon Sydney Turner. Some younger members now gained admittance: David Garnett, Francis Birrell, Raymond Mortimer, Sebastian Sprott – possibly E. M. Forster and some others. The original group has been greatly influenced by a Cambridge secret society called the Apostles, and by the ideas of the philosopher G. E. Moore. The Apostles, described by Leonard Woolf, a member, was a discussion group of an élite and esoteric nature, demanding absolute candour from its members and with a tradition of banter.

No consistency was demanded with opinions previously held – truth as we see it then and there was what we had to embrace and maintain ... the gravest subjects were continually debated, but gravity of treatment was not imposed ... though sincerity was ... it was ... a point of the apostolic mind to understand how much suggestion and instruction may be derived from what is in form a jest.†

All the original members of the Bloomsbury group came from or married into what has been described as an intellectual aristocracy: an élite network of Oxford and Cambridge academic, intermarried families, attached to establishment norms and principles of high-minded reformism, imbued with the values of the Protestant ethic even if they did not still profess its

* For example, Orage was the first London editor to publish a poem by Dylan Thomas.
† H. Sidgwick, quoted in L. Woolf, *Sowing, An Autobiography*, London, Hogarth Press, 1960, p. 150.

beliefs.* They were united by their belief in a public service open to talent and in freedom of access to the universities. The brothers of Virginia and Vanessa Stephen, Adrian and Thoby, were members of the Apostles, based on Gordon Square. Hence they were described as 'the Bloomsberries'.† By the 1920s, the two married sisters were still living in Bloomsbury, Virginia established as a stream-of-consciousness novelist, holding formidable evenings where new members were tried out, despised and discarded, or accepted. Their snobbishness and their assumed superiority were resented by many.

Clive Bell decries the stereotype formed by 'Bloomsbury-baiters', insisting that they were only a group of friends, that there was no 'movement', no doctrine or common language.‡ But D. H. Lawrence, son of a miner, wrote in a letter to David Garnett after a visit to Cambridge: 'I feel I should go mad when I think of your set, Duncan Grant, Keynes and Birrell. It makes me dream of beetles . . . I had felt it slightly before the Stracheys . . . you must leave these friends, these beetles . . .' Lawrence's stress on 'feeling with the blood' was incompatible with the intellectualism and nervous febrility of Bloomsbury. He was supported here by F. R. Leavis, who has done much to establish Lawrence as a major writer. Like Lawrence, Leavis sees the established order as hopelessly corrupt, but considers all active programmes to replace it to be useless.

Neither did the Bloomsbury group stand for trying to replace the established order; their formidable hold on the literary and intellectual life of the time was another factor restraining an active interest in politics among writers of the twenties. Virginia Woolf's novels are of the stream-of-consciousness school. The extreme subjectivity of this approach seemed inimical to active Marxist beliefs: its practitioners tended to be increasingly isolated and introverted, subject to physical and mental stress and, in the case of Virginia Woolf, to suicide. We can see how this movement was influenced by the aesthetic movement and by the view of art and the artist quoted from Thomas Mann. The

* N. Annan, 'The Intellectual Aristocracy', in *Studies in Social History*, ed. J. H. Plumb, London, Longmans, Green, 1955.
† For the first time by Mrs Desmond Macarthy, in a letter written about 1911.
‡ C. Bell, *Old Friends*, London, Chatto & Windus, 1956, ch. 8.

writer looked on himself as a being apart, possessed of a sensitivity superior to the majority, an observer and recorder of his own perceptions of the world: obscure, oblique, and ironic in his commentary on persons and events.

The decline of the gentry class to which many of these writers were attached via birth or education (public school and university) is an important factor in any understanding of changing values. The 'rentier' class was ceasing to have any real relationship with the land; the decline of agriculture and the rise of urbanization precluded this. A pessimistic and snobbish distaste for the new commercialism, for the urban proletariat and lower middle-class way of life, is characteristic of this group. Intellectuals coming from the gentry class felt particularly threatened. They derived anxiety from their parents; this was reinforced by the suspicion they received as intellectuals. English anti-intellectualism, always a feature of English cultural life, was fostered by the public schools. Many writers from this class reacted to these two sources of anxiety by mourning their lost rural roots, idealizing the lost organic pastoral society, or by attacking the new society, exposing its evils and hypocrisies (retreat or aggression). Combined, these feelings of loss and regret plus revulsion for the commonplace and vulgar are a clue to the values apparent in many novels of the twenties; withdrawal contributed to their isolation, apparent neurosis and lack of any coherent world view of writers – from Virginia Woolf to A. E. Housman.*

The sudden swing leftwards of many writers at the beginning of the 1930s was clearly influenced by the impingement of crude economic and political facts into the private worlds and coteries of British intellectual and literary life. Unemployment rose throughout the 1920s and hunger marches were organized through the streets of London. The Labour influence continued to grow: both in terms of gaining working-class votes (192 members of parliament by 1924) – and in terms of mobilizing sympathy from middle-class liberal supporters. But Baldwin's reactionary government produced the Samuel Commission on the coal-mines, recommending a wage reduction for miners in

---

* Another reaction was the hearty beer-drinking of J. S. Squire and others in a vain attempt to recapture the value of 'Old England'. See G. Orwell, *Inside the Whale and Other Essays*, London, Penguin 1957, pp. 21 and 28–9.

1926. This resulted in a wave of strikes and lockouts based on the miners' slogan 'not a penny off the pay, not a second on the day'. In May 1926 the T.U.C. came to the miners' assistance by calling a general strike; unfortunately the government had control of the radio, over which Baldwin's portrayal of the strikers as attackers of the community was broadcast, backed up by articles in *The Times*. A new alignment of values was presented to the 'ivory tower' writer: no longer was an intellectual literary élite facing crude bourgeois, middle-brow philistinism; another factor had come into focus, the oppressed and struggling working class. Withdrawal from politics became much more difficult for the younger writer, and a combination of a romantic Marxist-flavoured crusadism with literary activity was increasingly adopted. Most of these writers were from the upper middle classes and Oxbridge, many from the public schools, and their Marxist sympathies took shape accordingly.

The political situation impinged increasingly on the private worlds of writers as events abroad developed. Hitler achieved power in Germany and became Chancellor in 1933. The Reichstag fire and trial, and the persecution of the Jews in 1934 were ignored by many people in this country, but could not escape the condemnation of the 'intellectual élite' – even Bloomsbury was shaken. Leonard Woolf was a Jew: clearly the Nazi movement stood for a negation of liberalism and intellectualism. Stephen Spender writes in his autobiography:

Hitler forced politics on to non-political groups . . . the intellectuals . . . through sympathy with their colleagues . . . acquired an intensity of vision and a fury in their non-political politics which the professional politicians did not share. The intelligentsia had more sinister reasons for understanding Hitler. These were the elements of pure destructiveness, of attraction to evil for its own sake, and of a search for spiritual damnation which had been present in European literature for the past century, and which were fulfilled in Nazi politics . . . The cultured Europeans recognized in this political movement some of their own most hidden fantasies. Hatred of it was deeply involved with their own sense of guilt.

And he notes 'critics like Virginia Woolf' (of whom he was a great admirer) 'who reproached our generation for writing too directly out of a sense of public duty, failed to see that public events had swamped our personal lives and usurped our personal experience'.* Christopher Isherwood's early novels had given a picture of the spread of the Nazi ideology in Germany; the Spanish Civil War was an opportunity for writers to participate actively. Spender and others had already joined the Communist Party, if only nominally; W. H. Auden, Louis MacNeice, and Cecil Day Lewis were part of this anti-fascist trend. Ralph Fox, Christopher Caudwell, Julian Bell, Tom Wintringham, Humphrey Slater, and others actually joined the International Brigade, some to be killed fighting in Spain. But individualistic writers found it hard to come to terms with the outlook of the British Communist Party, or to concur with Edward Upward,† who asserted in 1937 that good books could from then on only be those written from a Marxist standpoint. Few read deeply into Marxism, the commitment to Stalinism by the Communist Party was hard to accommodate. Exceptions include Christopher Hill, historian of the Puritan Revolution and the producer of sophisticated studies of Marvell and *Clarissa Harlowe*, and George Orwell, who although educated at Eton struggled to understand the working class and working-class values. Orwell's pessimism about Soviet communism is expressed in *Animal Farm* and *Nineteen Eighty Four*.

When the Second World War broke out, writers experienced considerable uncertainty. A wave of pacifism had produced the 1937 vote not to fight for king or country in the Oxford Union, and the Russo-German pact of 1939 was hard to accommodate. Some, such as Aldous Huxley, Christopher Isherwood, and W. H. Auden, retreated to California: the former two to adopt a form of Eastern mysticism, the latter to return to Christianity. Spender resorted to the Fire Service and journalism, Orwell joined the Home Guard, and worked for *Tribune* and the *Observer*. Others were conscripted into the armed services – all felt the inevitable conflict of an artist in time of war. The horrors of the Second World War were on such a scale that the belief in short-term human progress, enlightenment, and morality was finally dispelled. The mass bombing, the revelations of the concentration camps, and finally the atomic destruction of Hiroshima and Nagasaki, completed the disillusion with official

* S. Spender, *The World Within*, London, Hamish Hamilton and the Book Society, 1951, p. 190.
† E. Upward, op. cit.

explanations which had begun with the social and economic changes of the 1880s and 1890s. The writer after the war tended to reflect feelings of nihilism and pointlessness in a variety of ways. George Steiner notes how Beckett has derived from his personal association with Irish letters a distinct note of comic sadness. But he doubts whether Beckett is writing drama in any genuine sense; it is rather 'anti-drama', proclaiming in *Waiting for Godot* with painful vividness the infirmity of our moral condition: the incapacity of speech or gesture to countenance the abyss and horrors of the times.* William Barrett writes of this play: 'Nothingness circulates through every line from beginning to end,' yet it runs for more than sixteen months to packed houses in Europe because the characters are placed in a predicament which is our own.† We are too close to post-war literature to know which writers – if any – will be remembered.

The English Stage Company at the Royal Court Theatre (where Bernard Shaw's plays were performed) gave scope for a new 'theatre of the absurd' by Harold Pinter, N. F. Simpson, John Arden, and others. In some of this drama it seems as if fragmentation has reached its zenith: Beckett's last play, *Breath*, contains only a living and a dying breath accompanied by a recorded baby's cry (performed three times). The anti-hero has been followed by the anti-play and the anti-novel: Robbe-Grillet's literary universe of objects expresses ultimate meaninglessness and 'reification'. However, the sixties show some renewed political committal in writing; translations of non-fiction works by writers such as Herbert Marcuse, Franz Fanon, and Régis Debray are available, and are accompanied by some social commentary novels: James Baldwin and Joseph Heller in the U.S.A. are examples.

The very act of writing can be compared with exile in that it involves a critical scrutiny of the assumed. The early Lukács writes that the modern novelist faces the loss of earlier certainties, recording the tensions between a problematic individual and a contingent world. These are resolved in an overview transcending the limitations of the protagonist, a final state of enhanced

* G. Steiner, *The Death of Tragedy*, London, Faber, 1961, pp. 349–50.
† W. Barrett, *Irrational Man*, *A Study of Existentialist Philosophy*, U.S.A., Doubleday and Co. Inc., 1958, p. 55.

self-awareness which may be termed irony.* It is this self-awareness which in writers like Joyce has been promoted by geographical exile; it enabled them to avoid feeling overwhelmed by the complexities of their experience – bringing them enough freedom to write. Such writers seek an environment which may itself contribute to their growing self-awareness, providing emancipation from provincial constrictions and shibboleths. Unfortunately for writers like Joyce, exile has only been possible over space and not time; if Joyce were writing today, the constrictions which still beset him in exile, in the form of censorship, would not have so harassed and distracted him. An exiled writer is often dependent on single-figure patronage or promotion to meditate his work with the home audience and market.

3

English written literature in North America developed in a situation where there was very little or no patronage by single figures to promote sales at home or in the home country. The earliest settlers were mercantile men of the English Renaissance, soon followed by men of the Reformation of a puritan biblical outlook. From the beginning, commerce and Calvinistic puritanism dominated the northern colonies: hardly an ideal climate for the encouragement of the arts. Although the spread of rival sects encouraged the production of theological pamphlets and the pioneer society welcomed practical manuals of a utilitarian nature, aristocratic and courtly patronage was entirely absent. Pirated books came from England to some extent, and there was some indigenous religious poetry, but 'Conversations with Muses that are no better than Harlots, which excite and ferment impure Flames' were heavily discouraged. In the absence of material encouragement, most writing was by ministers, schoolteachers, and women, and most of a didactic nature. In the southern colonies an aristocracy of a sort did develop among the larger planters; more descriptive and elaborated writing, which aimed at elegance of expression rather than at exhortation, found some market here, but it was mostly imported from England. Pennsylvania, the Quaker settlement,

* G. Lukács, *La Théorie du Roman*, pp. 70–89, Paris, Gonthier, Collection Mediation, 1968.

produced *Woolman's Journal* and the writing of William Penn, but the middle colonies had many non-English settlers, and the reading public was constricted. In all areas two distinct types of literature tended to develop: the one deriving from puritanism, on the 'otherness' of events, or spiritual significance of objects; the other stemming from the practical needs of the colonists, producing, for example, the writings of Benjamin Franklin. Sometimes these two tendencies fused – as with Mark Twain and Thoreau. Plays and novels were not admitted until the mid eighteenth century: feelings of unity among the colonists, stemming from resentment with England, then produced also a spate of political writing, often reflecting the ideas of the enlightenment, of 'right reason', and of science.

The position of writers in American society was arduous because of the small and scattered reading public, poor transportation, the lack of patronage, and the absence of a copyright law. A 'Connecticut Wit' writing in 1783 notes: 'as we have few Gentlemen of fortune sufficient to enable them to spend a whole life in study or induce others to do it by their patronage, it is more necessary in this country than in any other, that the rights of authors be secured by law ...'* Connecticut was the first state to obtain copyright protection – in 1790 the first Federal Copyright Law guaranteed copyright in all states for fourteen years, renewable for another fourteen. This protected the literary property of writers who suffered from the absence of monetary gifts from patrons, sinecure jobs such as tutor or secretary to a literary figure, and privileges arising from being identified with a protecting upper class. Publishers rarely took the risk of paying for publication: the author paid and the publisher served as his distributor on a commission basis. The author often tried to get promises to buy from his friends before he embarked on the expense of publishing: almost all literary works before 1800 were published in this manner, with a list of buyers at the back. Publishers often went bankrupt; in spite of copyright protection there was little professional authorship before 1820. International copyright came in 1891. Hence the crucial role of journalism in the United States: writers relied more exclusively on

* Letter from Joel Barlow to the President of Connecticut Congress, quoted in W. Charvat, *The Profession of Authorship in America 1800–1870*, Ohio State University Press, 1968.

the journals and magazines than was the case in England. Throughout the nineteenth century the consolidation of the reading public by journals slowly enabled the writer to become more self-supporting.

Many members of the reading public were first generation immigrants trying to learn English. The short story and light magazine article met their needs and increased further demand for magazine reading. The magazine habit remains today: A German immigrant to America was amazed at the limited number of bookshops and the fact that newspapers and magazines seemed more important than books. In America, he states, the book has a 'somewhat patronized dependence on the periodical press', relying on advertisements and reprints in periodicals. The magazine takes priority and few households own numbers of books. Whereas in Europe 'book-printing in settled communities nourished thought', and the bookshop was the focus of the intellectual life of the town, in the U.S.A. printing was a factor of colonization and an instrument of active westward expansion. There was little leisure for book-reading and so the periodical press became dominant, supplemented by the public library. The magazine became 'the characteristic expression of American Democracy'.*

Until the 1880s, then, writers were part-time amateurs or if, as in the case of Edgar Allan Poe (1809–49), they attempted literature as a profession, they suffered extreme poverty – eked out by journalism. The Puritan climate, particularly in New England, restricted their field: much English Restoration literature, for example, was proscribed. New England, originally a theocratic community, was the centre of American transcendentalism, a potent influence which still survives.† This literature was introspective and symbolic; later inroads were made on religious belief but the symbolic emphasis remained. Subjects of human love and relationships were not encouraged: man is seen as a lonely figure struggling with elemental forces – frequently of a sinister Gothic kind. Herman Melville's *Moby Dick* shows this transcendental influence. The increased publi-

* Lehmann-Haupt *et al.*, *The Book in America – A history of the making and selling of books in the U.S.A.*, New York, R. R. Bowker & Co., 1952.
† See L. Fiedler, *Love and Death in the American Novel*, London, Jonathan Cape, 1967, Introduction.

cation of magazines, together with a slowly widening reading public after 1850, began to encourage increased openings for literary activity. But there was no market situation in the United States comparable with that in England in the nineteenth century, and writers were not attached to the perspective of a social class, as in a more traditional society.

A feature of American literature is a fondness for violence and death which is expressed within an adolescent and even homosexual context. Heterosexual relationships are either absent, denigrated, or sentimentalized. These tendencies can be discerned in a stream of imaginative and impelling 'anti-novels' of the highest intensity, such as *The Scarlet Letter*, *Moby Dick*, *Billy Budd*, *Huckleberry Finn*, *The Red Badge of Courage*, and the stories of Edgar Allan Poe. Philip Rahv points to two polar influences in American writing: the 'redskins' or lowbrows, reflecting the world of the frontier and war, anti-intellectual and masculine – and the 'palefaces', stemming from the sensitive symbolic culture of New England, of the cities of Boston and Concord. In the twentieth century, he alleges, the redskins, led by Dreiser, Lewis, Wolfe, Caldwell, Sandburg, Steinbeck, Farrel, and Saroyan, managed to overthrow the palefaces. Certainly a change came when a wider reading had developed, together with growing organization and affluence of publishers, protected now from pirating by copyright laws.* The often brutal conditions of the immigrants in the industrialized cities, together with the wretched plight of the descendants of the slaves, were subjects of a movement which has been called American social realism. This was influenced by French and Russian writing, and found an audience among the growing population.

A clear dichotomy between outward-turning and inward-turning writing, or between romantic and realist writers, is obviously an oversimplification: Henry James, for example, had been an early protagonist of 'realism', of writing about the familiar environment with strict regard to its actual properties, but by 1886 he had left to live in England and was writing in a very different way and meeting new influences. Henry Harland wrote novels about Jewish immigrants in New York, but later

* P. Rahv, *Image and Idea, Twenty Essays on Literary Themes*, London, Weidenfeld & Nicolson, 1957, pp. 1–6.

emigrated to London and edited the *Yellow Book*, writing in the aesthetic manner. In the present century, William Faulkner's *The Sound and the Fury* is a highly psychological work in the stream-of-consciousness style, but the author is also obsessed by the social conditions of the southern states, by the racial conflicts and by their evil history and consequences. Any attempt to link American writing with the concept of world vision attached to a social class in the Goldmann sense is difficult: the class identifications of the writers are confused with immigrant loyalties. During the 1950s, McCarthyism dispersed the growing Marxist interest and was a factor impeding the development of a socialist movement.

The twentieth century has seen a remarkable output in American writing. This is a fertile field for sociological analysis: only a very brief indication of the field is possible here. The poets include Vachel Lindsay, Robert Frost, Ezra Pound, Theodore Roethke, E. E. Cummings, Allen Ginsberg, Lawrence Ferlinghetti, and a generation of modern poets influenced by beat and hip culture, such as Robert Creeley and Kenneth Patchen. But Leslie Fiedler* writes:

The old order is basically unchanged; the colleges brim full and overflow; the curriculum is expanded to include Burroughs and Kerouac; what was shuddered at yesterday is today anthologized and assigned ... our basic consciousness remains unaltered though new kicks have been added to old, marihuana to martinis, mescalin to bourbon on the rocks.

Novelists range from Sherwood Anderson, Sinclair Lewis, and Scott Fitzgerald at the beginning of the century, through Hemingway, Dos Passos, Steinbeck, and Faulkner in the middle years, to Salinger, Saul Bellow, Bernard Malamud, and John Updike today. Dramatists include Eugene O'Neill, Arthur Miller, Tennessee Williams, and Edward Albee – the theatre after a late start has enjoyed a remarkable vitality since the First World War, with New York as the main centre. The considerable body of literary criticism, which includes Leslie Fiedler and Harry Levine, has benefited from the work of European immigrants such as Erich Auerbach and René Wellek. There is a growing public for works on sociology and psycho-

* Leslie Fiedler, *Waiting for the End*, the American literary scene from Hemingway to Baldwin, London, Penguin Books, 1967, p. 172.

analysis: Theodore Reich and Herbert Marcuse have become best sellers.

The American book trade was once referred to as a 'tragedy' played out between the publisher, who sits upon mountains of books, and the man in the giant country who would gladly buy them.* This is because the number of retail bookshops is still so small: the distribution network consists of only 1,400 bookshops, the same number as in the much smaller West Germany. In fact, the 2,500 American publishers offer the book-buying public of approximately 10,000,000 people the surprisingly high figure of around 30,000 titles a year, averaging at seven titles bought per head a year. These books are bought by mail order, libraries, institutions of education, and include an enormous sale of paperbacks available outside bookshops. Paperbacks enable publishers to offer large advances to authors: such as $500,000 for Truman Capote's *In Cold Blood* and $350,000 for Philip Roth's *Portnoy's Complaint*. Paperbacks also now contract with authors for original publications, bringing out, for example, Norman Mailer's *American Dream* in paperback simultaneously with a hardback publication. So the financial situation for the American writer can show an improvement, that is if the writer can find a paperback publisher to back him.† This has been a relevant factor in the upward trend of novel publication in the States and may have been conducive to the diverse quality of fiction which obtains publication.

The teeming cities, the climate of violence at home and abroad, prolonged college life, the Negro activist movement – these are only some of the factors in a total context of social inequality and competition which have produced tension in American society. This ethos seems to be productive of attempts at self-expression and at an articulation of the social environment, in however debased or fragmented a form. At the apex of this pyramid of expressive activity stand those who can transcend the din and confusion of modern American life while retaining sufficient self-awareness and objectivity to translate this tension into works of literary merit. We ourselves are too

* L. Shatzkin, quoted by F. Raddatz, 'The Future of International Publishing', *The Times Literary Supplement*, 25 September 1969.
† Joseph Heller found difficulty in finding a publisher for *Catch-22*, subsequently a best seller.

close to these works to judge their quality with impunity, but a sociological study of their genesis can help us understand some of their meanings and something of the society from which they have sprung.

Part Three:
Towards the Sociology of the Novel
by Alan Swingewood

Introduction

The first two parts of this book tentatively explored both theoretically and empirically the kinds of relationships which exist between the production of literature and its social background. A major theme was the repudiation of any mechanical relation; the sociology of literature must concern itself with literature as *literature*, not solely as the simple, or complex, reflection of social structure. It was suggested that purely socio-economic factors as the major determinant of literary creativity must be analysed in close conjunction with actual literary texts: the texts themselves should never be dissolved into environment.

But there is here a major problem. To date the sociology of literature has tended to analyse literature solely in terms of the so-called conditioning factors, such as the writer's social status, the availability of markets, the dictates of types of publication, the structure of the audience. Now there is no doubt that these elements do exert a crucial influence on the ways in which literature is actually produced, but by itself this emphasis tells us nothing of the *significance* which a particular literary work exerted and continues to exert on widely different audiences, both in the past and today. It is necessary, for example, in providing an adequate *explanation* of the development of particular genres, or a specific novel, to include the cultural environment as part of the antecedent chain of causation which led to its appearance. But to analyse a literary work wholly from this one-sided perspective would distort its *meaning*, since such an approach must imply a reductionist conception in which literature reflects society and its different aspects. The whole point about literature, however, is precisely its creative activism, the fact that literary creation is a process which struggles with the world it sets out to depict; positivistic sociology in its extreme forms renders literature as a passive cultural object.*

At once this distinguishes great literature from the merely commercial, from the second-rate. Minor literature, which sets out to entertain and to render the social world non-problematic, is precisely the kind of literature which can be discussed solely in terms of its socio-economic determining factors. There is a sociology of literature which can analyse these literary productions, but in the third part of this book we will be concerned with more significant works, not because this orientation is necessarily more important but rather because, in a book of this nature, actual textual analysis of the kind which the structuralist method emphasizes can only be carried out on important literary works, on literature which is constantly striving to understand and go beyond the obvious, transient features of a culture. Literature, let us say, finds itself in conflict with the conventional, with the accepted norms and values of its socio-economic-political environment and actively struggles with them. The result is literature which is significant beyond its own time, literature which helps man towards a greater understanding of his social world. As such, this literature can be seen as a structural unity, a whole.

Thus the sociology of literature which we are advocating must be based securely on the texts themselves so that the critical activism which literary creativity naturally engenders is part of the analysis. Unlike literary psychoanalysis, which freely infers the significance of myths and symbols from outside the text in order to understand the text, structural analysis infers nothing which cannot be related to the actual literary work itself or its environment. The conception of world vision involving both social groups, social classes and social structure, together with problematic values and a reaching out beyond the conventional, is part of a method which allows literature to be discussed sociologically without losing its status as literature.

We are not, however, engaged in a work of original intention. In the works we have chosen to analyse, there is an attempt to

* This extreme positivism is best exemplified in the work of R. Escarpit, and his Centre of the Sociology of Literary Facts at the University of Bordeaux. For a convenient summary of this approach, see R. Escarpit, 'Sociology of Literature', *International Encyclopedia of the Social Sciences*, New York, The Macmillan Company, 1968, vol. 9, pp. 417–25.

relate literary texts in terms of their structure and values with the values and social structure of their society. But the analysis serves *only* as an introduction to the possibility of a literary sociology, one based on literature as a critical activity involving problematic values. Thus there is no attempt at a detailed analysis of a particular work, in the way Goldmann has discussed Malraux's fiction, nor is there a panorama of the great names with bits of analysis sticking to each. The three chapters deal in some detail with each writer and certain of his works in a way which we hope is suggestive.

The choice of the novel over drama and poetry was made not merely because the novel has enjoyed and continues to enjoy a greater popular appeal than the other genres, but for its more complete depiction of man's life in society. It is, too, a more convenient choice for illustrating the structuralist approach and some of the problems which were discussed in Part One. Ideally, a sociology of the novel should include a discussion of nineteenth century realism, the great landmark of the novel form – Balzac, Dickens, George Eliot, Flaubert, Tolstoy – and it may seem a perverse sociology which omits any analysis of this genre. In the chapters on Fielding and on alienation some reference is made to bourgeois realism, but that is all. In defending this omission we cannot claim overabundance of critical interest, for this would equally apply to Fielding, Sartre, Camus, and Orwell, the writers we have chosen to discuss. No, the reason is simply the pragmatic one of theme, for in deciding to follow Lukács and Goldmann we have engaged ourselves to some extent in a debate with their approach and analysis, especially the concepts of problematic hero and the status of alienated literature.

As we have seen, part of Goldmann's argument is that the hero, the central figure of bourgeois realism, gradually disappears from the novel under the impact of capitalist economics. Goldmann, in fact, correlates liberalism with the development of the novel form; capitalism engenders the liberal individualistic values of personal liberty, equality, tolerance, the rights of man, and the unhindered free development of personality upon which 'the category of individual biography' as 'the constitutive element of the novel' develops, taking the form of problematic hero seeking 'authentic' values. The decline of the hero thus parallels the decline of liberalism. The hero either vanishes and is replaced by the collectivity (the Communist Party in Malraux's *L'Espoir*) and the organization,* or turns into the anti-hero, the individual who is isolated from any kind of human community. But what exactly is a hero? Is Dostoevsky's underground man a hero, or Flaubert's Frederick Moreau? They are hardly related organically to their community and if they are anti-heroes, they fail to fit Goldmann's connection of novel form with the stages of capitalist development. And what of the modern picaresque hero, Salinger's Holden Caulfield, Bellow's Augie March,† and the absurd Yossarian of Heller's *Catch 22*? There is, too, the problem of the American realist tradition which flowered during the inter-war period when, according to Goldmann, it should have collapsed; Dick Diver is still a recognisable hero, as is Eugene Gant‡ and the masculine protagonists of Hemingway's fiction. Indeed, Wolfe's Eugene Gant and Fitzgerald's Dick Diver both exemplify what Goldmann demands as the two 'essential elements' of the novel form, heroes searching hopelessly for genuine values in a world dominated by the conventional.

Thus it might be argued that Goldmann, from a specialized study of one French writer, has developed a general theory of the novel which fails to account for American fiction between the wars or during the post-war period. His analysis seems highly restrictive, applicable to Malraux, the *nouveau roman* and Samuel Beckett.§

Related to this criticism is the extreme ambiguity of the concept of world vision. If the novelist pre-eminently functions as a critic of capitalism, then he cannot express either the 'real'

* George Orwell observed the transition from detective novels based on individual initiative (Sherlock Holmes) to those in which the criminal is beaten by the overpowering weight of organization. G. Orwell, 'Raffles and Miss Blandish', in *Collected Essays*, London, Mercury Books, 1961.
† J. D. Salinger, *The Catcher in the Rye* (1951); Saul Bellow, *The Adventures of Augie March* (1953).
‡ The hero of T. Wolfe's *Look Homeward, Angel* (1929) and *Of Time and the River* (1935).
§ It is interesting that Goldmann has not developed his ideas in actual research since the publication of the Malraux study in 1964. Since that date he has written on Genet, analysed Baudelaire's *Les Chats*, commented on two novels by the French-Canadian authoress, Marie-Claire Blais, and published numerous essays on Marcuse, Sartre, and the Enlightenment. (See *Sociologie de la Litterature*, Institute de Sociologie, Brussels, 1970.)

or 'potential' consciousness of the bourgeois class; the concept of the problematic hero makes this conflict certain. Thus if the novel form does express itself as a totality, as a world vision, then it must do so as the vision of a particular social class. But which one? It has already been suggested that in defining the novel according to the schema outlined in the young Lukács's *Theory of the Novel*, as essentially a 'demonic quest', the novel is largely equated with the picaresque form, although there is nothing to bar the concept of quest from traditional bourgeois literature. However, the picaresque tradition as such came to its close at the precise moment of bourgeois economic domination. It is for this reason that *Tom Jones* was chosen as a novel which might fit Goldmann's method of analysis and throw into relief the limits of this method. At the same time comparisons could be made between Fielding and his more obviously bourgeois contemporary, Richardson, for if the novel is simply the expression of the bourgeois class, then *Tom Jones* should in some measure reflect this simple class connection. Indeed, the influential study of the rise of the English novel by Ian Watt argues precisely for this kind of correlation, although, as we point out, in explaining the *differences* between the fictional worlds of Fielding and Richardson, Watt dissolves his crude sociological argument into one of mere individualism.

And what of modern literature and its possible world visions? Modern novelists are both ambiguous about their genre, as was the early picaresque novelist, and uncertain of the very vision which they strive to express. For Lukács, modern literature is simply decadent if it is not sympathetic to the challenge of socialism; bourgeois novelists are the ideologists of a declining social class. But taking the precept of critical activism as the basic impulse behind creative literature, it seemed worth while exploring, however tentatively, some of these pessimistic works. Sartre, Camus, and Nathanael West were chosen partly because they disclose a similar world, of man's extreme alienation from others, but equally for their contemporary relevance and artistic distance from the various species of social realism which dominated literature in the 1930s. They contrast sharply with the more conventional and popular, that is, less problematic writers such as Steinbeck, Dos Passos, Hemingway, and Aldous Huxley.

The book ends with a short discussion of George Orwell, a writer who, through his experiences during the Spanish Civil War, transformed his work from merely 'average' (his novels of the 1930s) to the truly significant (*Animal Farm, 1984*). Orwell is, moreover, a *political* novelist, one who confronts us with the basic questions of our time, and who in many ways is a natural continuation in terms of pessimism of the novelists of alienation. Orwell's fiction raises important questions of commitment and value, of political class consciousness.

8 Fielding, *Tom Jones*, and the Rise of the Novel

One of the striking themes of both the sociologists and historians of eighteenth-century literature is that the novel form is inextricably bound up with the growth of a commercial middle class. The argument is deceptively simple: the bulk of books published at the beginning of the eighteenth century were largely religious, with fiction forming a small fraction of total production – but by the 1720s secular fiction had increased substantially, at the precise moment, in fact, when the middle class was developing in size and in affluence.*

This connection between the middle class and the novel form has been and still is a widely held view.† It is certainly true that the novels of Henry Fielding (1707–54) and Samuel Richardson (1689–1761), which were published for the first time in the 1740s,‡ ushered in a new type of writing which may be indicative of a new form of social consciousness. Richardson claimed that his work represented a 'new species of writing', while Fielding described his first novel, *Joseph Andrews*, as a 'kind of writing, which I do not remember to have seen hitherto attempted in our language'.§

The new writing was realism. Thus Dr Johnson, comparing contemporary fiction with 'heroick romance', concluded that the novel represented a far more realistic depiction of social

---

* A. Hauser, op. cit., vol. 3, p. 40.
† Both Madame de Staël and Hegel accepted the connection, while the most recent defence has come from Ian Watt, in *The Rise of the Novel*.
‡ Richardson published three novels, *Pamela* (1740), *Clarissa* (1748), and *Sir Charles Grandison* (1754). Fielding wrote *Joseph Andrews* (1741), *The History of the Life of the Late Mr Jonathan Wild the Great* (1743), *Tom Jones* (1749), and *Amelia* (1751).
§ Fielding, Preface to *Joseph Andrews*, where he distinguished the comic prose epic from the genres of romance and burlesque, allying himself with Cervantes, Le Sage, and Marivaux as a historian recording the fundamental truths of humanity.

life, while Taine, nearly a century later, described the eighteenth-century novel as both new and eminently suited to its time, 'the work and the reading of positive minds, observers and moralists not intended to exalt and amuse the imagination . . . not to reproduce and embellish conversation like the novels of France and the seventeenth century, but to depict real life, to describe characters, to suggest plans of conduct, to judge motives of action'.* Realism becomes the literary expression of a secular-minded middle class, and Fielding and Richardson represent this class in terms of their innovations over previous prose fiction, but especially through their more concrete portrayal of period, events and people.

This is a point of some importance. It has been argued also, against Watt, that the novel is not connected in any meaningful sense with the eighteenth-century middle class but, on the contrary, represents a natural development from the seventeenth-century romances, from writers such as Nashe, Greene, Deloney, and Aphra Behn.† In the sense that a novel may be defined merely as prose fiction, then it is true that these writers did produce novels. But this is not the point: in the novels of Richardson and Fielding in particular there are marked and significant departures from this kind of writing which link it more directly with modern experience, with modern literature. The English novel of the eighteenth century is characterized by peculiar innovations and techniques not found in the earlier writers: the emphasis on the particularity of experience, place, time, the realistic naming of characters, and a deeper psychological awareness of human motivation. If the novel is defined as an 'authentic report' of character, milieu, of subjective and objective action, then both Fielding and Richardson developed significantly beyond the writings of their near contemporary, Daniel Defoe, for whom the novel was merely a 'report' on the state of society witnessed through the actions of particular individuals; there is no sense of time, for Defoe's novels (*Robinson Crusoe, Moll Flanders, Roxana, Captain Jack*) are simply sequences of chronological events, one following the

* In his Preface to *Joseph Andrews* Fielding wrote 'that everything is copied from the book of nature, and scarce a character or action produced which I have not taken from my own observations and experience'.

† For this argument, see D. Spearman, *The Novel and Society*, London, Routledge & Kegan Paul, 1966.

other, depicted in such a way that the passage of time, which is quite considerable in the novels, exerts hardly any effects on the characters. Moll Flanders loses her virginity, years pass, but her reactions to the many men of her life are virtually those of the first experience. Like Robinson Crusoe, the passage of years, the adventures, make hardly any impression on the personality.* Although he was one of the first writers to abandon plots based on mythology, legend, or previous literature, Defoe's portrayal of characters is flat and unconvincing: they have no inner life.

Fielding and Richardson are thus important because in their novels they depict man and his social and inner life more realistically than hitherto. The novel genre, in the eighteenth century, becomes increasingly penetrated by the material values of an urban, commercial society. There is, however, a problem, for while Richardson fits neatly into this perspective, Fielding does not. In two of his novels Fielding used the picaresque epic form and was strongly influenced by aristocratic rather than by urban, commercial values. His choice of the epic contrasts sharply with Richardson's wholly domestic milieu. But although seemingly writing in the epic tradition, Fielding rejected the introduction of unlikely events in favour of the possible and the probable; yet his use of coincidence, his mock heroics, and his persistently ironic comments on his characters and story tend to detract from the realistic presentation. Thus the 'fit' between Fielding, the middle class and the novel is at least problematic. Ian Watt concludes his assessment of Fielding by arguing that he 'departed too far from formal realism to initiate a viable tradition', but he was nevertheless a realist because his novels did portray life in the eighteenth century and he did strive to depict it as fully as possible.†

This brief discussion of the rise of the novel must now be supplemented with reference to the concept of world vision. The argument of Watt and others clearly involves social class and environment as crucial determinate factors for the development of the novel form. It would seem apposite, then, to correlate this evolution with a bourgeois world vision which, on

* David Daiches writes that Moll Flanders 'lives only as a figure in a social scene, not as a fully developed, doing and suffering human being' (*A Critical History of English Literature*, London, Secker & Warburg, 1960, vol. 3, p. 601).
† Watt, op. cit., p. 301.

Goldmann's terms, would give the individual works their inner coherence and validity. Most critics agree that *Tom Jones* is a great work of literature,* and it might seem therefore, from the evidence produced by Ian Watt, that this work has to constitute, in some measure, the literary consciousness of a rising bourgeoisie. As we have seen, Goldmann is not as deterministic as this formulation might suggest, for part of his argument involves situating the writer sociologically both in terms of the socio-economic structure as well as within the prevailing literary and philosophical traditions, since the writer's work, as literature, must in part result from these influences. But clearly there has to be a conjunction between the class aspect and these influences: the ways in which a writer transforms the inherited tradition will point to the world vision expressed in his work, as well as to his specific class position. The definition of class is thus important: class will be defined here not as mere aggregate of groups bearing a similar relation with the productive system of society, but rather as groups of individuals having a similar socio-economic status who can, and in some cases do, become conscious of themselves as a class as against another class. It is this fact of oppositional consciousness held and refracted through an exceptional individual within a group which conditions the kind of world vision that is expressed. We would expect to find, therefore, embedded at the heart of *Tom Jones*, a literary structure expressive of a middle-class world vision in opposition to the values and vision of the aristocracy and their supporters.

The problem, however, is more complex: in the 1740s the two major English novelists, Fielding and Richardson, produced novels so different from one another that it would seem most improbable that both were expressing a similar world vision. Fielding, for example, started his literary career by pub-

* '*Tom Jones* . . . after two centuries, remains among the handful of supreme novels' (W. Allen, *The English Novel*, London, Penguin Books, 1965, p. 60). F. R. Leavis, however, dissents from this judgement on the grounds that *Tom Jones* is a moral fable, not a novel (*The Great Tradition*, London, Peregrine Books, 1962, pp. 11–13). While it is true that Fielding dedicated *Tom Jones* to the 'cause of virtue', Jones, as a character and in his actions, is far more complex than this dismissal of Leavis's implies. Fielding's narrative technique is more realistic than Leavis would allow, even with the mock heroics. On this, see M. Irwin, *Henry Fielding, The Tentative Realist*, Oxford, Oxford University Press, 1967, ch. 7.

lishing a satirical attack on Richardson's novel *Pamela*, and followed this with a further, although less abusive satire, in his novel *Joseph Andrews*. Fielding's fictional universe is so different from Richardson's that if the latter is universally regarded as *the* middle-class author what of his denigrator? Ian Watt argues that Fielding cannot wholly be accommodated to his concept of formal realism, by which he means the attempt to imitate reality within the novel, its mimetic function, striving to depict as truthfully as possible the circumstances which surround an event or a person. Formal realism is the narrative method which embodies this fidelity to the truth, and, as already pointed out, Fielding, through his excessive use of coincidence, his mock heroics, reduces the authenticity of his novels. Thus if Fielding can be connected with the argument about the rise of the novel in an oblique manner, is it not possible to suggest that rather than being the expression, however ambiguously, of an incipient middle class, Fielding's works express a world that is essentially opposed to the middle class? How does Fielding's masterpiece, *Tom Jones*, fit into the middle-class novel nexus?

I

Tom Jones was first published in 1749. In content, style, and general intent, Fielding was writing against Richardson. Unlike Richardson, Fielding was a highly selfconscious novelist: *Tom Jones* is full of critical and ironic commentaries on the nature of the novel form, on society, its institutions, man, and literature. His scholarly detachment contrasts sharply with Richardson's straightforward portrayal of his experience.

Like Richardson, Defoe, and other eighteenth-century writers, Fielding set out to depict the social world as objectively as possible. Richardson's realism, by contrast, was less concerned with society as history, but rather with the individual's inner life, the subjective consciousness. In Fielding it is the values associated with the organic rural community which triumph over those of the corrupt urban areas. Richardson, on the other hand, supports these urban and middle-class values, setting his fiction within the middle-class home, and depicting middle-class man living out a life largely restricted to family affairs. The characters are ordinary types; there is neither heroic display nor pomp, but rather a measure of psychological depth, especially in the depiction of women. Fielding's epic arena is exchanged for a domestic milieu. The mode of expression, too, points to another important difference between the two writers, with Richardson's epistolary form expressive of a distinctive outlook, the 'transition from the objective, social and public orientation of the classical world to the subjective, individualist, and private orientation of the life and literature of the last two hundred years'.* There may be a direct connection between the largely middle-class values of Richardson's fiction and his objective social position as a wealthy printer, whose independence from the London booksellers was made possible through his intimate business connections with the Walpole government – he printed the Journals of the House of Commons – a government which Fielding ridiculed and despised.†

Fielding's view of the novel and social connections were wholly different. In both *Joseph Andrews* and *Tom Jones* it is the epic and historical character which dominate the structure. Fielding once wrote of his novels as 'comic epic poem[s] in prose' which, while adopting the formal technique of the epic, applied it to trivial, day-to-day incidents as well as to a wider choice of characters drawn from all parts of the social structure.‡ Fielding is not, however, a mere chronicler of events: like Defoe, his role is conceived as that of a historian who, striving to show man as a whole, which for Fielding meant man in action, will depict 'all ranks and degrees of men', 'high life and low life'. The novelist should aim at the universal.§

There is in this formulation a striking similarity with Balzac's conception of the novelist's role as the realistic portrayal of his historical period; this has led some critics to compare Fielding and Balzac as historians of bourgeois society.¶ Fielding certainly strives to create a totality, to grasp society as a whole.‖

* Watt, op. cit., p. 182.
† For details of Richardson's business and political connections, see A. D. Mckillop, *Samuel Richardson, Printer and Novelist*, Chapel Hill, University of North Carolina, 1936, especially pp. 297–305.
‡ See the Preface to *Joseph Andrews*.
§ *Tom Jones*, Book XI, ch. 1.
¶ On this, see Lukács, *Studies in European Realism*, op. cit., pp. 43–6; Wellek, op. cit., vol. 4, pp. 3–6.
‖ As Goldmann says, 'Any valid literary work takes in the whole of human life' (*The Hidden God*, op. cit., p. 99).

Fielding and Richardson, then, approach and practise the novel form in different ways, a 'dualism' at the heart of the development of the English novel. In seeking to explain this Ian Watt emphasizes their respective attitudes towards literary values. Fielding was a classicist, conspicuously embellishing his texts with learned references and drawing upon literary tradition for inspiration – the structure of *Joseph Andrews*, with its digressive interpolated stories and the descriptions of horseplay, is based on Cervantes's *Don Quixote* and other similar stories. Fielding was 'steeped in the classical tradition', and in *Tom Jones* he asserted that all aspiring novelists should develop 'a good share of learning' and that no writer was 'to be admitted into the order of critics, until he hath read over, and understood, Aristotle, Horace and Longinus, in their original language'.* Thus in Fielding there is the stress on the universal and the general, as distinct from the particular and trivial elements which largely constitute Richardson's fictional universe. In Fielding there are definite general types, universal figures (Tom Jones, Parson Adams), while in Richardson there are particular, concrete individuals. Finally there is in Fielding the epic genre, expressive of masculine, bellicose, and aristocratic values, clearly in opposition to parochial values of the rising commercial middle classes shown in Richardson.

This preliminary sketch is essential for understanding the novels of Fielding and Richardson. But although based on this kind of argument, Ian Watt's explanation is unsatisfactory. Fielding's peculiar orientation, his specific literary differences from Richardson, are analysed solely as a result of personal psychology, family background, education, or are seen merely as a more complex version of that same middle-class outlook which characterized Richardson's fiction. This latter explanation would seem untenable, since Fielding's values were diametrically opposed to Richardson's; and if class correlates are used in the explanation it would seem more apposite to argue that the significant literary differences resulted from opposed world visions and that the fiction of Richardson and Fielding represents the consciousness of conflicting social classes, that the two writers embody the values of antagonistic social groups.

* *Tom Jones*, Book 1, ch. 1.

In 1689, the 'Glorious Revolution' had brought absolutism to an end, and Parliament was now the effective political power, but the nobility were able to maintain their traditional domination through economic and social control over the franchise and over Parliament itself.* But the actual economic status of the nobility had shifted quite perceptibly. The protracted struggle during the seventeenth century between the Crown and the Court nobility on the one hand and the commercially-minded middle classes on the other, a conflict essentially over political power, had culminated in the 'compromise' of the bloodless revolution of 1689. The aristocracy now ruled England through Parliament but with the assistance of sections of the middle class; class compromise, not class conflict, characterized English history from this time onwards.

The English bourgeoisie had been unable to wrest political power away from the nobility. The English Civil War in the seventeenth century had ended with an alliance between parliamentary democracy and capitalism but within the political framework of the landed interest: 'The aristocratic order survived, but in a new shape, for money more than birth was now its basis. And Parliament itself became the instrument of landed capitalists, Whig and Tory both, and their connections and allies, whose interest the state now unswervingly pursued.'† Thus during the eighteenth century England was still largely a society which was dominated by the land and agriculture, and in its politics by the aristocracy. Economic expansion in England did not really occur until 1760, twenty years *after*

* Information on the social, economic, and political background of the late seventeenth and early eighteenth century has been drawn in the main from G. E. Mingay, *English Landed Society in the Eighteenth Century*, London, Routledge & Kegan Paul, 1962; C. Hill, *A Century of Revolution*, London, Nelson, 1961; *Reformation to Industrial Revolution*, London, Penguin Books, 1969; H. J. Habakkuk, 'English Landownership, 1680–1740', *Economic History Review*, February, 1940; A. Goodwin, (ed.), *The European Nobility in the Eighteenth Century*, London, Adam & Charles Black, 1967.
† P. Zagorin, *The English Revolution* (1955), quoted in B. Moore, Jr, *Social Origins of Dictatorship and Democracy*, London, Allen Lane The Penguin Press, 1967, p. 19. The strength of the great landowners is illustrated by the fact that, with only two exceptions, the great families of Northamptonshire and Bedfordshire still existed a hundred years after 1640 (Habakkuk, op. cit.).

the writings of the first major novelists. From 1689 until the French Revolution the landed interest ruled England in a period of economic and social stability; the incipient middle class, although slowly growing in size and influence, remained content to leave the major policy decisions in the hands of the nobility.

Thus although power hardly shifted during the eighteenth century, there were important changes occurring within the social structure. Social stratification, for example, became much more fluid. At the apex were the landed nobility, their power flowing from their ownership of large tracts of land; like all social classes they were more diversified than homogeneous. Within the class were wealthy land-owners, the effective ruling class, growing from approximately 170 in 1700 to 300 in 1800. But there were also the gentry, land-owners too, involving up to about 20,000 families who existed in the main on unearned incomes from rents, mortgages, and investments supplemented from various kinds of professional work. As distinct from the large land-owners, the gentry constituted a more diverse and less socially exclusive group. And finally there were the free-holders, who were either owner-occupiers, farmers, or absenteee owners.

During the course of the eighteenth century the dominant political position of the large land-owning class was never effectively challenged by other groups opposed to their policies. The middle class had been growing in size for many years but it was never able to constitute a viable alternative to the political authority of the landed interest. The political compromise which had been worked out in the seventeenth century between land and commerce meant that prominent members of the commercial bourgeoisie were simply absorbed into the landed ruling class. In the eighteenth century there was a substantial increase of mercantile and financial groups, their wealth drawn either from overseas trading or from mining interests such as coal, lead, tin, and copper. It was this class which bought out the holdings of those gentry who gradually became impoverished in their competition with the large land-owners and through rising costs and rents. New methods of crop rotation, the use of fertilizers and general agricultural improvement hit the small farmer and the gentry, who were unable to absorb these increasing costs from the dwindling profits of their small units. The eighteenth century was a golden age of the large estate with its high profits and low costs. Thus although there was an increase in parliamentary representation of merchants and lawyers, two-thirds of the members came from the land, and those who had connections with commerce frequently enjoyed family ties with the nobility. Mining deposits discovered on land held by the dominant class were worked jointly, a fact which points to the close economic connection which existed between the large land-owners and the commercial bourgeoisie.

The social positions of the small and the large land-owners are extremely significant. In the eighteenth century the large owners grew increasingly wealthy, while the gentry and the owner-occupiers gradually declined in both economic and social importance. With the advantage of incomes drawn from holding real and honorific government posts, from mortgages, etc., the large owners were able to develop and diversify their estate revenues. The smaller gentry, on the other hand, whose sole source of revenue came from profits derived from rents and farming, could ill afford the increasing burden of war taxation, taxes on land, and general price increases as well as maintaining the patterns of conspicuous consumption which they felt their status demanded. There were many, too, who had little real interest in developing agriculture. These factors combined to push the gentry gradually into the margins of society as their wealth and status were eroded by the growth of a monopolistic landed interest.

The evidence, then, suggests that during the course of the eighteenth century the commercial middle classes were only slowly establishing a foothold in the political structure, and that although economically strong and viable they continued to be dominated politically by the aristocracy. An urban middle class simply did not exist as a cohesive and significant social class until well into the eighteenth century, some time after the publication of *Pamela*, *Tom Jones*, and *Clarissa*. Indeed, it may be possible to link the actual decline of the English novel after 1760* with the growth of a middle class, through its insatiable

---

* The English novel after about 1760 fell away from the high standards set by Fielding, Richardson, Smollett, and Sterne, whose 'work had been crowded into a span of forty years, which was followed by a relatively barren period of twenty years in which little of intrinsic literary merit was written

need for entertainment which resulted in the development of circulating libraries, women novelists and the remarkable popularity of the Gothic horror novel. Yet Ian Watt argues for a direct causal relation between the novel and the rise of a specifically middle-class public consisting of wealthy shopkeepers, tradesmen, administrative and clerical workers, who, through increasing affluence and leisure, especially for women, constituted a new reading public able to afford the high price of books.* Watt concedes that this audience was small but nevertheless it 'may have shifted the centre of gravity of the reading public sufficiently to place the middle class as a whole in a dominating position for the first time'.† One result was the broadening of literary appeal, the weakening of classicist influence on literature, and increasing emphasis on pure entertainment.

Another factor in this situation must be discussed – the question of patronage. Writers were increasingly forced, from simple economic expediency, to acquire a patron. After 1689 the British government lost its ancient monopoly of patronage to the political parties: Defoe and Swift, for example, became active and able political pamphleteers working in close relation with the political parties and in some cases writers were given direct political office – Addison, for example, became a Secretary of State. One result of this direct political patronage was to make literature far more militant in its explicit social intent: 'At no other time,' writes Hauser, 'and in no other country have writers been honoured with so many high offices and dignities as in England at the beginning of the eighteenth century.'‡ But with the accession of the Whigs to power in 1721 this system came to an end, for the Whigs, enjoying a powerful political

---

... though novels poured from the press in an ever-swelling flood' (W. Allen, *The English Novel*, pp. 80–81). The novel now became the sentimental tale exemplified by Henry Mackenzie's *The Man of Feeling* (1771), the Gothic horror such as Walpole's *Castle of Otranto* (1764), Mrs Radcliffe's *The Mysteries of Udolpho*, and the light, entertaining social comedies of Mrs Fanny Burney who published her first novel, *Evelina*, in 1778. It was only in the early years of the nineteenth century that the English novel recovered its poise and purpose.

* Watt, op. cit., pp. 42–3.

† ibid., pp. 49–50.

‡ Hauser, op. cit., p. 45.

position, had no need for a political literature, while the Tories, heavily defeated by Walpole, were unable to finance literary service. Patronage was thus forced back to aristocratic and private control.

Fielding's life was lived out against this background. From the point of view of the sociology of literature the problem is to discover the possible conjunction between significant biographical data and the specific historical milieu: a writer's work will be both a reflection of his personal fate and the history of his time. In what ways did the larger social, economic, and political changes which occurred during the eighteenth century penetrate the early and late experiences of Fielding, driving him to express certain of these tendencies in imaginative literature? In discussing the biography of a writer a clear distinction must be kept between the childhood years, the middle years, and the years of maturity. Early childhood experiences may exert an influence on a writer's choice of career or subject matter,* although it would seem improbable that they could persist in such a way as to determine the essential structure of his literature. In any case, there is usually a dearth of reliable material on the very early years.

Henry Fielding was born in Somerset in 1712 into a family of small land-owners. Through his father, a retired army officer, he was related to the aristocracy; his mother came from a family of well-to-do gentry. The Fieldings were not successful economically. Mr Fielding, who had been retired on half pay from the Army, had tried and failed as a gentleman farmer, finding gambling more to his taste. His frequent trips to London, together with his debts and general indifference to agriculture, gradually weakened the economic viability of the family. When his wife died, Mr Fielding, much to the dismay of the family, married a woman from a different social status and religion, a Roman Catholic and keeper of a London 'eating-house'. The Dorset property bequeathed to the Fieldings on marriage was reclaimed and arrangements for the education of the six children was left in the hands of their mother's family.

* Edmund Wilson has argued that Dickens's experience in the blacking factory was one of the decisive influences on his art, although it is doubtful if this fact (if true) aids in the *understanding* of Dickens's texts (*The Wound and the Bow*, London, Methuen, 1952, ch. 1).

Henry was given a generous allowance and completed his early education at the Dutch university of Leyden, where he studied literature.

In his 'apprentice years' Fielding lived mostly in London, gathering fame as a highly successful playwright and political satirist. Between 1730 and 1737 he wrote more than twenty plays, many of them critically aimed against the Walpole government, attacking its use of bribery both in Parliament and at election time. A careful internal analysis of these early texts shows quite clearly Fielding's awareness of the main political problems of his day: in his play, *Don Quixote in England* (1734), Fielding depicts an election in which the Mayor of a Borough is forced to ask the Don to be the opposition candidate since none exists. Fielding was one of the most politically conscious men of his age.* In 1736 he joined the anti-Walpole party, and a year later started the *Historical Register*, an ambitious project aiming to portray on the stage all the significant theatrical, social, and political events of the previous year. The point was political satire; the target was the Walpole government, its members being savagely denounced as ignoramuses or grasping profiteers. In the end the government retaliated with the 1737 Licensing Act, which effectively ended Fielding's career as playwright.†

With his critical viewpoint, then, one strongly opposed to the political status quo, Fielding did not belong to the leading literary clubs and salons, preferring instead the company of young, impoverished writers among the taverns and garrets of London.‡ After 1737, however, he was forced to find a new profession to support his wife and family. The Fielding estate had been sold and divided among the six children, and Henry's share, £260, financed a three-year study of law. In 1740 he joined the English legal circuit, but failed to make the money he needed. He was thus forced to work at all kinds of literary hack

---

* Two of Fielding's greatest friends were William Pitt and George Lyttleton, who were both to play important roles in future British politics. Fielding dedicated *Tom Jones* to Lyttleton.

† F. H. Dudden, *Henry Fielding*, Oxford, Oxford University Press, 1952, vol. 1, pp. 166–70.

‡ It was often believed that Fielding lived a 'life of vice' during this period, but as W. Cross, *The History of Henry Fielding*, New Haven, Yale University Press, 1918, showed, this view was wholly unfounded.

work, pamphlets, articles, and so on. But throughout this period Fielding retained a keen political acumen and in 1740 he became the editor of a new opposition newspaper, the *Champion*. Here he resumed his attacks on Walpole and it is at this point that the biographies of Fielding and Richardson intersect. Unlike the impecunious Fielding, Richardson was a prosperous printer, 'plump, smug, middle-class and middle-aged',* a supporter of the Walpole government, the publisher of Walpole's newspaper, the *Daily Gazeteer*, and a man enjoying friendly relationships with the leading politicians within the government.

Walpole's government fell in 1742. The new administration contained many of Fielding's friends; now his relationship was similar to Richardson's connection with Walpole. In 1745 the Jacobite rebellion threatened the Constitution, and Fielding, through a series of pamphlets and the editorship of a weekly newspaper, the *True Patriot*, defended the government, the Constitution, and the Protestant religion. His reward was the office of Justice of the Peace firstly for Westminster and then for Middlesex.

Fielding and Richardson can thus be seen as politically conscious writers although on opposite sides. In terms of social origins it was the gentry against the middle class, one relatively poor and the other reasonably affluent, one critical of the political structure, the other wholly satisfied with it; and while Richardson accepted the values of commercial urban society, Fielding, forced by necessity to accept the private patronage of Ralph Allen,† constantly attacked the economic and the social consequences of commercial civilization. In 1747 Fielding wrote that society was becoming increasingly dissipated and immoral; everything apart from politics which, since the defeat of Walpole, lay in trustworthy hands, was in decline: 'No age or nation was ever sunk to a more deplorable state', with the desire for luxury giving rise to 'every kind of corruption and prostitution, no man being ashamed of anything but the appearance of poverty'.

* Dudden, op. cit., p. 308.
† In 1742 Fielding was saved from increasing debts by Ralph Allen (1694–1764) the 'Man of Bath'. A former official in the Post Office whose wealth came from limestone quarries on his estate near Bath, he patronized many prominent literary figures – Pope, Warburton, Garrick. From 1742 Fielding spent most of his time at Allen's country house, where he wrote *Tom Jones*.

Morals, art, music, architecture, and literature, all had declined; in the 1730s it had been the political system which was corrupt, but now in the 1740s it was society itself, and in the many articles written on this theme of social disintegration Fielding pointed to a growing concern with money, profit, and greed.

The background of an expanding middle class which was politically inert contrasts strongly with Fielding's political consciousness. If the middle class of the eighteenth century created the novel, then it did so as an expression of the social rather than the political world. The novelists who immediately followed Fielding are curiously silent on politics; nor are they especially critical of their society. The middle-class consciousness is expressed in this oblique manner precisely because as a class it lacked political confidence, for having formed an alliance with the commercially-minded elements of the aristocracy it remained politically subordinate to the land. But with the expansion of commercial capitalism and the actual growth of a middle class, its consciousness could express itself only outside politics, in the realm of ideas, in the cultural superstructure. It is undoubtedly true that during the course of the eighteenth century a specifically middle-class 'mentality' begins to emerge, confronting the aristocratic 'mentality' which had dominated culture for centuries. Historically, the middle class would finally assert itself politically in the nineteenth century, but in the eighteenth century its claims as a rising class capable of generating commercial and industrial expansion, of confronting the landed interest, could be met only in terms of a challenge to the dominant culture. A social class which strives towards some form of economic and political supremacy in circumstances which inhibit its claims will seek to assert itself through culture: as a rising class it must negate the values of the class it seeks to supplant. Thus during the eighteenth century the aristocratic and middle-class 'mentalities' coexisted, generating a certain tension. They were fundamentally opposed: the aristocratic stress on classicist taste in literature, 'the cool, sceptical intellect, witty, clever, a highly skilled technique, a purity of language', constituted the literary norms prevalent to about 1740. Classicist taste dominated literature. In Defoe for the first time these norms are challenged, and art is defined in terms of reportage, not the embellishment of the real.* In social terms, aristocratic culture accepted as normal the subordinate status of women; marriage was largely the subject of jokes. For the middle class, the family and marriage were almost sacrosanct; in literature tenderness and sentimentality became increasingly the norm in the eighteenth century: wit and heroic display are replaced by the novel of sensibility.†

3

Fielding's first two novels, *Joseph Andrews* and *Jonathan Wild*, follow the satirical pattern of his theatrical period; both novels are 'entertainment', far too satirical to succeed as great literature. Above all, the novels fail as aesthetic wholes: in *Tom Jones* all the numerous, apparently inconsequential episodes conduce ultimately to the dénouement – in *Joseph Andrews* the various episodes serve merely to bring out idiosyncrasies of character and do not have the same importance for the actual *development* of the plot, nor are they organically linked with the novel's end. Fielding's grasp of the novel as a unified whole is not yet apparent. This is especially brought out by comparing the technique, popular during the eighteenth century, of interpolating two independent stories, digressions, in the manner of the Spanish and French writers. In *Joseph Andrews* there are two digressions, both long and rambling and serving no apparent function within the novel. In *Tom Jones* the interpolated story of the man on the hill is situated at the centre of the novel and serves to link the rural scenes with those of the last part of the book in London. The end of *Joseph Andrews* with the foundlings restored to their heritage is artificial, it has been engineered; the various episodes which make up the novel are too often mere absurdities and not organically related to the development of the plot.‡ In *Tom Jones*, on the other hand, all the

* Watt, op. cit., p. 252, for this point.
† In *Gulliver's Travels* (1726), Jonathan Swift depicted family life among the Houyhnhnms in aristocratic terms – children are taken from their parents at twenty months and entrusted to public boarding-schools, and parents see them twice a year for a single hour. The family hardly exists. For a discussion of the differences between aristocratic and bourgeois culture in the eighteenth century, see L. L. Schucking, *The Puritan Family*, London, Routledge & Kegan Paul, 1969, ch. 5.
‡ See Dudden, op. cit., pp. 351–3.

apparent loose ends are tied together and this makes for an aesthetic whole. Many novels – Smollett's *Peregrine Pickle*, Dickens' *Pickwick Papers* – are built around a hero who passes through various episodes in which he meets many people who themselves do not exert any great influence on his subsequent career. Walter Scott's remark on Fielding as the 'father of the English novel' was probably bestowed for the plot of *Tom Jones*, a 'classic example of a perfectly coherent story, most carefully planned from the very beginning, progressing slowly but surely through a succession of strictly relevant characters and events and terminating in a logically appropriate catastrophe'.* All incidents in the novel are subordinated to the plot; the characters perform a particular function and they are never introduced simply because they might be interesting. At the same time, they are real living people, struggling with genuine moral problems.†

The novel is divided into eighteen books: six deal with the country, six with journeying on the road, and the final six with the town, London. In its structure *Tom Jones* is manifestly superior to the similarly picaresque *Joseph Andrews*, for all its numerous incidents conduce to its end: in *Joseph Andrews* the two highway robberies exercise no significant role in terms of plot, while the comparable incident in *Tom Jones*, in which Jones, hearing of the robber's economic distress, gives him money, is important because the robber is the cousin of Jones's landlady in London who, for this kindness, supports him at a crucial moment in his fortunes.‡

The plot hinges on the ambiguity of Jones's birth. The novel begins with Squire Allworthy, a wealthy Somerset land-owner, discovering a baby in his bed. He adopts the child, giving him his own christian name and the surname of the suspected mother. A local schoolmaster, Partridge, suspected of being the father, and refusing to confess, is dismissed from his employment.

---

* Coleridge compared the plot of *Tom Jones* with the *Oedipus Tyrannus* and Johnson's *Alchemist* as one of 'the three most perfect plots ever planned', while Thackerary wrote that 'as a work of construction' it was 'quite a wonder'. Quoted in Dudden, op. cit., p. 616.

† Although we would agree with Watt that 'the importance of the plot is in inverse proportion to that of character', there is nevertheless a strong didactic element which is worked out through the characters.

‡ See Irwin, op. cit., p. 100, on this point.

Squire Allworthy's sister, Bridget, marries Captain Blifil, who dies two years later, leaving behind a son who becomes Jones's main enemy. Young Jones and Blifil grow up together, in competition, under the guidance of the clergyman, Thwackum, and the philosopher, Square. Jones falls in love with Sophia Western, the daughter of a fox-hunting neighbour, Squire Western, who sees a marriage between Blifil and Sophia as economically as well as socially desirable. Jones, uncertain of Sophia, has an affair with the gamekeeper's daughter, Molly Seagrim. When Sophia refuses to marry Blifil, Jones's love for her is discovered and he is asked to leave the estate. Sophia, threatened with an odious marriage, flees and, like Jones, takes to the road. Meanwhile, Jones has met Partridge, now a barber surgeon, and the two travel to the inn at Upton. Here Jones rescues a Mrs Waters, actually Jenny Jones his suspected mother, from an attempted murder and becomes her lover. At Upton many of the characters meet without knowing it. When Jones hears that Sophia has left for London he follows. In London Jones becomes the paid lover of Lady Bellaston. Lord Fellamar, a 'rake', is encouraged by Lady Bellaston to seduce Sophia whom she suspects Jones loves. An attempt to pressgang Jones fails. Later, a Mr Fitzpatrick, suspecting that Jones has had an affair with his wife, is wounded by him in a duel. Jones is arrested and Sophia breaks off all relations. Meanwhile his friend Nightingale and his landlady Mrs Miller, together with Partridge, successfully work to clear Jones's name and the dénouement reveals that Jones is the illegitimate son of Bridget Allworthy and thus free to marry Sophia.

This brief summary of what is in fact a highly intricate plot serves merely to point out its essential basis in ambiguity.

4

Fielding was much more than a prose fiction writer: in both *Joseph Andrews* and *Tom Jones* he dwells at some length on the nature of the novel form. His intention is to portray a totality, historically and concretely grasped. Thus his repeated emphasis on experience: our history, he wrote of *Tom Jones*, must strive to the universal, to know 'all ranks and degrees of men'. In

Tom Jones this ambition is fully realized, for the novel depicts a remarkable gallery of social types, urban and rural, teachers, ministers, publicans, tradesmen, aristocrats, criminals. The art of writing, Fielding argued, was to show man in general, 'not man but manners', not an individual but a 'species'.* The literary vehicle for achieving this ambition was the epic, a significant choice, for if the epic is to create a true picture of human life then it must reflect in some measure the relationship between freedom and necessity, that is, it must depict men's actions as circumscribed by time and place but show how they still result from human initiative. But the human deed as an integral part of epic action has never been achieved: in the classical epic it is the Gods, not men, who embody its driving force, and 'the greatness of the epic hero emerged only in his . . . tenacious and cunning resistance to these forces'.† In *Tom Jones* the hero is rarely called upon to exercise any form of initiative, and his progression through the novel is wholly the result of the unintended consequences of his actions and does not flow from his personal efforts: things happen to Jones and he accepts his fate with resignation and humour. Tom Jones has no tenacious cunning: Allworthy turns him out of his house and all he can do is write a pathetic letter to his love accepting his social rejection; he then becomes involved with a military unit, cheerfully agreeing to move north and fight the Jacobites; he is the paid lover of the corrupt Lady Bellaston; and finally his true paternity is discovered *by others* and he is saved from the gallows and reunited with his Sophia. The only occasion where Jones actually exerts initiative is when he criticizes Nightingale's callous treatment of his mistress, an incident wholly unconnected with his own personal fate.

The function and role of the hero is crucially important for understanding the development of the novel form. During the eighteenth century the world was increasingly grasped in secular terms: the social world was man's work and not the result of divine intervention; the prevailing trend in philosophy became the desire to free the individual from the restrictions imposed on his understanding by custom and tradition. In literature this took the form of setting the individual free, alone

* *Joseph Andrews*, Book 3, ch. 1.
† G. Lukács, *Goethe and His Age*, London, Merlin Press, 1968, p. 147.

in the world, to work out his own personal salvation.* This
conception of freedom is closely bound up with the ideology of
individualism, itself a reaction against the 'corporate loyalty
and customs' which permeated pre-industrial societies.† Thus
when Jones is rejected by Allworthy and Squire Western as a
proper suitor for Sophia, he sets off to discover his fate, to
realize himself through some form of action. But his freedom to
do this is severely circumscribed. He is portrayed as a victim,
not hero, of a world in which events are outside the control of
the individual; his rare intentions are never properly realized
and, unlike the hero of the nineteenth-century novel, he lacks
a genuine concrete aim – Stendhal's lower-class hero, Julien
Sorel, for example, possessed a concrete social ambition.
Sorel's aims placed him in conflict with society, while Jones,
although rejected socially, never constitutes a threat to the social
structure. It was not until after the French Revolution that the
modern hero emerged as one demanding that society accept
him, the 'hero by will rather than by birth'. His social ambition
was clearly linked with the idea of equality which the Revolution had fostered; expectations replaced privilege and the hero
saw society in terms of conflict rather than consensus.‡ Thus
Jones can think of joining the Navy at one moment or the Army
to fight the Jacobites – but he finally goes to London in vague
pursuit of Sophia. What Goethe called the 'retrogressive motif',
the process of distancing the action from the goal, dominates the
novel. The force of circumstances proves to be superior to the
vaguely defined intentions of Jones. Social necessity, not freedom, asserts itself, for although he acts in conformity with his
character, the results of his actions are always contrary to his
intentions.§

* See Lukács, *La Théorie du Roman*, ch. 1. Fielding's religious affiliations
are important here: he was a Christian of the Low Church, Latitudinarian
tradition, which stressed the rationalist and mystery-dispelling aspect of
Christianity. Man was by nature potentially good, but he was free to choose
between virtue and vice: works, i.e. action, were more important than faith.
See Irwin, op. cit., ch. 2, for a discussion of Fielding's moral views, and
M. C. Battestin, *The Moral Basis of Fielding's Art*, Middletown, Wesleyan
University Press, 1959.
† See C. Hill, *Puritanism and Revolution*, London, Mercury Books, 1958.
‡ I. Howe, *Politics and the Novel*, New York, Meredian Books, 1960, pp.
27–8.
§ Since the novel is built around the plot, to which the characters are largely
subordinate, they cannot *know* the others, and thus the structure is based 'on

Jones can hardly be claimed as a modern hero. A bourgeois world vision would not have endowed him with his excessively modest ambitions, his largely negative character. Pamela, Becky Sharp, Julien Sorel, Rastignac, are characters endowed with thrustful, ambitious personalities, wholly positive in their concrete, social aims. To depict him in a 'bourgeois manner' would have created obvious difficulties for Fielding, leading him into criticism of a system of social stratification and inequality which he saw as essentially natural and necessary. Tom Jones is more the hero of a declining gentry whose prestige and power was steadily being undermined by the development of large landowners and the impoverishment of the smaller owners, farmers, and tenants. This factual loss of status is the condition for social marginality and for the marginal hero, the first 'superfluous man', the first modern anti-hero.

5

Many writers have observed the close relation between the development of the novel and the freedom of women. Before the novel could claim status as a viable literary genre, the concept of romantic love had to be a part of its structure. During the eighteenth century, middle-class women were increasingly freer, having a voice in marriage decisions although the whole relation was still strongly bound up with property.* The aristocracy's low estimate of marriage and contempt for women contrasts strongly with the middle-class, Puritan view of marriage as a sacrosanct institution in which women were formally equal.† The ideology of the middle classes stressed above all else pre-marital chastity and the absolute fidelity of the wife to the husband. This became the predominant eighteenth-century attitude: Dr Johnson was explicit in drawing the connections existing between sex and property, arguing that a woman's chastity was 'of the utmost importance, as all property depends upon it'. The increasing significance of landed property

---

an elaborate counterpoint of deception and surprise, and this would be impossible if the characters could share each other's minds and take their fates into their own hands' (Watt, op. cit., p. 288).
* Hill, *Puritanism and Revolution*, p. 371.
† Schucking, op. cit.

for conferring status underlines the reasons for the popularity of marriage through mergers. A chaste wife would guarantee unsullied family succession. Given this as the background, how did Fielding depict sex and love in *Tom Jones*?

Ian Watt argues that Fielding's treatment of sex is one of his 'general organizing themes'. Much of the action in *Tom Jones* flows from Jones' sexual adventures, their pleasures and pains. Jones is characterized by Fielding as a highly-charged individual possessing 'naturally violent animal spirits', a 'thoughtless, giddy youth, with little sobriety in his manners, and less in his countenance', but nevertheless with a 'gallantry of temper which greatly recommends men to women'.* Jones is physically appealing, 'a charming figure', young, healthy, fresh, strong, resembling, if men can, 'an angel' – in short, one of the 'handsomest young fellows in the world'.† With such attributes Jones is naturally a success with women: Molly Seagrim, Mrs Waters and Lady Bellaston all discover in Jones significantly attractive properties. It is interesting to note that in his relations with these women Jones is initially passive, the seduced rather than seducer. Although not yet in love with Sophia, he cannot seduce Molly because she is far too young, and thus it is Molly who seeks Jones – he nevertheless attributes the conquest to himself.‡ Similarly in his relation with Mrs Waters: unlike Molly, Mrs Waters is middle-aged and not too attractive, but with her clothes torn by her attacker, 'her breasts, which were well formed, and extremely white, attracted the eye of her deliverer'. On the walk to Upton, helping her over the stiles, Jones finds these particular attractions too much to resist. But it is Mrs Waters, over dinner, who strives successfully to effect a conquest, not without some initial difficulty: 'Now Mrs Waters and our hero had no sooner sat down together, than the former began to play this artillery upon the latter.' Fielding describes with masterly comic skill the ensuing meal of meat, drink, and seduction:

First, from two lovely blue eyes, whose bright orbs flashed lightning at their discharge, flew forth two pointed ogles. But happily for our hero,

* *Tom Jones*, ed. R. P. C. Mutter, London, Penguin Books, 1966, pp. 235, 135.
† ibid., pp. 441, 453.
‡ ibid., pp. 166–70.

hit only a vast piece of beef which he was then conveying into his plate, and harmless spent their force.

Jones is only gradually affected by Mrs Waters' attentions:

And now, gently lifting up those two bright orbs which had already begun to make an impression on poor Jones, she discharged a volley of small charms at once from her whole countenance in a smile. Not a smile of mirth, nor of joy; but a smile of affection, which most ladies have always ready at their command, and which serves them to show at once their good humour, their pretty dimples, and their white teeth.

Jones at last understands: 'He then began to see the designs of the enemy, and indeed to feel their success. A parley now was set on foot between the two parties.' Sophia, far away and apparently lost, is forgotten and 'no sooner had the amorous parley ended, and the lady unmasked her royal battery, by carelessly letting her handkerchief drop from her neck, than the heart of Mr Jones was entirely taken, and the fair conqueror enjoyed the usual fruits of her victory'.[*] Again in London, Jones is the willing victim of the corrupt Lady Bellaston. He is certainly no Lovelace for whom the pursuit and conquest of the virginal Clarissa constitute the main motivating force of Richardson's novel.

Clearly Jones enjoys sex, but unlike Richardson, Fielding treats sex not as a means of social promotion (especially in *Pamela*), but rather as a necessary and genuine part of human relations. Fielding's concern is with virtue and the problem of values. His account of sex conflicts with the growing Puritan conception which is found in the novels of Richardson. In the course of the eighteenth century virtue was redefined in sexual terms. Like Malthus later, Dr Johnson, one of Richardson's most ardent supporters, argued that 'man's chief merit consisted in resisting the impulses of nature', a view clearly at variance with Jones's practice.[†] In Richardson sex is a mixture of Puritanism and prurience. Pamela, the servant girl who resists seduction and has her virtue rewarded by social elevation, typifies the Puritan horror of sexual love which is outside marriage.[‡] In *Clarissa*, the heroine resists the sexual advances of

[*] ibid., pp. 455–6.
[†] Watt, op. cit., p. 163.
[‡] Schucking, op. cit., pp. 138–40.

the rakish Lovelace before finally succumbing to his schemes in a brothel and then dying of shame.* One historian has commented that it was largely on questions of sexual behaviour that bourgeois and aristocratic values diverged so dramatically. The word 'prude', for example, appears for the first time in 1740, while a word such as 'indelicacy' becomes part of the new middle-class language of feeling.†

Fielding's wholly different conception of sex is particularly brought out in his treatment of Jones's fluctuating attitude towards Molly, whom he believes he has made pregnant. At first, thinking he was her sole lover, he decides he has responsibilities, but when he finds her in bed with his tutor, Square, remarks, 'What can be more innocent than the indulgence of a natural appetite or more laudable than the propagation of our species.' And when, a little later, meeting Molly walking in a 'delicious grove', Jones, although thinking of Sophia, none the less has intercourse with Molly, Fielding comments: 'Some of my readers may be inclined to think this event unnatural. However, the fact is true; and, perhaps, may be sufficiently accounted for, by suggesting that Jones probably thought one woman better than none, and Molly has probably imagined two men to be better than one.' In any case, Jones is partly excused because he has been drinking wine; but he does indulge his natural appetites.‡ It must be said that Fielding is not subscribing to the view held by many eighteenth-century philosophers that man was simply an animal dominated by insatiable appetites.

---

* David Daiches has pointed out the violent and violating aspects of Richardson's treatment of sex. 'None of Richardson's rakes seeks [sexual] satisfaction; they want to rape; they are not sensualists but competitive collectors of virginities.' Lovelace drugs Clarissa and the 'woman is sacrificed to male violence'. Sex is a 'matter of planning and stamina', without either pleasure or satisfaction (D. Daiches, 'Samuel Richardson', in his *Literary Essays*, Edinburgh, Oliver & Boyd, 1956).

† Hill, op. cit., pp. 372–3.

‡ *Tom Jones*, pp. 238–40. Ian Watt suggests that Jones has not yet achieved the 'continence of moral adulthood', op. cit., p. 290. Fielding's open, fresh portrayal of sex in his novels was often taken simplistically to indicate a personal predilection for loose living. Taine, for example, comparing Fielding and Richardson, likened his works to 'rough wine' while *Pamela* was a 'flower', going on to argue that for Fielding virtue was 'but an instinct', that he was a 'drinker', and that his novels merely created an awareness of 'the impetuosity of the senses, the upswelling of the blood' (Taine, *History of English Literature*, vol. II, p. 176).

Tom Jones is a novel built around the concept of romantic love: Jones has his affair with Molly *before* he is fully aware of his love for Sophia, and his relations with Mrs Waters and Lady Bellaston *after* he feels he has lost her. Fielding repeatedly argues that love is superior to mere physical passion, mere 'hunger'. Man has a 'kind and benevolent disposition, which is gratified by contributing to the happiness of others'; there is parental and filial affection and 'though the pleasures arising from such pure love may be heightened and sweetened by the assistance of amorous desires, yet the former can subsist alone, nor are they destroyed by the intervention of the latter.* When Jones and Sophia finally marry, Fielding comments that Jones was the 'happiest of all human kind: for what happiness this world affords equal to the possession of such a woman as Sophia, I sincerely own I have never yet discovered'.†

Unbridled sexuality is bad simply because of its corrupting power, as with Lady Bellaston and Lord Fellamar. Fielding's moralizing attitude is especially brought out in Jones's criticism of his friend Nightingale who, to please his father, agrees to marry a women he does not love instead of Nancy, his mistress. 'You have gone far beyond common gallantries,' says Jones, to which Nightingale replies by pointing to Jones's apparent sexual incontinence. Jones's answer is that he is no 'canting hypocrite', or virgin, but that in his affairs with women he has neither consciously injured them nor simply gained pleasure for himself. Women are friends, not enemies, not objects to be conquered.‡ Thus when Nancy is discovered to be pregnant and Nightingale argues against marrying 'a whore', Jones angrily retorts that 'when you promised to marry her, she became your wife, and she hath sinned more against prudence than virtue'. Nightingale is frightened by what others would think, he would be 'ashamed of ever showing my face again'. What is this world, says Jones, 'but the vile, the foolish, and the profligate? Forgive me, if I

* ibid., p. 252.
† ibid., pp. 871–2.
‡ ibid., pp. 667–9. In Richardson's novels women attempt to assert themselves as the equals of men, but it is always men who overpower them. In his depiction of Mr B. (in *Pamela*), Lovelace (in *Clarissa*), and Sir Charles Grandison, Richardson made certain that his heroines would not go unpunished for their assertion of equality. The male must dominate women, humiliating her, sometimes beating her.

say such a shame must proceed from false modesty, which always attends false honour as its shadow – But I am well assured there is not a man of real sense and goodness in the world, who would not honour and applaud the action.'* There is nothing here which suggests either an aristocratic or middle-class conception of sexual love; it is motive, not social conventions, which for Fielding determines an action's moral worth.

6

The notions of birth and honour exercise an important influence on the structure of *Tom Jones*. His suspected illegitimate lower-class origin is the initial cause for Jones's ejection from the All-worthy household and the motor force of the whole novel. The plot hinges on Jones's ambiguous birth, for if he is indeed a lower-class bastard then marriage to Sophia will threaten social status and undermine the basis of the class structure. But Jones's saving grace is his conception of honour, that 'monstrous, vile word' as Richardson described it; for while a bastard he is yet a true gentleman. Stendhal's Julien Sorel has little conception of honour, but for Jones it acts as an important motive for action. He enters his affair with Lady Bellaston not only for money but also because it represents a challenge to his honour; as a true gentleman he loves Sophia for herself and not, like Blifil, for her wealth; he rescues Mrs Waters; he upbraids Nightingale.

But while these actions point to a generous and worthy man, Squire Western, while accepting Jones as an equal of sorts, cannot allow the 'blood of the Westerns' to be contaminated through an alliance with a bastard; it is blood not ceremony which matters for the Westerns and for the gentry for whom status was ascribed, not achieved. For Fielding, social stratification was necessary, inevitable, and immutable, conceived as a system of fixed statuses adding up to an organic unity in which all social classes worked for the benefit of the whole. Government is based on the principle of subordination; each individual has the duty of contributing to the whole:

The gentleman ought to labour in the service of his country; the serving man ought to wait diligently on his master; the artificer ought to

* *Tom Jones*, p. 680.

labour in his work; the husbandman in tilling the ground; the merchant in passing the tempests; but the vagabonds ought clearly to be banished, as is the superfluous humour of the body.*

Social structure is essentially static; each individual has an allotted role and function and should know it:

Those members of society, who are born to furnish the blessings of life [i.e. labourers, artificers, servants] now begin to light their candles, in order to pursue their daily labour, for the use of those who are born to enjoy these blessings.†

Jones is fully aware that as a lower-class bastard he has no chance of marrying Sophia, but his consciousness of this fact does not place him in an antagonistic position with society, rather his position is one of passive acquiescence. Fielding solves this problem of irreconcilable love by disclosing Jones's true paternity, as part of the gentry: for Stendhal, the resolution of the conflict between Julien Sorel and society came through death. But Fielding's vision conceived a society which was closed, not open, in which social classes accepted their status as fixed. The basis of this rigid vision of stratification is not challenged by Fielding's resolution: the lovers are united 'without subverting the basis of the social order'.‡

For Richardson the class structure was far more fluid. Pamela captures her Squire B. and marries successfully into the squirearchy, her sound bourgeois virtue both confounding and leavening aristocratic lechery; Clarissa Harlowe's wealthy middle-class family strive to consolidate their status through marriage into the aristocracy. Pamela, unlike Jones, *achieves* her status.

Fielding's static conception of the class structure, his vision of a closed organic, that is, pre-capitalist, rural society could not

* Quoted by G. Sherburn, 'Fielding's Social Outlook', in J. L. Clifford, *Eighteenth Century English Literature: Essays in Criticism*, New York, Oxford University Press, 1959, pp. 251–73. In his 'Essay on Conversation', Fielding wrote that 'Men are superior to each other . . . by title, by birth, by rank in profession, and by age'. Quoted in Irwin, op. cit., p. 21. Although he accepted the validity of rank it is clear that he also saw society in terms of merit, of useful work, and his criticism of the aristocracy is couched in these terms. Beggars are excluded from society because they do not work.
† *Tom Jones*, pp. 542–3.
‡ Watt, op. cit., pp. 280–81. Fielding's vision of society had to be one of class rigidity in the end, since an open system threatened the basis of the gentry's status.

by itself constitute the basis for his new 'species of writing'. The novel in essence is to do with values which have been challenged, with moral ambiguity, with doubt and uncertainty, with change. But rural society is too ordered, secure, tradition-oriented, full of slow, undemanding growth, its organic community and unchanging order symbolized by its periodic harvests, its church, its village green. The picaresque form of the novel, such as *Tom Jones*, allows a contrast to be drawn between the rural and the urban, the pre-capitalist and the capitalist communities. It has often been argued that the influence of urbanism and commercial capitalism were crucial factors for the growth of the novel, since rapid social change facilitates comparisons between rural and urban in terms of life styles, social types, and values. As we have seen, England in the eighteenth century was changing slowly into a commercial society, but it remained predominantly agricultural. This fact hides the rapidity of urban development: by 1750, for example, London held 11 per cent of the population, compared to Paris with $2\frac{1}{2}$ per cent and Amsterdam with 8 per cent.* London's remarkable growth in the eighteenth century fostered an overall change, with a more fluid social structure in which the ethic of individualism, of individual effort, was challenging status by ascription and threatening the status of gentlemen, as well as making it more indefinable.† But Fielding's vision refused to accommodate these changes to it. In *Tom Jones* the contrast between rural and urban is in favour of the former. Urbanism is identified with corruption.‡

Tom Jones is divided into two equal parts. In the first part Jones's upbringing and early life on the Allworthy estate are depicted, followed by his adventures on the road to Upton; the action of the second part of the novel occurs in London. Dividing these two sections is the story of the man on the hill. For many critics this interpolated story seems irrelevant and boring, included by Fielding because he was writing in the picaresque tradition. Such criticism is misdirected, for the story serves to

* E. A. Wrigley, 'London's Importance in Changing English Society and Economy, 1650–1750', *Past and Present*, no. 37.
† Allworthy, for example, comes from a humble background, the son of a gamekeeper.
‡ For Fielding the values of the town are anathema and, as Irwin says, 'the superior happiness of rural life is a constant theme . . .' (op. cit., p. 20).

bind the two separate parts of the novel together into a unified structure. The man on the hill is the story of urban corruption and the subsequent retreat to rural life, to peace and tranquillity. It looks backward to Jones's relatively uncomplicated rural life, and forward to London, its problems, its corrupting power, where Jones is degraded to the status of kept lover and where Lord Fellamar, one of the novel's few positive males, attempts to rape Sophia.* Fielding's actual technique of writing changes in his urban scenes:† there are no more humorous speeches, no discussions of principle, and he continually remarks that many things are being omitted because the reader would only find them dull – the characters are depicted as dull-witted, the upper class have vice and no wit, numerous illicit love affairs occur, there are plots against Jones and Sophia, even hints of incest (Mrs Waters and Jones).‡ The gloomy urban scenes end with the discovery of Jones's true origins and his marriage to Sophia.

7

Tom Jones is a novel of a hero who eventually triumphs materially through moral worth. Jones can marry his Sophia because others have been convinced that he is worthy and are prepared to work for him, against those like Blifil and Fellamar who intrigue to prevent his union with Sophia. This has to be, for the hero in this novel cannot hope to challenge successfully a social system as corrupt as Fielding's London. The intricate, highly artificial plot serves to pilot the 'worthy' Jones to a happy dénouement. As Ian Watt has observed, the plot's basic direction is to 'return to the norm', to the status quo, its inner structure determined by Fielding's vision of a legitimate social structure beyond challenge. It is thus difficult to resist the conclusion that while Fielding was critical of certain aspects of the social structure, especially the aristocracy, the Church of England, and the medical profession, he seems finally to assert the virtues of a traditional rural England over the secular,

* Richardson's rape scenes are, by contrast, filled with horror.
† 'Whenever he writes about London his tone becomes grim, hard, distressing' (Sherburn, op. cit.).
‡ See A. D. McKillop, *The Early Masters of English Fiction*, Lawrence, University of Kansas, 1956, p. 134.

advancing urban capitalist areas.* It is hard to see how Fielding can be situated in the history of the novel as a bourgeois writer; in *Tom Jones* society and the need for social order exercise priority of individual motivation and action – the plot functions as a kind of 'magnet' pulling 'every individual particle out of the random order brought about by temporal accident and human imperfection and puts them all back in their proper position'.† Fielding's flat portrayal of character, his lack of interest in the subjective aspect of life, flow from his acceptance of the neo-classicist emphasis on the priority of the plot over character. 'Our province,' he wrote, was 'to relate facts, and we shall leave causes to persons of a much higher genius.' *Pamela* and *Clarissa* are subjective explorations into the dark recesses of reality; *Joseph Andrews* and *Tom Jones* range outwards, encompassing a panorama of English society. In Fielding's *Tom Jones*, as many writers have pointed out, there is little conception of the complex subjectivity of human feeling; love and sexual passion are depicted simply, while Richardson conveys a complex matrix of feeling, as in Lovelace's experience of love for Clarissa which is mixed with a desire to humiliate her.‡ This marked lack of subjectivity puts Fielding in opposition not merely to Richardson but to much of the literature which followed. Richardson, like Jane Austen and Proust, is inward-looking, embodying a rejection of the 'great world' in favour of the humanely superior 'little world of the bourgeoisie',§ and directly counterposed to Fielding's aristocratic, panoramic, external, and generous view. Jones, it might even be said, represents a last stubborn attempt to reassert a vision of the world which was rapidly vanishing, a

---

* Fielding's last novel, *Amelia*, set exclusively in an urban area, is more cynical and critical of eighteenth-century society than the other novels.
† Watt, op. cit.
‡ McKillop, op. cit., p. 129. On this, see also M. Praz, *The Romantic Agony*, London, Fontana, 1960, pp. 114–16. R. Alter has recently argued for a more ambiguous element in Fielding, citing Jones's indiscretion with Molly and commenting that Blifil gratified 'his desires with the aid of his own right hand'. Fielding's text reads: 'The charms of Sophia had not made the least impression on Blifil; not that his heart was pre-engaged; nor was he totally insensible of beauty, or had any aversion to women; but his appetites were, by nature, so moderate, that he was easily able, by philosophy or by study, or by some other method, to subdue them' (*Tom Jones*, p. 263). R. Alter, 'Fielding and the Uses of Style', *Novel*, Fall, 1967.
§ Lukács, *Goethe and His Age*, p. 243.

world not yet 'degraded' by commercial values,* a world where it was still possible for epic action to take place, where there was no rupture yet between the hero and his world, no problematic values, and no quest for personal identity. Goethe's Werther and Stendhal's Julien Sorel are seized by life's apparent emptiness and lack of genuine values, heroes engaged in some measure in searching for values and meaning. We cannot claim that for Tom Jones.

The social, economic, and political background of the early English novel was that of an expanding bourgeois society in which the continued power of the aristocracy hinged on its highly concentrated system of family property and entail. The political compromise with the bourgeoisie had been worked out in the seventeenth century. Is it possible to argue that in the realm of ideas there would be no automatic and mechanical correlation with the new social structure, but rather that the ideas would tend to lag behind the social changes, and that by the 1740s the political compromise was still in the process of being worked out in the superstructure of ideas and culture? Thus the novel has this contradictory history – that although both Richardson and Fielding subscribed to realism, their visions were wholly dissimilar.

All great literary works express some kind of world vision, the product of a 'collective group consciousness', a complex of ideas, aspirations, and feelings which place them in real and theoretical opposition to other groups, other classes. The world vision will express itself in literature as a coherent whole, precisely because of the writer's identification with certain 'fundamental social tendencies' of the period. In *Tom Jones* Fielding created a coherent whole, an integrated structure, and not a collection of amusing episodes. Each part has a place in the emerging pattern and the final result is a totality, a rich, comic novel which mourns the death of the English gentry and hesitantly accepts the emerging bourgeois society. His realism of presentation, as it has been called, is *not* aristocratic; the novel form demanded a realistic dimension and this Fielding accepted, but within the novel the values are not those of the bourgeoisie. When Fielding turned to writing a novel about social reform in

* This is a constant theme in Fielding's entire literary and political writings. See Irwin, op. cit., pp. 17-18, for some early statements.

the urban areas, *Amelia*, the narrative technique is not picaresque but based on ordinary contemporary life in the town, and in this sense it is more realistic than the other novels. Jones, for example, is depicted as lacking intimate social contacts for the first twenty years of his life, but in *Amelia* hero and heroine are placed far more concretely in the social context, a married couple with three children, heavily in debt. There is more detail of domestic life, there are no picaresque adventures, and the dialogue is more realistic. In short, General Booth and his family lead a specific kind of social life. Fielding's vision in this novel is wholly pessimistic, and the social system is characterized in terms of extreme moral decay. But having shown that contemporary society was incapable of allowing a 'gentleman' to make a genuine life, Fielding ends the novel artificially, by an arbitrary happy ending, the Booths leaving the town for the quiet life of the country. Virtue is preserved by leaving society.*
Fielding's vision would not allow him to come to terms with commercial capitalism, and he could portray urban man only as grasping and egoistic.† The unity of the novel suffers and the artificial end indicates its failure as an integrated totality. For Fielding, the novel was essentially a means of expressing values which were gradually becoming obsolete; *Amelia* is the pessimistic, one-sided view of this vision.

* One of the main themes in *Amelia* is that of public corruption, the motor force of the plot being the inability of General Booth to save his family from financial ruin by gaining a deserved status; but his prison sentence for debt completely prevents this. See Irwin, op. cit., ch. 8.
† Thus Booth's characterization of country life, is one of perfect contentment in comparison with his nerve-racked urban existence: 'I scarce know a circumstance that distinguished one day from another. The whole was one continued series of love, health and tranquillity ... who can describe the pleasures which the morning air gives to one in perfect health; the flow of spirits which springs up from exercise ...' (quoted in Battestin, op. cit., p. 93).

9   Alienation, Reification, and the Novel

Twentieth-century literary critics have been vocal in claiming the death of the novel. The Spanish critic, Ortega y Gasset, in his 'Notes on the Novel' (1924) wrote that any literary genre may at some point reach exhaustion: 'There exist a number of possible themes for the novel. The workman of the primal hour had no trouble finding new blocks – new characters, new themes. But present-day writers face the fact that only narrow and concealed veins are left them.'* The rise of the subjective novel ('the stream of consciousness novel') and the decline of nineteenth-century realism seemed to support the view that modern writers such as Proust, Virginia Woolf, and James Joyce had brought the novel form to its logical end. Henceforth the novel could function as clear reportage (the non-fiction fiction of Norman Mailer) or as intense, subjective explorations of the alienated consciousness.

To the French novelist Alain Robbe-Grillet it would be artistically and sociologically impossible for anyone today to write a novel in the manner of Balzac and Dickens, the two great representatives of nineteenth-century realism,† for the stable reality of that bourgeois world has been replaced by a world of ambiguity, of unstable, shifting values. Character is no longer a fixed, stable entity, but has become something highly problematic; the bureaucratic twentieth century has rendered identity ambiguous, personality incomplete, and in modern fiction it is the notions of anguish, of doubt, and of absurdity which have replaced the stable structure of bourgeois values. For while bourgeois realism depicted life as hard, full of conflict and tension, it was nevertheless *meaningful*; bourgeois society was critically accepted, together with its values, a generalized liberal humanism which worked against the portrayal of genuine

* Ortega y Gasset, *Notes on the Novel* (1924).
† A. Robbe-Grillet, *Towards a New Novel*, London, Calder & Boyars, 1966.

anguish. The individual protagonists operated within a fictional universe which defined them as part of a community, as an organic part of the social structure. In a novel like Barbusse's *Hell* (1908), this sense of community has disappeared: the anonymous hero lives as a spectator, a voyeur who, through the hole in the wall of his hotel room, observes the moments in the lives of those who pass through it. He witnesses death, adultery, love; the characters have neither a past nor a future for they exist merely as the objects of his perception. Both they and the observer are alone, even in the act of love itself:

Once again the mingling of bodies and the slow, rhythmical, endless caress took place. And once again I watched the man's face while he was pre-occupied with his pleasure. Oh, it was obvious he was alone!*

In this particular novel the absence of an identifiable community leads to an ambiguous identity (the narrator frequently asks who he is), and the sense of others as strangers:

Up there on the top of a tram, a young girl was sitting; her dress rose a little and billowed out ... From underneath, it must have been possible to see right inside her. But a traffic jam separated us. The tram moved on, vanished like a nightmare.†

There is no deep contact with others. In this novel, as in many others written during the last years of the nineteenth century and the opening decade of the twentieth, there is a deep anguish, a sense of the fundamental purposelessness of life: isolation and despair form the basic structures.

Related to this shift in structure is the increasing alienation of the writer himself. Novelists have become more self-critical of their role as writers, as artists, not merely in terms of their potential audience but in the practice of their art. Novelists are nowadays critics of the novel. They still seek fidelity to the truth, as did the nineteenth-century realists, but argue that reality is a far more complex matter than the old realists assumed; reality has neither a beginning, a middle, nor an end, and novels which *impose* this kind of order on a reality which is in constant flux are thus artificial and *unrealistic*. After all, *life*, reality, is stranger than fiction, even though it has few heroes or

* Barbusse, *L'Enfer*, trans. as *Hell* by R. Baldick, London, Panther Books, 1969, p. 81.
† ibid., p. 62.

dramatic moments, and is dominated by the insignificant details of ordinary human existence. The 'subjectivist' trend in fiction, the 'end of the novel' hypothesis, occurs at the moment when creative writers *sense* that life perhaps is absurd, meaningless, arbitrary, and petty.

The classical heyday of the novel, 1750–1920, correlates with the rise and then the hegemony of the bourgeoisie. *Tom Jones* was one of the last picaresque novels and although the genre took many forms after 1750 – the Gothic horror novel, the sentimental domestic comedy – its main direction was towards realism, the faithful depiction of what was, the portrayal of a social world and character essentially non-problematic. If serious faults did mar the industrial system of nineteenth-century capitalism – and Dickens, Flaubert, and Zola showed this – they were nevertheless secondary to the problems of the individual. In *New Grub Street*, Gissing portrays his novelist hero Reardon failing not so much because he is crushed by society but rather because he cannot rise to its challenge. The nineteenth-century novelist depicted a social world in which the individual floundered and often failed, but not because of society. The classical novel with its characteristic plot, its concrete portrayal of character and its general air of optimism (Zola's ending of *Germinal*) constituted the firm literary vehicle for liberalism and the middle class; the realist novel develops precisely in a society in which the ideology of individualism embodies the notion of a free individual who, realizing his own interest, facilitates the interests of the whole. 'Equality, freedom, justice' are the bulwarks of liberal ideology, but they are individual, not collective values. The optimism of the realist novel is clearly related to this ideology, the values of a 'rising class' which, under the banner of abstract rights, acts for all segments of society. The values of the nineteenth-century novel are basically humane and rational; life is meaningful, and only occasionally ambiguous.*

* Cf. E. Knight, *A Theory of the Classical Novel*, London, Routledge & Kegan Paul, 1969. Not all nineteenth-century novelists fall into this category, for Stendhal and Turgenev portray a social world and character equally as problematic. In Stendhal's case, he never fully accepted the bourgeois class as rulers, while for Turgenev the *absence* of a politically viable bourgeois class in Tsarist Russia helps to explain his presentation of the 'superfluous' man, especially in his novel *Rudin* (1856).

But not all creative writers produced literature within this framework. In the eighteenth century, Denis Diderot, a great admirer of Richardson, produced the first genuine anti-hero, a sponger whose nihilist values directly challenged the dominant bourgeois values of rationalism and humanism, while in Dostoevsky's *Notes from the Underground* (1864), the petty official who narrates the story and openly calls himself an anti-hero proclaims his envy of others and his hatred of reason and 'enlightenment'. The 'self-expressing pessimism of the self-consciousness', as Hegel called Diderot's hero, is the darker side of bourgeois reality, already hinted at in Richardson's perverse treatment of sex and de Sade's open contempt for humane values.

At the end of the nineteenth century these incipient tendencies in bourgeois culture are more pronounced. Robbe-Grillet is right to say that Flaubert created the new novel of the 1850s, for his portrayal of bourgeois life is far bleaker than his predecessor Balzac.* Any argument, therefore, which puts forward a mechanical relation between society and its literature must be rejected; the connections are elusive and far less concrete than is sometimes appreciated. To argue for a bourgeois world vision which expresses itself in the literature of the nineteenth century is at once correct and yet misleading, for what characterized the great bourgeois realists was precisely their criticism of society articulated in a framework of values which made their criticism financially successful. Dickens could pillory the factory system and point to the abuses of the legal system and poor relief without curbing his remarkable popularity. For his criticism is muted; it is not so much society which depraves man but man himself. If the sanitary conditions were improved, the debtors' prisons abolished, the legal system reformed, then society and man would be more in harmony, there would be less to criticize. This 'reformism', so characteristic of the nineteenth-century bourgeois realists – George Eliot, Gissing, Zola, Mrs Gaskell – tended to deflect and flatten any awareness which these writers may have had of the alienation within society, which political economy and philosophy had clearly analysed. In Flaubert the hero is alone – but the world is not yet hostile, he is not alienated. Human relations are not yet the relations of objects, although

* Robbe–Grillet, op. cit.

in Balzac's novels and Flaubert's *Sentimental Education* money undoubtedly functions as one of the major structures through which human relations are mediated – but not exclusively. In Henry James's *The Spoils of Poynton* (1897), human relations do take on a more reified form and are made to revolve almost exclusively around the Poynton legacy. This artistic rendering of the fetishist character of bourgeois consciousness undoubtedly represents a foretaste of the alienated fiction of the twentieth century.

The pervasive sense of alienation which now dominates the modern novel had not yet entered bourgeois realist literature. It does so at the moment the novelist begins to lose his secure position within his class, a process which had been developing since the late eighteenth century, and from within this highly problematic situation he communicates an overpowering sense of alienation. Twentieth-century literature actually strives to humanize the alienation of life which it depicts; the novelist himself, the 'teller of the tale' in novels such as Barbusse's *Hell* and Gide's *Counterfeiters*, is more acutely conscious of his *presence* and the artificiality of the form itself. In the nineteenth-century novel there are no novels within novels, the writer does not reflect on his role as writer, for he feels a more stable relation between himself and his audience, and thus his reality. The eighteenth-century picaresque novel, too, evinced uncertainty, its practitioners frequently deliberating on their function – especially Fielding – but then the novel and its class basis had not yet been stabilized.

Thus the 'decline of the novel' means only the dissolution of classical bourgeois realism and the development of a neurotically self-conscious genre which continually questions its right to exist at all. In B. S. Johnson's novel, *Albert Angelo* (1964) in which a young architect is forced to do supply teaching for a living, there is a sudden, violent transition from the straightforward narrative mode to one of acute self doubt:

Albert lazed at his drawingboard before the great window. Nearly seven weeks' summer holiday lay ahead of him in which to work; and he could not work today, always tomorrow was the day he was going to work. Part of the trouble, he thought, was that he lived and loved to live in an area of absolute architectural rightness, which inhibited his own originality, and resulted in him being – OH, FUCK ALL THIS LYING.

The novel that Johnson is writing is a lie and in the fourth part, called 'Disintegration', he dwells on this lying:

– fuck all this lying what im really trying to write about is writing not all this stuff about architecture trying to say something about writing about my writing im my hero though wat a useless appellation my first character then im trying to say something about me through him albert an architect when whats the point in covering up covering over-pretending pretending i can say anything i would be interested in saying.

The writer's relation to his craft and his audience has thus become highly problematic. The nineteenth-century writer on the whole enjoyed a stable relationship with his class, his audience, and his genre. But with the development of 'mass society', an all pervasive commercialism, and an organized working class and its ideology of socialism, the genuine creative writer finds himself more and more alienated from his society, his increasingly problematic situation reflected in the strong sense of alienation within his work. From the 1880s the main tendency within bourgeois literature has been to portray man as essentially alone, isolated; the dominant theme of modern literature becomes the unhappy, pessimistic consciousness of man, depicted subjectively, as anguished, seeking his real self and others.

This concept of alienation has been discussed earlier. Originating in the writings of eighteenth-century political economy and the philosophical idealism of Hegel, the notion of alienation was given its most concrete form in the early economic and philosophic writings of Marx.*

Marx defined alienation as a process by which man is turned into a stranger in the world his own activity has created. The social division of labour has the effect of creating vast accumulations of wealth but at the cost of a progressive devaluing of human life. Capitalism transforms man's labour into a commodity to be bought on the market and used against the worker: 'This fact,' writes Marx, 'implies that the object produced by labour, its product, now stands opposed to it as an alien being, as a power independent of the producer. The product of labour is labour which has been embodied in an object and turned into

* The following discussion is based on Marx's *Economic and Philosophical Manuscripts* (1844).

a physical thing; this product is an objectification of labour.'* Man's labour produces commodities which are the direct result of human activity and participation; they should not be regarded as alien objects.

Marx identifies three main characteristics of alienated labour. First, the worker's alienation from the product of his own labour ('alienation of things'), in which the product becomes an alien thing; the more he works the greater is the worker dominated by the world of objects his own labour has created: 'The worker puts his life into the object, and his life then belongs no longer to himself but to the object. The greater his activity . . . the less he possesses.' Man's 'self-confirming essence', his labour, is turned against the worker, alienating him from productive activity itself ('alienation of self'). For within the capitalist mode of production, man's work becomes a 'forced activity', an 'external thing' which acts to deny rather than to fulfil man, stunting his faculties, inducing misery, exhaustion, and despair. Work is wholly instrumental, a mere means to acquire the basic necessities of life and a few consumption luxuries.

Since work, labour, is thus intrinsically unrewarding, man feels free only outside work, with his family, in his leisure; he is free as an individual. Man is thus alienated as a 'species being', for he now lives entirely for himself, no longer producing for the whole of nature – an act which differentiates man from animals according to Marx – but existing as an isolated activity, a wage, a commodity; capitalism transforms species man into individual man.

Marx's early writings are thus remarkably prophetic in their basic theme of man creating the social world through his activity but experiencing it as an alien and hostile place. In so far as capitalist production turns man's activity into an object, a thing, then all art, literature, philosophy which reflects this tendency

* Marx makes an important distinction between objectification and alienation. Objectification is the process in which man externalizes himself in nature and society, becoming an object for others, a social being in other words; alienation occurs when man, having externalized himself, finds his own activity, his labour, operating upon him as an external and alien force. Marx argues that some form of objectification is necessary if society is to develop at all, but in itself it is not the same process as alienation, which is the direct expression of a society based on the private ownership of property and is historically specific. And since society can be changed, alienation can be conquered.

will itself be alienated. When the human world is portrayed as a world of objects, when society is depicted not as a product of human labour but as an 'external thing', something which is fundamentally non-human, hostile, then this is a process of reification.* Marx had argued that man progressively transforms nature, humanizing it through his labour, conquering it through science and collective social life. Yet man finds society an alien environment in which he sees himself and his work as 'other than himself'. In pre-capitalist society it was possible for craftsmen to be genuinely creative in work, but the tendency of capitalism is to crush the spark of creativity through its machines, extended division of labour and accumulated capital.

It is not the case, however, of the worker alone experiencing alienation. For Marx alienation is a total process, one which pervades every aspect of society. The worker, the capitalist driven by necessity to make more and more profit and to regard human needs as secondary, and the writer producing for instant consumption, are all alienated.

Marx's analysis was made in the 1840s. He was not so much disclosing alienation as a total condition then existing, as arguing for a progressive development of it with the growth of capitalism. As capitalism became a total system, turning the vast mass into mere wage earners, the fact of alienation and reification would threaten the foundations of both bourgeois liberal ideology and its humanism. Literature, in reflecting this alienation, would break away decisively from the stable framework of values of nineteenth-century bourgeois realism. Thus the rise of the new picaresque (Kafka), and the intense subjective anguished novels of the modern period depict an isolated man pitted against other men, against society, sometimes engaged in a hopeless quest for his identity or in a self-conscious exploration of the act of writing itself.† Alienation and reification now inform the basic structures of contemporary literature.

* Man's activity fulfils a keenly felt 'inner need', to express his humanity in his labour – none more so than writers, who *consciously* strive after self-expression, to render the social world meaningful. But the main tendency within commercial culture is to define the act of cultural creation exclusively in market terms, as fulfilling a commercial, a profitable, function, not 'inner needs'.

† For comments on the rise of the new picaresque, see Knight, op. cit.

But this is not to argue that *all* modern literature is an artistic depiction of alienation or that all literature can be meaningfully understood in terms of this concept. As we have said, the nineteenth-century realists developed a novel form which tended to ignore the basic fact of nineteenth-century capitalist society, its system of alienated labour. In bourgeois realism alienation is not the dominant structure, for the critical acceptance of bourgeois values deflected artistic awareness of its crucial importance. Thus in modern literature there are those writers who, through their break with the tradition of realism, engage themselves in a struggle with alienation. The modern writer as an intellectual is himself alienated; the stream-of-consciousness technique of fiction reflects both an artistic criticism of the limits of realism as well as the isolation and uncertainty of the modern intellectual, no longer securely, if critically, anchored in the bourgeois class.

Not all writers, however, break with realism or its modern variant, naturalism (Hemingway, Dos Passos), or become aware of the alienated nature of modern social life to the extent that it becomes the major structure in their work. Scott Fitzgerald's two greatest novels, *The Great Gatsby* (1926) and *Tender is the Night* (1934), are pre-eminently about class and money and document Fitzgerald's gradual awareness that no 'aristocracy' existed in American society which would defend creative intelligence; Dick Diver's tragedy is that he actively strives to be part of a society which can only corrupt him. Gatsby and Diver are thuse minently sane heroes; they are non-problematic in that society is their milieu and is in no sense deeply conceived as hostile and strange. Life is neither absurd nor alien. Life is purposeful and meaningful; they fail because society, that is, the upper class, reject them. It would be therefore pointless to analyse these texts from the point of view of alienation, as it would be to use the term as a blanket concept applying to all contemporary creative literature.

Alienation, too, is not always grasped as alienation. In the 1930s Sartre, Camus, and Nathanael West experienced alienation as nausea and the absurd. The absurd is often defined as the loss of secure, traditional values: Ionesco in an essay on Kafka defined it as 'that which is devoid of purpose ... Cut off from his religious, metaphysical, and transcendental roots, man is lost;

all his actions become senseless, absurd, useless.'* The literature of the absurd is the literature of the twentieth century, and is not exclusively bound to a philosophical and religious impasse towards which science, nuclear war, and 'mass' society has driven its intellectuals, but is specifically related to a social structure which succeeds in alienating its artists as it has alienating its productive workers. When Sartre and West tear away the apparently ordered nature of reality to disclose the unreason and chaos beneath, they do so within a specific socio-economic setting; they are novelists not of the human condition as such but of its specific contemporary form.

I

Sartre's first novel, *Nausea*, published in 1938, is pre-eminently a philosophical essay on the nature of man's alienation from the world; Sartre's 'hero' is obsessed by the overwhelming presence of an object world which stands in opposition to the social and human world created by man. Clearly a novel as conceptual as *Nausea* raises many problems for the sociology of the novel. Is the book to be understood as a curious fictional outgrowth of Sartre's philosophical position in 1938 and then related to the social position of French intellectuals between the wars? Or is it to be grasped as a *general* statement on the nature of human life, that man, using a term Sartre employs in his philosophy, is condemned to be free,† but also condemned to be alone and outside?

On one level *Nausea*, like Camus's *Outsider*, skilfully communicates an acute, anguished sense of alienation and social isolation: the dedication at the beginning of the novel is from the 'anguished' Céline, Sartre's contemporary. 'He is a fellow without any collective significance, barely an individual.' On another level, the novel presents itself as an essay in epistemology, seeking answers to the fundamental philosophical question of the nature of reality, the function of the 'I' within this reality, and its relations with the object world. And finally, *Nausea* poses as a self-conscious literature structure, question-

* Quoted in M. Esslin, *The Theatre of the Absurd*, London, Penguin Books, 1968, p. 23.
† J. P. Sartre, *Being and Nothingness* (1943).

ing the reality, the nature and purpose of the novel form itself. Sartre goes further than Zola who, in a celebrated passage, had enjoined writers to 'kill the hero' and replace him by the average person.* Sartre kills more than the hero – he kills the concept of plot as a structure with beginning, middle, and end. The nineteenth-century realist novel had worked within this traditional framework; all the loose ends were neatly tied together in the dénouement, and the novel could be closed by its bourgeois readers with a profound sense of completion – the hero, heroine, the minor and the major figures, had received their just deserts, their identity was rendered secure, either in terms of their actions within the novel or in the final comments of the omniscient author. There was nothing more to add; the 'adventures' had worked themselves out to a logical end. But for Sartre's 'hero', Antoine Roquentin, 'there are no adventures', for life is seen as an endless flux in which reality has neither beginning nor end; thus the novel, if it is to depict this reality faithfully, must discharge the arbitrary framework used by the nineteenth-century novelists, substituting for the artificial beginning, middle, and end, the 'real'. And since both the hero and the author have been 'killed' there cannot be a third-person, objective, point of view, 'the all-knowing author' pulling his strings, imposing his artificial plot on a reality which was in constant movement, but rather the first person singular, whose consciousness grapples with this flux and the question of meaning and significance in human existence.

Nausea is the diary of Antoine Roquentin, an itinerant scholar who comes to the dreary provincial town of Bouville to continue his research into the life of the Marquis de Rollebon, a minor figure of late eighteenth-century French political life. Roquentin has been living in Bouville for three years when he begins keeping a diary. The previous day, watching children throwing stones into the sea he decides to copy them: he picks up a pebble but then drops it.

There was something which I saw and which disgusted me, but I no longer knew whether I was looking at the sea or at the pebble. It was a flat pebble, completely dry on one side, wet and muddy on the other.

* E. Zola, *Le Roman Expérimental*, Paris, 1880. Translated extracts in G. J. Becker, *Documents of Modern Literary Realism*, Princeton, Princeton University Press, 1963.

I held it up by the edges, with my fingers wide apart to avoid getting them dirty.*

This is Roquentin's first experience of the nausea which, as he says on the first page, 'concerns objects'. Later, when he hears a man from Rouen, who stays each weekend in the hotel, coming up the stairs, Roquentin feels better, and the feeling of disgust and unease leaves him: he is not insane after all. 'What is there to fear from such a regular world? I think I am cured' (p. 11). Thus at the start of the novel, in the fragmentary undated pages, Sartre states his two basic themes: the sense of disgust, of nausea, and the yearning for some kind of order, a 'regular world'.

Roquentin thinks he is cured, but as the diary shows, this is an illusion. A few days after his first experience he picks up a lined piece of paper from a puddle:

I stayed in a bent position for a moment, I read: 'Dictation: The White Owl', then I straightened up, empty-handed. I am no longer free, I can no longer do what I want. Objects ought not to touch, since they are not alive. You use them, you put them back in place, you live among them: they are useful, nothing more. But they touch me, it's unbearable. (p. 22.)

He now knows the feeling – a 'sweet disgust' – which emanates from the object into his hands, 'a sort of nausea in the hands'. Gradually the nausea becomes all pervading. His face in the mirror appears 'fish-like', inhuman, while his hand is 'crab-like'. The world becomes an alien place because the objects within it appear to have no reason for existing; there are no necessary links between objects, no essential ordering to an 'existential randomness'.† Rocks, sand, paper are all objects which cease to bear this random character when *classified* by the human mind, when they become assimilated to man himself, to his purposes. It is this process of humanizing the world of objects, reflected in the anthropomorphism in literature itself,‡ which disguises the contingency of the object world. Working in the Bouville library one day, Roquentin experiences 'a sort

* J. P. Sartre, *Nausea*, trans. R. Baldick, London, Penguin Books, 1965, p. 10. Subsequent references are to this edition and are indicated by page numbers in parentheses.
† Cf. D. I. Grossvogel, *Limits of the Novel*, New York, Cornell University Press, 1968, p. 239.
‡ A phrase like 'the valley nestled' implies a human character to something non-human, for only humans nestle (Robbe-Grillet, op. cit.).

of unsubstantiality of things', in which the fixed landmarks of the library, the books, the shelves, are fixed no more, and 'it seemed that their very existence was being called into question' (pp. 112–13). At this moment nothing is real; Roquentin's surroundings seem completely false as if the world was 'waiting for its attack of nausea'. And he thinks suddenly: 'Anything can occur, anything can happen.' He leaves the library in desperation, thinking that as long as he can 'fix objects', keep them in the order which man has given them, nothing can happen: 'I looked at as many as I could, pavements, houses, gas lamps; my eyes went rapidly from one to the other to catch them out and *stop them in the middle of their metamorphosis*' (our italics).

For Roquentin, reality is now entirely formless; there is no necessary pattern to human existence like that within a novel. There is no meaning while we live through an experience, an event, only when we reflect upon it and place it within some overall pattern: through his increasing sense of nausea, Roquentin comes to realize the futility of his own existence which, like the objects around him, has no reason for being. An object simply exists, is there, in space and time; so with his life. In the Bouville art gallery he feels the questioning gaze of the bourgeoisie whose portraits look down on him, their faces exemplifying order, firmness, coherence, and he realizes the difference between himself and these worthy people – they would challenge his right to exist: 'And it was true ... I hadn't any right to exist. I had appeared by chance, I existed like a stone, a plant, a microbe. My life grew in a haphazard way and in all directions.' He was unclassifiable, worse than the stones and the pavement, for he was neither a father nor husband, he didn't vote, pay taxes or work. He concludes: 'My existence was beginning to cause me serious concern. Was I a mere figment of the imagination?' (pp. 124–7). Well, no, for he can taste himself actually existing: 'I exist. It's sweet, so sickly sweet, so slow. Sweet, soft sweetness. My mouth is full of light frothy water.' But although he feels he exists, the existence seems absurd: Roquentin cannot retain his past, it appears to him in images, as something insubstantial. If he cannot recapture his own history, what of the subject of his study, Rollebon? He abandons the biography the moment he realizes what he calls 'the true nature of the present' – 'that which exists ... all that (which) was not present did not exist. The past did not exist. Not at all. Neither in things nor even in my thoughts.' The past was no more than a form of 'pensioning off', a 'holiday' with each event having been experienced neatly packed away to become 'a honorary event', since man cannot stand nothingness. Now Roquentin knew: 'Things are entirely what they appear to be and behind them . . . there is nothing.' The past simply does not *exist*: M. de Rollebon thus dies for the second time (pp. 138–40).

All this occurs in Bouville. The diary records the dreariness and the pettiness, especially of bourgeois life, in this provincial town. The ritualistic bourgeois Sunday parades, its museum full of its bourgeois notables who, as one native puts it, 'made Bouville what it is'. Roquentin meets the self-taught man, the 'auto-didact' whose activity is in working alphabetically through the reference books of Bouville library, a humanist with what Roquentin cynically calls 'a naïve and barbaric love' of mankind. Roquentin sleeps occasionally with the woman who runs the hotel where he lives, making love on 'an au pair basis', for her, pleasure, for Roquentin, a necessary purging of his melancholia. Before coming to Bouville he enjoyed a permanent relationship with Anny; he feels that she would dispel his nausea, but when he visits her in Paris he discovers that she, too, has changed. Before, he recalls her 'love of perfection', her need for 'perfect moments', but now, like Roquentin, she experiences only disgust with life. She tells Roquentin of the origin of her perfect moments, reading Michelet's *History of France* as a child and being captivated by the illustrations: 'I had an extraordinary love for those pictures; I knew them all by heart, and when I re-read one of Michelet's books, I would wait for them fifty pages in advance.' These pictures were the perfect moments of the book, chosen from so many, depicting events of special significance; they were the 'privileged situations', like love and death in life itself. In the book the pictures had been ordered, the sequence followed a certain coherent pattern – life should be like that, its 'raw material' put in a certain order: 'First,' says Anny, 'you had to be plunged into something exceptional and feel that you were putting it in order. If all these conditions had been fulfilled, the moment would then have been perfect . . . You had to transform privi-

leged situations into perfect moments. It was a moral question.'
But now all this is over: life cannot be controlled in this way, for
life is flux, and is not order. Both Anny and Roquentin are disgusted with life; they remain isolated from each other, and
Roquentin returns to Bouville.

At only one point does Roquentin feel free of his nausea:
when he listens to an old jazz record, *Some of These Days*, for
the notes follow each other, rigorously, necessarily, and then die
away. 'Existence is a degeneration,' he says, but melodies like
circles 'retain their pure and rigid contours', they simply *are*,
they do not *exist*. Having abandoned his book on Rollebon,
Roquentin sits for the last time in the café listening to the old
record. He thinks of the Jew who wrote the song, the Negress
who sang it: they had transcended existence through creating
out of their misery, their nausea, a song. Why not Roquentin:
he resolves to make of his misery a record, a book, and the novel
ends at the moment when Roquentin begins writing it.*

2

Nausea, then, constitutes at once a highly complex philosophical
and self-conscious literary structure. Some critics have argued
that to understand the novel some knowledge of Sartre's actual
philosophical position in 1938 is essential. In *Nausea*, Sartre is
in fact attacking the philosophy of the phenomenologist,
Edmund Husserl.†

Sartre had accepted phenomenology originally for its concern with things, with the objects of perception, and its radical
rejection of metaphysics. All that is certain according to the

---

* Cf. Grossvogel, op. cit., pp. 235–6.
† Edmund Husserl (1859–1938) developed the science of phenomenology in
opposition to the various metaphysical tendencies then current in philosophy.
His basic argument implied an external world which was knowable, in which
objects communicate themselves to those individuals who perceive them.
All knowledge is based on experience, on the ways in which the object is
presented to the consciousness. Husserl believed that each object possessed
its own essential quality, its essence, and the problem for phenomenology
lay in determining the means whereby these essences are known by the
consciousness. Phenomena, therefore, as essences, are the content of consciousness, and Husserl's aim lay in the investigation of a pure consciousness
and its correlative, the phenomenal essences. See E. Husserl, *Ideas: General
Introduction to Pure Phenomenology*, New York, Macmillan, 1931.

phenomenologists is the phenomenal world, the world of objects, the *given*, and we know this through consciousness of that world; thus phenomenology tended to become the study of consciousness itself, and moved away from the things, the objects. And if consciousness is merely its contents, how does it preserve any kind of unity? Husserl's answer was a 'transcendental ego', an 'I'. In his criticism, Sartre argued that this 'I' would lie 'behind each consciousness, a necessary structure of consciousness whose rays would light upon each phenomenon presenting itself in the field of attention'.* This 'transcendental consciousness', Sartre argued, does not exist; it is a figment of Husserl's own imagination, for the 'ego is neither formally nor materially in consciousness: it is outside, in the world. It is a being of the world, like the ego of another.'† Sartre argues that the 'I' implies reflection, that there cannot be an ego, an 'I' which is unreflected:

When I run after a streetcar, when I look at the time, when I am absorbed on contemplating a portrait, there is no I. There is consciousness of the streetcar having to be overtaken, etc. . . . In fact, I am then plunged into the world of objects; it is they which constitute the unity of my consciousness; it is they which present themselves with values, with attractive and repellent qualities – but me, I have disappeared; I have annihilated myself. There is no place for me on this level. And this is not a matter of chance, due to a momentary lapse of attention, but happens because of the very structure of consciousness.‡

Sartre is describing here Roquentin's nausea, the sense of the world at an unreflective level, a life at the level of existence, not of being. Unity is shaped not by the consciousness but by the objects: in the novel, Sartre portrays a man with no enduring social relationships, utterly self-centred, a man who becomes an object to himself because his consciousness is shaped by objects. The 'I' is an object; it is not transcendental. But in grappling with Husserl's philosophy, Sartre goes further, for in depicting a socially isolated individual whose reflective consciousness is shaped by objects, he suggests the sheer *artificiality* of social life itself: once the individual becomes involved in a matrix of

* J. P. Sartre, *The Transcendence of the Ego*, New York, Noonday Press, 1957, p. 37. This long essay was written against Husserl and first published in *Recherches Philosophiques*, 1936–7.
† ibid., p. 31.
‡ ibid., pp. 48–9.

social relations, the underlying nothingness of human existence is hidden from him.

Roquentin realizes this forcefully one evening in Bouville's park. He is studying the root of a chestnut-tree when he finds he no longer remembers it is a root: 'Words had disappeared, and with them the meaning of things . . . the feeble landmarks which men have traced on their surface.' The 'black, knotty mess' of the root frightens him; and then comes a revelation, for he now knows what it is to exist:

I was like the others, like those who walk along the sea-shore in their spring clothes. I used to say like them: 'The sea *is* green; that white speck up there *is* a seagull', but I didn't feel that it existed, that the seagull was an 'existing seagull'; usually existence hides itself. It is there, around us, in us, it is *us* . . . (p. 182).

The verb 'to be' reverberates through Roquentin's mind; what is it to exist:

If anybody had asked me what existence was, I should have replied in good faith that it was nothing, just an empty form which added itself to external things, without changing anything in their nature. And then, all of a sudden, there it was, as clear as day: existence had suddenly unveiled itself. It had lost its harmless appearance as an abstract category: it was the very stuff of things, that root was steeped in existence. Or rather the root, the park gates, the bench, the sparse grass on the lawn, all that had vanished; the diversity of things, their individuality, was only an appearance, a veneer (p. 183).

The 'veneer' discloses for Roquentin a disorganized mass, 'a frightening, obscene nakedness'. For like the root of the chestnut-tree, individuals themselves are 'a heap of existents' without any reason for being there; the tree is 'superfluous' in its relation with other trees, the park gates, pebbles – it exists on its own, as a thing. The arbitrary character which is imposed on the world of 'existents' by humans, such as measures, quantities, bearings, has collapsed completely: objects are superfluous because they have no necessity to exist; they simply are! And as an object himself, Roquentin too is unnecessary:

I dreamed vaguely of killing myself, to destroy at least one of those superfluous existences. But my death itself would have been superfluous. Superfluous, my corpse, my blood on these pebbles, between these plants, in the depths of this charming park. And the decomposed flesh would have been superfluous in the earth . . . and my bones, finally, cleaned, stripped, neat and clean as teeth, would also have been superfluous; I was superfluous for all time (pp. 184–5).

Roquentin, the 'superfluous man', has now 'found the key to existence, the key to my nausea, to my own life' – *absurdity*. The root is absurd in relation to any other object; it exists simply for itself. It is an alien object, existing independent of Roquentin, in its own right. Thus, confronted by an alien object world, Roquentin ends by defining himself as an object, and, like objects, superfluous. The meaning of existence is tersely stated in his diary: 'Nothing. Existed' (p. 241).

Temporal unity and order have collapsed; but it is bourgeois order which strikes Roquentin most forcefully. He has seen through to the underlying nothingness of the object world once that world has been stripped of its language, man's classification of it, and *that* is his nausea – but not quite: counterpointed to this structure is another, bourgeois stability, its ordered purposiveness, its mindless routine. When he returns from his fruitless visit to Anny in Paris, Roquentin feels utterly alone, 'alone and free', free because he knows that in life one always loses, for only the 'swine' think they can win: 'Eat, sleep, sleep, eat. Exist slowly, gently, like . . . trees, like a puddle of water, like the red seat in the train.' The nausea is his 'normal condition', and the heart of existence is a 'deep, deep boredom' (pp. 223–4). The final pages of his diary show Roquentin's deep sense of anguish and despair. He looks down from a hill upon Bouville; its people seem to belong to another species:

They come out of their offices after the day's work, they look at the houses and the squares with a satisfied expression, they think that it is *their* town . . . They are given proof, a hundred times a day, that everything is done mechanically, that the world obeys fixed, unchangeable laws. Bodies released in a vacuum all fall at the same speed, the municipal park is closed every day at four p.m. in winter, at six p.m. in summer, leads melts at 335° C., the last tram leaves the Town Hall at 11.05 p.m.

'The idiots,' says Roquentin, to live within the illusion of laws; nature obeys no laws, only habits, which it might change tomorrow. Nature and its objects simply exist – 'vast, vague Nature has slipped into their town, it has infiltrated everywhere, into their houses, into their offices, into themselves', it is everywhere, all around us. Roquentin dwells on nature's freedom to allow anything to happen. What if nature started to palpitate?

That may happen at any time, straight away perhaps: the omens are there. For example, the father of a family may go for a walk, and he will see a red rag coming towards him across the street, as if the wind were blowing it. And when the rag gets close to him, he will see that it is a quarter of rotten meat, covered with dust, crawling and hopping along, a piece of tortured flesh rolling in the gutters and spasmodically shooting out jets of blood. Or else a mother may look at her child's cheek and ask him: 'What's that – a pimple?' And she will see the flesh puff up slightly, crack and split open, and at the bottom of the split a third eye, a laughing eye, will appear ... And somebody else will find something scratching inside his mouth. And he will go to a mirror, open his mouth: and his tongue will have become a huge living centipede, rubbing its legs together and scraping his palate ... And hosts of things will appear for which people will have to find new names – a stone-eye, a big three-cornered arm, a toe-crutch, a spider jaw, and somebody who has gone to bed ... will wake up naked on a bluish patch of earth, in a forest of rustling pricks, rising all red and white towards the sky ... with big testicles half-way out of the ground, hairy and bulbous, like onions. (p. 226)

Nature is not arbitrary, only the man-made world: so let things change, cries Roquentin, 'then everyone will be plunged into solitude', alone and pursued by monsters scourging their science and their humanism (p. 227).

Roquentin's 'unhappy consciousness', his sense of nausea, his anguish, is saved not only through his absorption in the jazz record but by his act of writing a diary, the novel. Unlike the characters in a novel of Virginia Woolf, who are also alienated, Roquentin refuses to accept his absurdity; he feels the world should be wholly different. Thus the thought of writing at the close of the diary implies some purpose, a meaning. The novel Roquentin will write will provide a structure to his moments, 'the plain record of moments, people, objects', written without the omnipresent, mediating author, for like the jazz record it will not interfere with the reader's perception. Like nature, events will simply happen, simply exist, and they will be written as they happen, in a wholly impersonal manner.

Thus at the close of the novel, Roquentin is faced with purposive activity. He has been portrayed as alienated, both from objects and the social world, a form of alienation which is historically specific. Because nature is seen as external and oppressive, with no fixed boundaries, the social world is merely the veneer of an underlying, pristine *existence*. In the novel, human relations are turned into relations of things; humans become objects as with natural objects and there is a complete identification of the natural with the human world. Thus if the root seems superfluous so too is the individual. But if this were so, then it would be most unlikely that Roquentin could save himself. His own activity, the act of writing the diary, shows clearly enough that he is not an object in the same sense as a tree – a natural causality creates trees, while human procreation implies a degree of consciousness, of purpose. But by confusing this, Roquentin turns human relations into things: they are observed coldly, clinically, from the outside (the woman he sleeps with, the auto-didactic, the bourgeoisie on their Sunday ritual). Because he is isolated, Roquentin sees relationships only as relations of things, of objects; they are not mediated through the human community. The woman he sleeps with is experienced as an object which assuages his melancholia; Anny and himself remain isolated individuals, objects to each other, unable to come together; the self-taught man is merely an interesting specimen, a good example of the 'provincial humanist'. The 'superfluous man' in Roquentin's terms has no community, no deeply-felt human connections.

This reified structure is closely linked with the rejection of humanism and science. 'But there are people,' cries the self-taught man, and Roquentin merely laughs at such a 'naïve' justification of life. He has seen through humanism; man is simply alone in a meaningless world, hiding from the nausea or bravely confronting it. Science, with its order and coherence, further masks the underlying nothingness. Both must be rejected. But Roquentin is not simply negating the values of science and humanism – he is fundamentally rejecting their *social use* by the bourgeoisie; it is their meanings which he rejects, their ritualistic, ordered, humane social world. Like Barbusse, Gide and Céline, Sartre has written a novel which arraigns the values of bourgeois society, a novel which does not express a bourgeois world vision. But in rejecting bourgeois values he has rejected *all* values; man's relation with his world is simply *nauseating*. *Nausea* has no 'progressive' element; yet as an aesthetic structure it is saved by the keenly experienced anguish of Roquentin, the result of facing an apparently value-less world, and by his determination to struggle against it. The shallowness of bourgeois life has been clinically exposed, its crushing mediocrity and ritualism; but the pessimistic structure which should follow this rejection together with the contempt for socialism ('left-wing humanists')* is saved by the anguish. The novel 'works' for this reason: Roquentin affirms his existence through the act of writing, thus transcending a total negative pessimism.†

3

Four years after *Nausea* was published, Camus's first novel, *L'Étranger*, appeared in France. Camus had written it in Algeria during the period of his creative life which produced the philosophical essay on the notion of the absurd, *The Myth of Sisyphus*.‡ Like Roquentin, Camus's anti-hero Meursault experiences life as essentially meaningless; he lives in isolation from other human beings, indifferent to the values which others place on the ordinary routine of living. Meursault has often been seen as a nihilist, a sensualist living entirely for the present, devoted to the sun, the sand, and the sea.§ Roquentin had found life to be nausea; Meursault finds it absurd.

In *The Myth of Sisyphus* Camus defined the absurd as the realization by man that there could not be any reconciliation between his reason and the fundamentally irrational nature of the world itself. This theme, of course, is common to many writers of the inter-war period, especially Malraux and Sartre: in Malraux's early work, *La Tentation de l'Occident*, there are many references to the idea of a metaphysical absurdity which dominates human life; existence is not in any sense ordered,

* See Roquentin's conversation with the auto-didact, pp. 155–78.
† Sartre himself clearly developed beyond the extreme pessimism of *Nausea* in his trilogy of novels, *The Roads to Freedom*, and in his gradual acceptance of a Marxist philosophical position.
‡ Camus was born in Algeria in 1913. His father died in 1914 from wounds inflicted at the battle of the Marne and he was brought up by his impoverished and illiterate mother. He studied at the University of Algiers, joined the Communist Party in 1934, leaving it in 1937 and founding the Théâtre du Travail. He was an actor, journalist, goalkeeper. In 1938 he wrote his play, *Caligula*, and started work on *L'Etranger* and *Le Myth de Sisyphe*.
§ 'Meursault ... is an Algerian Frenchman, totally devoid of human sympathies or tenderness. He lives as in a hard shell, impervious to human touch' (S. Finkelstein, *Existentialism and Alienation in American Literature*, New York, International Publishers, 1965, p. 114).

but a chaotic stream of events and things irreducible to reason itself – this is the absurd, 'an unbridgeable gulf between rationality and experience'.* For Camus the absurd is a form of anti-rationalism in which reason is utterly powerless when opposed to the randomness, the diverse multiplicity of experience – we are reminded of Roquentin, things simply exist, without reason, beyond reason. Thus the world, which clearly cannot be grasped by reason, is essentially unknowable: in his philosophical essay, Camus writes:

I said the world is absurd, but I was being too hasty. All one can say of the world is that it is not amenable to reason. The absurd, however, is the confrontation of this non-rational world by that desperate desire for clarity which is one of man's deepest needs. The absurd depends as much on man as on the world for its existence.†

The absurd, then, is a relationship between man and things, and does not inhere in things, in the world alone. Camus develops this conception in the first chapter of *The Myth of Sisyphus*, in which he defines four major types of the absurd. There is the absurd routine way of life, catching the same train each day, performing the same duties week in week out, refusing to pose the question of meaning and purpose to life; there is the sense of time passing, bringing man nearer to death; there is the sense of the arbitrary character of life, the sheer contingency of existence, the sudden awareness of the alien nature of the object world, its essential inhumanity; and finally there is the absurd as the experience of utter isolation from other human beings, for although they possess some kind of human essence, mechanical routine existence drives them to mechanical, ritualistic responses to other persons. Life is fundamentally absurd because man cannot know others or the world. But he demands to know, to understand, to be conscious of his experiences, and it is this desire to grasp what Camus regards as fundamentally unknowable which leads to what Robbe-Grillet calls the fatal complicity, the affirmation of freedom in the face of an indifferent, hostile, and alien world.‡ Sisyphus, condemned by the Gods to roll a heavy stone up a hill only to see it roll down again,

* See J. Cruikshank, *Albert Camus and the Literature of Revolt*, London, Oxford University Press, 1960, pp. 48–9.
† A. Camus, *The Myth of Sisyphus*, London, Hamish Hamilton, 1955.
‡ Robbe-Grillet, op. cit.

embodies a futile labour which is the symbol of an absurd existence; yet in the very task which enslaved him, Camus argues, Sisyphus finds his freedom:

Sisyphus, proletarian of the Gods, powerless and rebellious, knows the whole extent of his wretched condition: it is what he thinks of during his descent. The lucidity that was to constitute his torture at the same time crowns his victory. There is no fate that cannot be surmounted by scorn.*

Like Rameau's nephew, Sisyphus finds his freedom in scorning his absurd existence, as does Meursault, in the condemned cell, who realizes that the world is indifferent to men and that his own indifference to life is the truth of life. Sisyphus and Meursault are both free because they have penetrated to the heart of reality, a reality which is utterly absurd.

Meursault works as a clerk in an Algerian shipping office, and the novel opens with the sudden death, in an old people's home, of his mother. The first scenes depict an indifferent Meursault: during the three years his mother has been in the home he has visited her infrequently, not wishing to give up his Sundays or bother with bus fares and a tedious journey. He refuses to observe the usual formalities associated with death; he neither looks at his mother's face when he first arrives at the home, nor when the coffin is finally screwed down. After the night vigil beside the coffin a bored Meursault welcomes the dawn without grief: 'There was the promise of a very fine day. I hadn't been in the country for ages, and I caught myself thinking what an agreeable walk I might have had, if it hadn't been for mother.'†
He returns to Algiers, goes swimming, meets an old girl-friend, Marie, visits the cinema, and then sleeps with her. Later he becomes friendly with a fellow lodger, Raymond, and agrees to write a letter to a girl who has let Raymond down, full of insults and couched in such a way that she will be sorry for what she has done. When the girl visits Raymond there is an argument and then violence; she calls the police and Raymond is accused of assault. Meursault agrees to act as witness for Raymond against the girl and the police drop the charges. Marie

* Camus, op. cit.
† A. Camus, *The Outsider*, trans. S. Gilbert, London, Penguin Books, 1961, p. 21. Subsequent references are to this edition and are indicated by page numbers in parentheses.

asks Meursault if he loves her; he replies by saying that the question has no meaning but he supposes not. She thinks him odd, but later asks him to marry her, and he agrees. Raymond invites Meursault and Marie to a beach house; they are followed by two Arabs, one of them the brother of the girl Raymond has beaten, and later, on the beach, there is a fight in which Raymond is injured. Afterwards Meursault is walking along the beach alone with Raymond's loaded gun when he meets the Arabs:

Then everything began to reel before my eyes, a fiery gust came from the sea, while the sky cracked in two, from end to end, and a great sheet of flame poured down through the rift. Every nerve in my body was a steel spring, and my grip closed on the revolver. The trigger gave, and the smooth underbelly of the butt jogged my palm. And so, with that crisp, whipcrack sound, it all began . . . I knew I'd shattered the balance of the day, the spacious calm of this beach on which I had been happy. But I fired four shots more into the inert body, on which they left no visible trace. And each successive shot was another loud, fateful rap on the door of my undoing. (p. 64)

The second part of the novel contains the account of Meursault's trial for murder. The events of the first part dominate the trial; he is not on trial for killing an Arab, but more for not respecting his mother. Meursault is found guilty because he refuses to compromise, because he does not observe the semblances of convention or simulate feelings of tenderness and affection. Meursault is condemned to die, Camus wrote, 'because he doesn't play the game. In this sense he is a stranger to the society in which he lives; he drifts in the margin, in the suburb of private, solitary, sensual life.' Camus means here that Meursault refuses to lie, to say no more than what one feels: 'He refuses to disguise his feelings and immediately society feels threatened. He is asked, for example, to say that he regrets his crime according to the ritual formula. He replies that he feels about it more annoyance than real regret and this shade of meaning condemns him.'* Thus although Meursault can lie to the police he will not deceive himself; he will not take an easy refuge inside the accepted norms of the society and it is this aspect of his character which makes him an outsider. But the term 'stranger' has another meaning: Meursault is a French

* Quoted in C. O'Brien, *Camus*, London, Fontana, 1970, p. 20.

Algerian rooted in a French culture in which the Arab presents a potentially alien force – in both *The Outsider* and *The Plague* (1947) there are no fully realized Arabs or Africans, only French Algerians.* It is not surprising, then, to find Camus depicting the French Algerians, the Europeans, living in an essentially alien society, as isolated and apathetic. In *The Plague* this is put most forcefully:

In this extremity of solitude, none could count on any help from his neighbour; each had to bear the load of his troubles alone. If, by some chance, one of us tried to unburden himself or to say something about his feelings, the reply he got, whatever it might be, usually wounded him.†

But the novels are more than simple reflections of a peculiar colonial situation, and while it might be interesting to connect up Camus's working-class background with his apparent insensitivity in portraying the Arab as mere background to the fates of the Europeans, it would not help us to understand a novel like *The Outsider* which is only explicable in terms of a more general conception of 'strangeness'.

In *The Outsider* Camus is clearly making a statement on the human condition generally, not its specific state in Algeria. Meursault's alienation, like Roquentin's, takes a number of forms, but both are in rebellion against bourgeois values, although in Meursault's case not against bourgeois society. Meursault may be alienated but unlike Roquentin he seems to have little awareness of his position or to experience the anguish which should result from it. Meursault is utterly *indifferent* to the world; this total alienation is especially brought out in the narrative method Camus employs.

Like *Nausea*, *The Outsider* is written in the first person singular. This form of narration should mean greater insights into the motives and actions of the main and subsidiary characters; Sartre uses the technique to explore, through Roquentin, the

* Commentators on Camus frequently fall into kinds: those who ignore this aspect of the novels or those who give it some prominence. O'Brien, for example, argues that in the court scenes Camus is perpetuating a myth, that of French Algeria, in presenting a trial of a white man who has killed an Arab in terms of strict judicial impartiality. No Algerian court could be impartial between Arab and European, although Camus depicts this as a reality (ibid., p. 23).
† A. Camus, *The Plague*.

intense *subjectivity* of human experience – but Camus has a narrator who lacks all the qualities so necessary for a rigorous, subtle introspection. Meursault is intellectually dull, has little or no psychological insight, and is indifferent to other human beings, seeing them wholly externally in the same way as he sees objects and events. The vocabulary employed in the novel supports this wholly objectivist perspective; it is non-analytic, descriptive, merely stating in concrete terms, and with little imagery, what in Meursault's experience happens outside. The result is to sharpen the impact of Meursault's alienation, for merely describing life as a succession of random events, each as important or insignificant as any other, implies both an incoherent view of the world as well as an acceptance of it. Roquentin, like Meursault, experiences the world as unknowable diversity, as something strange, alien, but he struggles against it, while Meursault accepts the incoherence as the norm, and life as essentially non-problematic. The objectivist narrative method embodies Meursault's alienation in depicting, through Meursault, life as a series of events with no pattern or meaning to them in which the narrator, the 'omniscient' 'I', makes no attempt to reflect on the course of his life or life in general. Barbusse and Sartre have 'heroes' who experience anguish when life seems suddenly to be without meaning and purpose, but Meursault merely regards the futility of life with indifference.

Meursault has no ambition. When his employer offers him a post in Paris, he replies that he really 'didn't care much one way or the other', since 'one life was as good as another and [the] present one suited [him] quite well'. As a student he had realized the pointlessness of ambition and thus abandoned his university studies (p. 48). His life is colourless, and is depicted as such. He has never 'cared for Sundays', for example; it is a day to be endured, to be got through. Camus's account of one such Sunday in Meursault's life illustrates his total lack of subjectivity. He rises from his bed, eats, pastes an advertisement from an old newspaper in an album kept for this purpose, and then spends the afternoon on his balcony looking down at people and events in the street:

I turned my chair round and seated myself like the tobacconist, as it was comfortable that way. After smoking a couple of cigarettes I went back to the room, got a tablet of chocolate and returned to the window to eat it. Soon after, the sky clouded over and I thought a summer storm was coming. However, the clouds gradually lifted. All the same they had left in the street a sort of threat of rain, which made it darker. I stayed watching the sky for quite a while. (pp. 30–31)

He sits at his window and Sunday draws to its close. He eats some food; the night turns cold:

As I was coming back, after shutting the window, I glanced at the mirror and saw reflected in it a corner of my table with my spirit-lamp and some bits of bread beside it. It occurred to me that somehow I'd got through another Sunday, that Mother now was buried, and to-morrow I'd be going back to work as usual.* (p. 32)

The sober, objectivist narrative mode is quite deliberate. Meursault is a spectator, an observer on a world which is alien to him, and he looks at people as he would any object, as possibly interesting, as something which may provide him with pleasure and thus help in getting through another day. Unlike Sisyphus he does not reflect on his estrangement and it is not until he is sentenced to death that Meursault actually becomes conscious of himself as a thinking being. Throughout the first part of the novel he is depicted as wholly dominated by the physical qualities of human life. He deliberately describes trivial detail: 'Before leaving for lunch I washed my hands. I always enjoyed doing this at midday. In the evening it was less pleasant, as the roller-towel after being used by so many people was sopping wet' (p. 33). Meursault has an obsessive concern with the physical, external world, its sights, sounds, smells; it is a world which has not been fully humanized.† And when he shoots the Arab it is not intent which impels him to pull the trigger but the sun, the sand, the heat (pp. 63–4).

His relations with people reflect this alienation. Humans are observed, and like other objects they are strictly functional. Raymond is 'interesting', someone to eat with and who saves

* There are many other examples of Meursault's addiction to the physical – in his cell he is 'seized with a desire to go down to the beach for a swim' (p. 79), and later, he thinks of the moment during the day which he loved more than any other: 'The shouts of newspaper boys in the already languid air, the last calls of birds in the public garden, the cries of sandwich-vendors, the screech of trams at the steep corners of the upper town, and that faint rustling overhead as darkness sifted down upon the harbour . . .' (p. 98).
† Thus his description of Paris as a 'dingy sort of town' where the people have 'washed-out, white faces' (p. 49).

Meursault the trouble of cooking; Marie is someone to sleep with, whom he agrees to marry if that is what she wants, for he has no desires one way or the other; in a restaurant he observes 'an odd-looking little woman' who, waiting for her meal, makes ticks against radio programmes in a magazine, reads while she eats and continues to tick off items 'with the same meticulous attention' – she is described as having 'abrupt, robot-like gestures', 'the little robot', clearly an 'interesting object' (pp. 49–50). Meursault's indifference to the social, human world is total; he is committed only to the physical moments of existence. In his relations with Marie it is her body which communicates with him, her physical presence: she is described in terms of her 'pretty dress', leather sandals, her 'firm little breasts', her 'sun-tanned face' (p. 41); she is the brine left by her head on Meursault's pillow. In his human relations Meursault is outside the world, for he lives more or less according to his animal, not to his fully human, functions.*

During his trial, Meursault comes to reflect for the first time on his life. He finds no room for regret, for he has 'always been far too much absorbed in the present moment, or the immediate future, to think back' (p. 101). He lives as an animal, but, unlike animals, he is aware of death; he justifies his animal existence on the grounds that all men die and are therefore equally condemned: 'From the dark horizon of my future a sort of slow, persistent breeze had been blowing towards me, all my life long, from the years that were to come. And on its way that breeze had levelled out all the ideas that people tried to foist on me in the equally unreal years I then was living through.' All men are condemned to die, and therefore 'nothing had the least importance'; there are no values which transcend this world and existence is its own justification (p. 118). Meursault, the alienated man, lives by no values, except a stubborn refusal to compromise with a social world he is not part of; he refuses to 'play

* In his manuscript on alienated labour, Marx wrote that the alienated man feels only free in his animal functions, eating, drinking, procreating, 'or at most also in his dwelling and in personal adornment – while in his human functions he is reduced to an animal . . . Eating, drinking, procreating are, of course, also genuine human functions. But abstractly considered, apart from the environment of human activities, and turned into final and sole ends, they are animal functions' (Marx, *Early Writings*, ed. T. B. Bottomore, London, Watts, 1964, p. 125).

the game', to abide by a formal adherence to bourgeois values. This is the meaning of the trial. He is not on trial for killing an Arab; he is found guilty because he is honest in that he speaks and acts as he *feels*. Thus he says openly that he had nothing in common with his mother, that she was much better off in the old people's home, and that he regrets nothing. At the trial the prosecutor emphasizes Meursault's 'great callousness', shown at his mother's funeral, that he drank coffee and smoked during the night's vigil beside the coffin when, in the eyes of the prose-cution and the courtroom audience he should have refused 'out of respect for the dead body of the poor woman who had brought him into the world' (pp. 91–2).* He is guilty because he does not conform to the values which hold bourgeois society together; his rejection of these values and his refusal to pretend condemn him, because bourgeois society sees him as a threat to its own existence. No hero can bury his mother one day and go swimming with a girl, visit the cinema, and then sleep with her the next, and hope to survive the judgement of bourgeois values (p. 95). He is found guilty, too, for his association with the pimp, Raymond, for not rejecting a man whose values are hostile to those of respectable bourgeois society. In his summary the prosecutor puts the case against Meursault quite simply: 'I accuse the prisoner of behaving at his mother's funeral in a way that showed he was already a criminal at heart' (p. 97).

Thus at the close of the novel, the man whose 'animal' existence had led to 'crime', the alienated man who is the ob-server of events and the spectator even at his own trial (p. 86), comes to understand the 'truth' of life: his own callousness is the truth, his own indifference to values by which men usually live. His scorn, like that of Sisyphus, is his freedom; Meursault *knows* he will die, he *knows* the indifference of the world to man, that the world is meaningless, a succession of experiences with-out pattern or purpose. Roquentin had struggled against his alienation through the self-conscious activity of the diary/novel; Meursault simply accepts the 'absurdity' of his alienated exis-tence. Thus the two basic structures within the novel – death rendering life absurd, and the agnostic standpoint towards

* Earlier Meursault had perturbed his lawyer by remarking that 'all normal people . . . had more or less desired the death of those they loved, at some time or another' (p. 69).

values leading to rejection of bourgeois formal values and humanistic values too – provide Camus with a bleak, pessimistic and *individualistic* vision, a vision which becomes increasingly less critical of bourgeois society and its thought in his later works.*

Camus has often been described as a rebel, as the embodiment of revolt, but his depiction of Meursault in essentially non-social terms, as alienated without anguish, together with Camus's own indifference to the indigenous population of Algeria, indicate clearly enough the limits of his 'revolution'. But *L'Étranger* will remain a remarkable statement on man's alienation from the social world and its community.

4

L'Étranger and *La Nausée* were both written during the late 1930s, at a time of increasing political instability, with the rise of fascism and its challenge to the Western democracies. These novels, however, do not obviously reflect this crisis; like other European intellectuals writing in this period, Sartre and Camus depict a general sense of instability which may perhaps be related to the specific historical crisis. Their sense of pessimism, of the general absurdity of human existence, is a structure which dominates many of the great post-1918 novelists (Hesse, Musil, Kafka, Céline), a pessimism which is subsumed too often under the rubric of a revolt against mass civilization and technology. This revolt is more properly characterized as alienation; it is historically specific in its literary form and is closely bound up with the productive forces of capitalist economy.

This sense of alienation is not found in all the literary works produced in this period. American novelists such as Hemingway, Dos Passos, and Steinbeck were certainly critical of society, and although they portrayed a world which was occasionally hostile it was nevertheless a recognizably *human* world, one essentially non-problematic in which there is little awareness of genuine human anguish. There is nothing of the absurd in Hemingway's

* In particular the political essay which brought about the final rupture between Camus and Sartre, *The Rebel* (1951), in which Marxism is identified with Stalinism.

masculine bellicosity, in Steinbeck's sentimental rendering of the Joad family's trek to California, or in Dos Passos's inflated social reportage.* More problematic are the novels of Scott Fitzgerald, Faulkner, and James T. Farrell.† But it is only in the work of Nathanael West that alienation is genuinely grasped artistically. In West there is a sense of overpowering alienation, of an intense, dominant pessimism about man's world, more powerfully rendered even than in Sartre and Camus.

West wrote four short novels, *The Dream Life of Balso Snell* (1931), *Miss Lonelyhearts* (1933), *A Cool Million* (1934), and *The Day of the Locust* (1939). At the time they failed both critically and financially: *Balso Snell* was hardly reviewed, the publishers of *Miss Lonelyhearts* went bankrupt immediately after the book received some favourable reviews, while his last two novels sold very few copies. Depressed by his lack of success, West, like Faulkner, Fitzgerald, and many other American writers, went to Hollywood where he wrote scripts for B films. He died in a car accident in 1940.

West's reputation as a major American novelist has grown considerably in the last few years. He has been rediscovered, and while most critics would perhaps not wholly concur in Alan Ross's judgement of *Miss Lonelyhearts* and *The Day of the Locust* as novels which 'rank with any ... that came out of America in the 1930s, more condensed, penetrating and poetic than many ...'‡ there is now a general consensus on West's significance.§

West's novels are ironic, satirical, and pessimistic. There are no 'ordinary' people in his universe, and his characters are

---

* Dos Passos's trilogy, *U.S.A.* (1930–36), strives to a totality in depicting American history from 1900 to 1927, involving fictitious and real persons in his mixture of biography, newsreels, newspaper reports, etc. It is a dossier on American life; it describes what happens to people in certain situations but does so *externally* and superficially.

† Especially Faulkner's *Sanctuary* (1931) and *The Sound and the Fury* (1929), and Farrell's *Studs Lonigan* (1932–5). Faulkner is concerned with the abnormal, the pathological, while Farrell depicts the fundamental hopelessness of working-class life. See later, for comments on Fitzgerald.

‡ A. Ross, Introduction to *The Complete Works of Nathanael West*, London, Secker & Warburg, 1957, p. xxii.

§ West's fiction has been the subject of a number of full-length studies published in the last few years. See especially V. Comerchero, *Nathanael West: The Ironic Prophet*, Seattle, University of Washington, 1967; R. Reid, *The Fiction of Nathanael West*, Chicago, University of Chicago, 1967.

grotesque and horrifying; his vision is extraordinarily harsh. He observes neither a strict fidelity to the surface exterior of life (realism) nor to the interior life of characters (Proust, Joyce). This fact perhaps explains his comparative critical and commercial failure in the 1930s, for writing at a time when even such a non-political writer like Hemingway could feel sympathy with the ideas of 'social realism',* West's obvious lack of artistic identification with the dominant literary models could only lead to neglect. Not that he was hostile to communism. He actually accepted its political doctrines, but objected to the idea that art must necessarily function as the expression of the socialist state rather than of the individual author. He could never accept the crude Stalinist argument that art is propaganda, useful in resolving the class struggle. In *Miss Lonelyhearts* he originally intended a chapter called 'Miss Lonelyhearts and the communists', but could never bring himself to finish it. Yet at the 1935 American Writers' Congress he signed the manifesto which proclaimed that 'the revolutionary spirit is penetrating the ranks of creative writers'.† The crucial influence on his work, however, was not the ideals of socialism, but, through his years spent in Paris during the 1920s, the work of the surrealists (Breton, Éluard), the French symbolists, and Baudelaire and Rimbaud. This is not to argue that these literary influences explain West's work; a writer is clearly under the impress of other writers and artists, of certain traditions, style, emphasis, but only in proportion to the needs of his own individual vision. To explain West's pessimism, 'a blend of sordid realism and nightmarish fantasy', as 'probably influenced by Baudelaire's own created half-world' is to ignore the writer's own critical activity; he *chooses* the influence positively and not mechanically because his own experience, his vision of man's world, can be harmonized and enriched by the influence. Of course, West was indebted to Baudelaire, Huysmans, Rimbaud, as well as to other literary influences such as Kafka and Dostoevsky. Miss Lonelyhearts, for example, reads *The Brothers Karamazov* because the problem which obsesses Dostoevsky, the fact of human suffering in

* Especially emphasized in Hemingway's *To Have and Have Not* (1937), a crude novel of the class struggle, set in Florida.
† Quoted in J. F. Light, *Nathanael West: An Interpretative Study*, Evanston, Northwestern University Press, 1961, p. 149.

a world which has lost God, is Miss Lonelyhearts' problem too. But West is writing from within American society about that society in which human suffering and human alienation take on particular forms and which puts them outside the simple remedy of Christian panaceas.

On one level *Miss Lonelyhearts* is a straightforward tale of urban alienation. Miss Lonelyhearts is a male reporter (he is never named) who accepts the job of agony columnist for the promise it holds for his career. But he soon discovers that the suffering which his correspondents write about is real and that his facile suggestions for remedying them are simple deceptions. The novel begins with this awareness:

Although the deadline was less than a quarter of an hour away, he was still working on his leader. He had gone as far as: 'Life *is* worthwhile, for it is full of dreams and peace, gentleness and ecstasy, and faith that burns like a clear white flame on a grim dark altar.' But he found it impossible to continue. The letters were no longer funny. He could not go on finding the same joke funny thirty times a day for months on end. And on most days he received more than thirty letters, all of them alike, stamped from the dough of suffering with a heart-shaped cookie knife.*

Miss Lonelyhearts now becomes the seeker after new values; he struggles agonizingly against the conventional clichés by which the majority live. In this quest he becomes involved with two of his correspondents, a sexually starved, promiscuously inclined lady, Mrs Doyle and her husband, a crippled gas-meter reader. Mrs Doyle hates Mr Doyle because he is not really a man; Mr Doyle hates his job and finds life intolerable. To both, Miss Lonelyhearts advocates Christ, not clichés. But Mrs Doyle, who has previously seduced Miss Lonelyhearts, only laughs and sends her husband out for drinks hoping for further sex. Miss Lonelyhearts instead shouts Christ at her, and struggling out of her embrace, knocks her to the floor. Mr Doyle, already suspicious, returns to find his wife apparently raped and seeks out Miss Lonelyhearts who, obsessed by Christian charity and love, rushes towards him, convinced that Doyle has been sent from God as a sign that he 'could perform a miracle' and by embracing the cripple, make him 'whole again'. Unfortunately, as Miss

* Nathanael West, *Miss Lonelyhearts and A Cool Million*, London, Penguin Books, 1961, p. 7. Subsequent references are to this edition and are indicated by page numbers in parentheses.

Lonelyhearts falls on Doyle, the cripple struggles, thinking he is being attacked, a gun goes off and both of them roll down the stairs together.

Miss Lonelyhearts, then, discloses a world which seems fundamentally absurd. Life has no meaning or order, and in the course of this short, episodic novel West introduces a bizarre selection of absurd characters. Shrike, the hard-boiled features editor is the most important for he rejoices in the fantasy world which Miss Lonelyhearts must create for his suffering correspondents. Thus when Miss Lonelyhearts himself needs help Shrike savagely and gleefully strips to pieces the various fantasy escapes, the retreat to the countryside, the South Seas, a life of hedonism, art, suicide, drugs. Counterpointed to Miss Lonelyhearts' desperate quest for values, for a meaning to his life, is his girl-friend, Betty, the conventional woman, who personifies the order which is absent from his own life. She wants him to get a job in an advertising agency. When she sees that he is sick she suggests a walk in the zoo, amusing Miss Lonelyhearts by her evident belief in 'the curative power of animals'; she tells him, too, 'of how fresh and clean everything in the country is' and that 'he ought to live there and that if he did, he would find that all his troubles were city troubles' (p. 42). His concern with his suffering correspondents strikes her as ridiculous; she is totally lacking in anguish, preferring the cliché to genuine thought. She is like Faye Greener in West's novel of Hollywood, *The Day of the Locust*, who invents and lives off a necessary romantic image of herself and her life in order to survive,* and like Mrs Shrike who 'thinks in headlines'.

West's attack on clichés can be seen as part of the novelist's critical activism. The cliché has an undoubted positive social function: it prevents us from thinking of the real situation; we can hide from reality in the cliché. *Miss Lonelyhearts* is the world of the cliché which finally defeats its tormented creator.

The world, too, is hostile. The language which West uses embodies a vision of overpowering alienation. The urban sky above a park is described as 'canvas-coloured and ill-stretched', while the skyscrapers 'menaced the little park from all sides' (p. 37). The shadow of a lamp-post is like 'a spear' and the

* For West's attack on the cliché, see the discussion in Comerchero, op. cit., pp. 47–8.

ground is covered by 'decay', for 'May had failed to quicken these soiled fields. It had taken all the brutality of July to torture a few green spikes through the exhausted dirt' (p. 10). But more significant is the way in which the sense of alienation is rendered not only in the language of *Miss Lonelyhearts*, but in the depiction of the *conventional* world as essentially one of chaos unless arbitrarily ordered by human convention. As we have seen with Sartre, one of the major themes of the novelist of alienation is the awareness that norm-governed behaviour, ordinary social activity, which acts as the regulator of acceptable and non-acceptable conduct, constitutes something *artificial*, unnatural. Betty is the living embodiment of conventional order: 'She had often made him feel that when she straightened his tie, she straightened much more.' When Miss Lonelyhearts is sick she comes to restore order to his room, and as he becomes obsessed by suffering and misery, the secure world of objects seems to break down: in order to survive at all he has consciously made everything conform to a pattern, to some kind of order. But as he lies sick in bed the inanimate objects break free of arbitrary classification and 'take the field against him'.

When he touched something, it spilled or rolled to the floor. The collar buttons disappeared under the bed, the point of the pencil broke, the handle of the razor fell off, the window shade refused to stay down. He fought back, but with too much violence, and was decisively defeated by the spring of the alarm clock. (p. 18)

In the streets 'chaos was multiple'; the noise of the street-cars and the shouts of the crowd fail to 'fit' any 'rhythm and no scale could give them (the words) meaning'. But Betty's world is free of object alienation: 'Her sureness was based on the power to limit experience arbitrarily.'

When he speaks to her his tongue 'had become a fat thumb'. Miss Lonelyhearts' sense of anguish is remarkably like Roquentin's nausea. In his dream he thinks of order:

Man has a tropism for order. Keys in one pocket, change in another. Mandolins are tuned G D A E. The physical world has a tropism for disorder, entropy. Man against nature ... the battle of the centuries. Keys yearn to mix with change. Mandolins strive to get out of tune. Every order has within it the germ of destruction. All order is doomed, yet the battle is worthwhile. (pp. 40–41)

Thus with apparent chaos all-pervasive, Miss Lonelyhearts searches desperately for a solution. He turns to religion. As the son of a Baptist minister he has a 'Christ complex' and as a boy 'when he shouted the name of Christ something secret and enormously powerful stirred in him' (p. 15). Thus after one particularly horrifying letter from 'Broad-Shoulders', Miss Lonelyhearts suffers the final collapse, and on his visit to the Doyles desperately substitutes Christ for cliché:

'Christ is love' he screamed at them. It was a stage scream, but he kept on. 'Christ is the black fruit that hangs on the crosstree. Man was lost by eating of the forbidden fruit. He shall be saved by eating of the bidden fruit. The black Christ-fruit, the love-fruit . . .' (p. 62)

But his rhetoric, like everything else about him, is false: he is copying Shrike and his satirical diatribes on religion: 'He felt like an empty bottle, shiny and sterile.' The anguished sense of alienation has driven him to a religious, not social, solution of human suffering, but he knows how false even that is for him. Shrike has destroyed all illusions.

West is not, as some commentators have suggested, a religious novelist. To turn him, pre-eminently a novelist of alienation, into a Christian is, as Comerchero argues, to offer a reading 'diametrically opposed to everything West believed. It offers a solution to the human dilemma when it is clear that West had none and never attempted to pose one.'* West's use of irony, too, points to an anti-religious interpretation. The portrayal of Miss Lonelyhearts is as a totally *false* individual, lacking in spontaneous gesture and feeling. The spurious solutions he offers to his suffering correspondents are matched by the complete inauthenticity of his own responses to religion, love, and sex. Thus as he shouts of his 'Christ complex' he accompanies it with 'gestures that were too appropriate, like those of an old-fashioned actor' (p. 20), and to his audience, Betty, he says, 'What's the matter, sweetheart, didn't you like the performance?' Religion is a performance: for Shrike has blocked what he thinks is his only escape by teaching him to handle Christ 'with a thick glove of words' (p. 43).

Miss Lonelyhearts is utterly dead. He cannot respond to

* Comerchero, op. cit., p. 76. Some of the argument here is based on Comerchero's discussion.

ordinary human experience, he fails in his relations with others. This is the extent of his total alienation, more so than Sartre's intellectual hero who had at least struggled with his nausea through the act of writing. But like Roquentin and Meursault, West's hero is outside the experience of human love. Betty, who loves him, is seen as living by clichés; Mrs Shrike is too cold and unresponsive; while Mrs Doyle rapes him. Human relations do not endure with the novelist of total alienation.* For Miss Lonelyhearts, responses have been blunted and he has lost any ability to grasp life as joyous.† Thus in his relation with Mrs Shrike he has to force himself to think of sex with her: 'He tried to excite himself into eagerness by thinking of the play Mary made with her breasts. She used them as the coquettes of long ago had used their fans.' (p. 28).

He fails: 'the excitement refused to come'. West portrays alienated love as essentially the failure of sexuality; throughout his novels there are few consummations or genuine love relations. His passive heroes are either raped or idealize women from afar.‡ Sexual failure is used to emphasize the failure of a modern industrial society to provide man with genuine creative and human activity. This is especially brought out in his description of Mrs Doyle's seduction of Miss Lonelyhearts. Fay Doyle is presented quite deliberately in sub-human imagery: her

* Thus in a novel like Scott Fitzgerald's *Tender Is the Night*, human relations are possible and genuinely authentic although fraught with tragedy.
† Comerchero's interpretation emphasizes Miss Lonelyhearts' sexual passivity as a form of homosexuality, and the whole text of *Miss Lonelyhearts* as a form of Oedipal homosexuality. Thus the ending is seen on this view as Miss Lonelyhearts' acceptance of his castration: 'The religious conversion is really a conversion from latent to overt homosexuality; so is the ending. The final embrace between Miss Lonelyhearts and Doyle is a "homosexual tableau – the men locked in embrace while the woman stands helplessly by" [quoting S. Hyman, *Nathanael West*, University of Minnesota Pamphlets on American Writers, No. 21, 1962].' But as Reid points out, this is seriously to misread West's actual text, for not only does deadness characterize all of Miss Lonelyhearts' responses, including the sexual, but in the final scene Doyle actually struggles to avoid Miss Lonelyhearts' embrace (Reid, op. cit., pp. 81–3). The psychoanalytic approach as used by Comerchero and Hyman certainly imputes too much; the sociological approach does not set out to read into an author's work but to relate his text to verifiable external experience, and not to go beyond the text in order to understand it.
‡ Especially Tod Hackett, the 'hero' of *The Day of the Locust*, who admires and loves Faye Greener, the shallow, struggling actress who provides the single instance of consummated love in all of West's fiction, with a Mexican cowboy.

legs are like 'Indian clubs, breasts like balloons and a brow like a pigeon'. Her arm 'felt like a thigh' and following her upstairs to his room 'he watched the action of her massive hams; they were like two enormous grindstones'. As she undressed she made 'sea sounds' and 'something flapped like a sail; there was a creak of ropes; then he heard the wave against a wharf smack of rubber on flesh'. The use of sea metaphors to describe a human *not* animal relation is indicative of West's overpowering sense of alienation, and the passage ends with her calling him described as 'a sea-moan', and his experience like 'an exhausted swimmer leaving the surf' (pp. 37–8).

Mrs Doyle, Mr Doyle, and Miss Lonelyhearts fail sexually. Mr Doyle brings Miss Lonelyhearts back to his flat on his wife's instructions and half jokes that he's a 'pimp' bringing 'home a guy' for his wife. Mrs Doyle hits him with a newspaper but he growls like a dog, catches it in his teeth and falls to the floor and continues his imitation of a dog: 'Miss Lonelyhearts tried to get the cripple to stand up and bent to lift him: but, as he did so, Doyle tore open Miss Lonelyhearts' fly, then rolled over on his back, laughing wildly. (p. 61).

West's vision is thus one of total pessimism, agonizingly portrayed in Miss Lonelyhearts' hopeless quest for genuine values. In this sense West is pre-eminent among the American novelists writing in the thirties, and while it may be true that his was an ideological conception of the world and not an authentic world vision (thus his episodic plots, his fragmentary literary mode), *Miss Lonelyhearts* must remain as a genuine artistic rendering of man's alienation from his world and from his fellows.

5

The theme of man's alienation from a world his own activity has created, a world which is human for that reason, but one depicted by many contemporary novelists as inhuman and hostile, constitutes the basic structure informing much of the creative literature of the past fifty years. Joyce, Musil, Hesse, Gide, Sartre, Camus, and West are novelists whose world is deeply problematic and whose art reflects a crisis of values. Goldmann has argued that this crisis of values emerges only with the development of a capitalist society which is totally organized, in which a rigid homology exists between economic and literary structures, where market values dominate human values.* It has not been possible to analyse in any detail many of the works which embody this sense of alienation. Clearly its intensity and form will vary between writers. Robbe-Grillet is a contemporary novelist who carries the anguished sense of alienation of Sartre, Camus, and West to its logical conclusion. For him, as a scientific observer of man, things are things and must be described as such. His strong anti-anthropomorphism is wholly directed against the bourgeois realist novel which tended to humanize the world of objects, in other words, to humanize nature. Robbe-Grillet rejects this approach in favour of surface description, establishing the exteriority and total independence of the object world. In Robbe-Grillet's fictional universe man is totally alienated, for human relations take on the aspect of reifications. The traditional realist novel had drawn the world of things as functioning within a specific human context; the meanings of objects were derived from their human associations and man's use of them. This 'complicity', as Robbe-Grillet calls it, enabled the realist novel to depict relations between humans *as* relations between humans, mediated exclusively by the human community.

In his essay on Tolstoy, Lukács shows how an apparently insignificant detail reveals the dead love between Anna Karenina and Vronsky: '"She lifted her cup, with her little finger held apart, and put it to her lips. After drinking a few sips she glanced at him and by his expression she saw clearly that he was repelled by her hand and her gesture and the sound made by her lips."' Lukács comments that the cup, the detail, is rendered significant because it represents an objectification of the 'decisive emotional turning-points in the lives of people'.† In Robbe-Grillet, by contrast, details, objects, things, are described as wholly external and *indifferent* to man – Roquentin experienced his nausea through the visceral relations he felt with

---

* Goldmann, *Pour une sociologie du roman*, pp. 297–8.
† Lukács, *Studies in European Realism*, p. 174. Other examples would include the famous muff motif in *Tom Jones* which serves to structure the plot, Jones and Sophia drawn together and then apart through its various appearances.

objects, but Robbe-Grillet would regard this as a form of 'complicity' between man and things.* It must be argued, however, that things are never *things*, for not only do they function within a human environment, but their meaning is derived from their being structured within a human- and not thing-context.† Sartre and West depict man struggling with things; Roquentin affirms his human essence through the act of writing itself, while Miss Lonelyhearts sinks into madness and death *after* a struggle with a world apparently inhuman. It is the quality of this despair, that it is human and not thing-like, which differentiates these writers from Robbe-Grillet and other exponents of the *nouveau roman*. Robbe-Grillet has dehumanized alienation. His novels are certainly technically brilliant, full of allusions to the problems involved in the act of writing, to myth, to sexuality, psychoanalysis, and so on, and, like the novelists of alienation, he portrays man as totally isolated and alone. The husband in *La Jalousie*, for example, observes the growing relationship between his wife and another man and the novel becomes the construction of what might have happened at certain times and what he imagined happened or was happening in his presence, but whose actual involvement is non-existent. Robbe-Grillet depicts a world which is fundamentally the world of the spectator, a world which has no place for human initiative: things happen to individuals independent of their will – they have no choice. The jealous husband's actions are determined by external necessity: he owns a banana plantation which, because it is well organized and efficiently run, fails to occupy his mind fully. When his wife A., together with Franck, the imagined lover, returns from a trip to a nearby town, the husband/spectator/ novelist writes:

A. . . . asks for today's news on the plantation. There is no news. There are only the trivial incidents of the work of cultivation which periodically recur in one patch or another, according to the cycle of operations. Since the patches are numerous, and the plantation man-

* Robbe-Grillet, op. cit., especially the essay 'Nature, Humanism and Tragedy'.
† Albert Moravia has written that to call the sea the sea 'is equivalent to humanizing it, for the fact of indicating an object by a word involves withdrawing it from the anonymous objectivity of the pre-human and extra-human worlds and incorporating it in the human world' (quoted in B. Bergonzi, *The Situation of the Novel*, London, Macmillan, 1970, p. 39).

aged so as to stagger the harvest through all twelve months of the year, all the elements of the cycle occur at the same time every day, and the periodical trivial incidents also repeat themselves simultaneously, here or there, daily.*

Mathias the watch salesman in *Le Voyeur* rapes a girl on a sales trip to an offshore island but cannot remember if he really has committed the act; Wallas, the secret agent in *Les Gommes*, tracking down political murderers in a provincial town, is continually led astray by the local police and his own bureau and ends the novel killing the man whose supposed murder he was investigating.† In Robbe-Grillet's novels it is not so much the objective descriptions of objects and things which weaken the books' aesthetic structure, rather the failure to depict anguished human relationships: the husband simply observes the actions, real or supposed, of others, but his reflections, which are the novel, fail to communicate any sense of his own involvement in the relationship. Robbe-Grillet does not *struggle* with the problems of human relationships which attend the isolated human beings his novels portray; his characters do not have continuous human relations, their identity is never defined in terms of other humans, only as a function of the highly complex structures which constitute 'plot'. Personal identity has been rendered wholly ambiguous: who or what is Mathias, or Wallas, or any of Robbe-Grillet's characters? Character does not exist: humans are objects, and like objects, are isolated, without relations with others, and must be depicted as such.

But the most despairing comment on alienation comes from perhaps the most 'alienated' of contemporary writers, Samuel Beckett. In his novel, *Molloy* (1950), the first person narrative recalls the early life of an old, sick man, Molloy, and his relations with others. There was love and sex:

It was she made me acquainted with love. She went by the peaceful name of Ruth I think, but I can't say for certain. Perhaps the name was Edith. She had a hole between her legs, oh not the bunghole I had always imagined, but a slit, and in this I put, or rather she put, my so-called virile member, not without difficulty, and I toiled and moiled until I discharged or gave up trying or was begged by her to stop. A mugs game in my opinion and tiring on top of that, in the long

* Robbe-Grillet, *La Jalousie*, trans. R. Howard, London, 1960, p. 98.
† *Les Gommes* (*The Erasers*, 1953), *Le Voyeur* (*The Voyeur*, 1955).

run . . . Perhaps after all she put me in her rectum. A matter of complete indifference to me, I needn't tell you. But is it true love in the rectum? That's what bothers me sometimes. Have I ever known true love, after all? *

This is, indeed, a dehumanized alienation.

* S. Beckett, *Molloy*, London, 1966, p. 60.

10 George Orwell, Socialism and the Novel

The work of George Orwell (1903–50) – novels, literary, and social criticism – spans the period of Hitler, appeasement, the Second World War, and the beginnings of the cold war. Orwell wrote during the era of concentration camps, secret police, 'framed' political trials, and the total mobilization of whole societies for war. It was the time of the dictator, of the ebb-tide of revolution that had started with the growth in the Soviet Union of a bureaucratic apparatus working against the genuine international revolutionary perspectives of the Bolsheviks, substituting instead the nationalistic Stalinist concept of socialism in a single country. During the 1930s, socialism in Germany and in Spain was crushed by fascist parties while in Britain the economic slumps of the 1920s, coupled with the disastrous failure of the 1926 general strike, demoralized the working class socially and politically. Orwell developed in this period of increasing totalitarianism and successive defeats for the working classes of Europe. His concept of socialism, which in a paradoxical way was to determine the greatness of *Animal Farm* (1944) and *Nineteen Eighty-Four* (1950), was fashioned within this entirely pessimistic context.

I

Writing in 1940 on the American novelist Henry Miller, Orwell was convinced of the overpowering and irresistible development of totalitarianism; individual rights and freedoms would gradually be eroded and the individual be no more than a cipher of the total state:

Almost certainly we are moving into an age of totalitarian dictatorships – an age in which freedom of thought will be at first a deadly sin and later on a meaningless abstraction. The autonomous individual is going to be stamped out of existence.*

Totalitarianism would signal the final death of the novel, since of all literary genres, Orwell argued, the novel could only have developed and continue to persist in an atmosphere of 'mental honesty and a minimum of censorship'. As the product of the 'free mind' and the 'autonomous individual', the novel could not exist under a totalitarian form of government, except as the conformist mouthpiece of a political orthodoxy, for 'good novels are not written by orthodoxy-sniffers, nor by people who are conscience-stricken about their own unorthodoxy', but by writers 'who are *not frightened*'.†

Thus for Orwell, looking back on the writers of the 1930s, at a literature which was mediocre precisely because it had tied itself increasingly and uncritically to the ideology of the Communist Party, Orwell concluded that in order to sustain a genuine novel form the novelist must remain outside the control and the dictates of a political party. This is not to say that he should have no political commitments; on the contrary, without some form of social or political conviction great literature cannot be written at all. In his essay on Swift's *Gulliver's Travellers*, Orwell explicitly argued against the crude Marxist view, which defined 'good' literature in terms of its politically 'progressive' nature, by pointing out that history was characterized by a continuous conflict between 'reactionary' and 'progressive', and that 'the best books of any one age have always been written from several different viewpoints, some of them more palpably more false than others'. It is not the viewpoint which matters, whether fascist, communist, or conservative, but rather the *conviction* of the writer, always providing that he is medically 'sane' and not 'crankish' (for example, a spiritualist).‡ It is clearly a questionable point on the literary viability of fascism, which in essence is wholly irrational and inhuman and hardly the basis of a genuine novel. But Orwell's point remains: no genuine (serious) writer can hope to be associated too deeply with a political party and still remain an artist.

* G. Orwell, 'Inside the Whale', in *Collected Essays*, London, Secker & Warburg, 1961, p. 157.
† ibid., pp. 148–9.
‡ ibid., p. 398.

This attack on political attachment and the writer must be seen within its historical context. Before the First World War there had been little debate on the political commitment of the writer, and it was generally assumed that the novelist wrote of life as he experienced it, honestly, his political values constituting his own individual vision and not those of a political party. After the 1917 Bolshevik revolution, however, this question was brought sharply into focus. The existence of the first workers' state could hardly be ignored, and the fact of the apparently first successful workers' revolution entered the consciousness of writers. In general they ignored it, and wrote of pessimism and of alienation. But with economic depression the fate of capitalism seemed in the balance, and during the 1930s increasing unemployment and the menace of fascism drove many writers towards a more optimistic and socially progressive point of view – in England, Spender, Auden, Isherwood, Cornford, in France, Malraux and Aragon, in Italy, Silone, either joined or became the literary mouthpieces of the Communist Party. The writers' function became one of a non-critical acceptance of Russian communism coupled with a hatred of industrial capitalism. Art was harnessed to ideology, and socialist realism became the literary norm.*

The commitment proved unstable. For the most part writers had not grasped the real nature of the Soviet State or its cynical disregard for all socialist principles. The Moscow Trials in the late 1930s of old Bolsheviks tried as 'fascist agents', together with the Soviet–German pact (1939), broke the tenuous links which had held many writers to the Communist Party, and in their rejection of communism they tended to dismiss all varieties of socialism. Orwell stands out as an intellectual who, as a socialist, rejected Russian communism in the 1930s and after the betrayals continued to believe in a socialist perspective. He did not adopt a quietist stance, for he believed that the novelist was *involved* in the society he artistically renders; he is not a spectator, but must strive to communicate his own passion, his

* For a discussion on communism and the writer, see especially J. Ruhle, *Literature and Revolution*, London, Pall Mall, 1969. Possibly the only genuine revolutionary novel to come out of Britain during the 1930s was Lewis Grassic Gibbon's *Scots Quair*, set in Scotland, and depicting political activity, class conflict, exploitation both in farming and in industry portrayed through the lives of ordinary working-class people.

convictions, through his art. The paradox with Orwell is that while he attacked those writers who had involved themselves politically with the Communist Party, it was only when he himself embraced a socialist vision that he was able to create his two masterpieces.

In his early novels, especially *A Clergyman's Daughter* (1934) and *Keep the Aspidistra Flying* (1936), Orwell had portrayed life from the standpoint of the middle class. In a sense these novels anticipate the bleakness of *Nineteen Eighty-Four*, but they fail to function as integrated wholes, as aesthetic unities. Orwell himself was highly critical of them,* and with justification. In *A Clergyman's Daughter* the various episodes through which the sexless Dorothy passes – the hop-picking in Kent, the vigil with the homeless in Trafalgar Square, the private school with its fee-conscious headmistress and efficiency ritual which defines the secret of success as efficiency and the test of efficiency as success – are never successfully welded together as a unity. The ostensible theme of the novel, Dorothy's loss of religious faith, is not integrated into the main body of the novel, but merely suggested as a necessary consequence of her picaresque wanderings. Like *Keep the Aspidistra Flying*, *A Clergyman's Daughter* functions essentially as social comment, as a document of the harsh realities of lower middle-class life in England during the 1930s and of the generally depressing nature of life.† Their message is that money defines one's social status; character virtually revolves around this theme in a forced way, with genuine human relations a virtually hopeless possibility. The subjective experiences of the characters are subordinated to Orwell's social intent: Dorothy accepted her loss of faith but

---

* In a letter to George Woodcock, Orwell wrote that he was 'ashamed' of both *A Clergyman's Daughter* and *Keep the Aspidistra Flying*, the former 'an exercise . . . I oughtn't to have published . . .' and the latter because 'I was desperate for money' (G. Orwell, *Collected Essays, Journalism and Letters*, ed. S. Orwell and I. Angus, London, Secker & Warburg, 1968, vol. 4, pp. 205–6).

† '*A Clergyman's Daughter* contains Orwell's first nightmare vision and it has not changed radically by *1984* . . . Both worlds are "desolate", "dank", "windless", "bleak", "colourless", "grey". The "slummy wilderness" of capitalist civilization is succeeded by the slummier wilderness of totalitarianism . . . the later world is only a political translation of the earlier' (P. Rieff, 'George Orwell and the Post-Liberal Imagination', in I. Howe (ed.), *Orwell's 1984*, New York, Harcourt, Brace & World Inc., 1963, p. 229).

continues to work for the Church since she cannot imagine another alternative, while the struggling poet, Comstock, the hero of *Keep the Aspidistra Flying*, abandons art for a safe comfortable life in advertising. In these novels Orwell has no political perspective: there is clearly something seriously wrong with industrial capitalism and with middle-class life and its values, but as yet there is no awareness of any alternative. His characters simply submit. In *Coming Up for Air* (1939) this sense of futility fuses with a pessimistic political element. In this transitional novel the pessimism is becoming total; the cheerful cynicism of his middle-aged insurance agent contrasts sharply with the overpowering sense of hopelessness, with political solutions: the war is coming, capitalism is finished, socialism is a middle-class sham – these are George Bowling's thoughts as he returns to the village where he was born, hoping to fish and be free of his wife and two children for a few days. *Coming Up for Air* has a more integrated structure precisely because Orwell is not subordinating his characters to his desire for reportage. The sterility of lower middle-class life is communicated naturally through Bowling's cynicism and awareness that there is neither an alternative for him nor any point in struggling against the system. Through Bowling, Orwell is anticipating an era of totalitarianism.

In these novels, then, a political vision of the world is largely absent. In this Orwell is the reverse of Malraux, for although the early novels indicate a talented writer in themselves they would not suggest the greatness of *Animal Farm* or *Nineteen Eighty-Four*. In 1936 Orwell became a convinced socialist, a belief which survived his experience in the Spanish Civil War of being hounded from Spain as a 'Trotskyite-Fascist'[*] by the communists for whose cause he had fought. Orwell's refusal to reject his socialist vision, his awareness of the counter-revolutionary tendencies of Russian communism, combined with his overall social pessimism, constitute the basic elements of his creative genius.

[*] Orwell clearly understood the distinction between Stalinism and Trotskyism, in that the latter was a political tendency which based itself on revolutionary Marxism, on world revolution, while Stalinism represented a conservative denial of world revolution, substituting instead the theory of 'socialism in one country'. In Stalin's struggle for power, Trotsky and his theory of permanent revolution became the chief obstacle, and during the 1930s Trotskyism was hounded unmercifully by the Communist Party.

2

Orwell's life as a writer began in the late 1920s when he lived in London and Paris with the unemployed, the vagrants and tramps. Although born into the English middle-class and with the advantage of a public-school education at Eton, Orwell felt guilty about his privileged status. His significance as a writer undoubtedly stems from his shifting attitudes towards his own social class, the middle-class intelligentsia, and the working classes, and his deliberate attempt to understand the nature of socialism and the role of the working class in achieving it.

He was born, he wrote,* into the 'lower-upper-middle class', a social stratum which included those earning as little as £300 a year and those with £2,000 per annum. The class was defined for Orwell both in terms of money, since it was 'the quickest way of making yourself understood', and social status: 'a naval officer and his grocer very likely have the same income, but they are not equivalent persons', for one has tradition behind him, the knowledge that he belongs to a social stratum which is not defined exclusively by its work function, as the working class is defined in terms of contractual manual labour. For the ordinary middle-class person, his gentlemanly status was sufficient to distinguish him clearly from the few working-class individuals who earned as much as he or possibly more.

When Orwell left Eton he was, in his own words 'an odious little snob', convinced of his own superiority over the working classes. Serving in the Imperial Police in Burma he gradually fashioned a critical view of British imperialist policy and a warm attachment to the 'underdog'. His experience left him with a 'bad conscience', and on leave in England in 1927 he decided that he had had enough of an 'oppressive system' which had left him with 'an immense weight of guilt' in need of expiation:

I felt that I had got to escape not merely from imperialism but from every form of man's dominion over man. I wanted to submerge myself, to get right down among the oppressed, to be one of them and on their side against the tyrants.†

At this stage in his career Orwell was not a socialist; social inequality was grasped in the simplistic terms of *them* and *us*, those

* Biographical data on Orwell's life is in his *The Road to Wigan Pier*, London, Gollancz, 1937, part 2.
† ibid., p. 180.

in authority and those under its dictation. At this time, he wrote, 'failure seemed . . . the only virtue', and thus he sought out the socially deprived, those completely at the mercy of 'respectable' society, the tramps and the outcasts of his first book, *Down and Out in Paris and London* (1933). He described his experience as a time of great happiness; his guilt was being assuaged. But these social rejects were not the authentic working class and Orwell knew this. Although disinterested in socialism at this time, he was nevertheless aware of the rigid class divisions which marked the British social structure and which, we may hazard, left him uneasy. He desperately wanted to establish contact with the working class, as the submerged class, as the downtrodden. In 1936 he wrote a report for the left-wing publisher Victor Gollancz on the state of the working class in the north of England. In his novels he had ignored the working class except as peripheral figures in his explicitly middle-class milieus, but in this report he struggled to approach them. The result is important for the development of his later fiction. Orwell approaches them as a middle-class left-wing critic of capitalist society; he describes them from the outside, in somewhat idealized terms and turns necessity into a virtue.

In his early novels Orwell had attacked the middle class. In his report on the English working class it becomes clear that the middle class are in virtually all important respects the inferiors of the working class. Orwell depicts the worker as entirely free of any sense of status, of notions of 'getting on', which for him embodied the essence of the middle-class family; the worker is not 'badgered' to improve his social position. Orwell admired, too, their strong sense of community, of mutual aid and the absence of any fear of poverty by those who clearly could go no higher in the social scale. If the worker is in employment, Orwell argued, then he 'has a better chance of being happy than an "educated" man' for he will enjoy a far 'saner' family life:

Especially on winter evenings after tea, when the fire glows in the open range . . . when Father, in shirt sleeves, sits in the rocking chair at one side of the fire reading the racing finals, and Mother sits on the other with her sewing, and the children are happy with a pennorth of mint humbugs, and the dog lolls roasting himself on the rag mat – it is a good place to be in, provided that you can be not only in it but sufficiently of it to be taken for granted.*

* ibid., p. 149.

Orwell's admiration for the spontaneous elements of working-class life extended to a belief in their superior sexuality, simple and basic with no neurotic overtones, as well as to their sheer physical qualities and inherent 'good sense'. The middle-class socialists, on the other hand, are savagely pilloried, as cranks for whom the working man has only contempt: 'One sometimes gets the impression that the mere words "Socialism" and "Communism" draw towards them with magnetic force every fruit-juice drinker, nudist, sandal-wearer, sex-maniac, Quaker, "Nature Cure" quack and feminist in England.'* The working class, Orwell suggests, simply ignore such alien forces.

Orwell describes the working class in terms of an idealized community, putting up with life, that is, with unemployment, the dole queues, and poverty. The significant point about his characterization lies in the implications for socialism. The working class, Orwell repeats again and again, are not revolutionary, they have no deep commitment to the ideals of socialism, still less to communism: 'To the ordinary working man . . . Socialism does not mean much more than better wages and shorter hours and nobody bossing you about.' The revolutionary implications of socialism are missed. In Orwell's *Diary* of his experiences in the North of England, he commented on the working-class audience at one political meeting in terms which leaves no doubt that he saw the proletariat not as the agency of social change but as one of the supports of continued bourgeois rule and capitalism: 'I suppose these people represented a fair cross-section of t he more revolutionary elements in Wigan. If so, God help us. Exactly the same sheeplike crowd – gaping girls and shapeless middle-aged women dozing over their knitting . . . There is no *turbulence* left in England.'† Orwell could not grasp that the 1930s were a period of defeat for the English working class and that their apathy, indifference and seeming acceptance of the system were as much the result of prolonged economic depression as of political failures in the General Strike and the conservative rather than socialist legislation of the

* ibid., p. 206. Attending an Independent Labour Party meeting in London, Orwell typically observed, 'Are *these* mingy little beasts . . . the champions of the working class?' (ibid., p. 207).
† *Collected Essays, Journalism and Letters*, vol. 1, p. 181.

second Labour Government (1929–31).* Orwell's *political* conception of the working class was thus forged at a time when the
class was *demoralized*: it accepted a second-class life out of
necessity, not choice. The cinema, radio, 'strong tea', football
pools and fish and chips were not solely the social forces which
averted revolution in England in the 1930s, as Orwell argued; a
revolutionary class must have confidence, it must believe in itself, as a revolutionary force, as a viable oppositional unit. The
workers' lack of interest in politics, a theme which runs through
all of Orwell's writings,† was not necessarily an inherent tendency of the working class but rather the consequence of dis-
believing in themselves as a potentially revolutionary class.

For the paradox here is that Orwell retained a belief in the
socialist future and a *theoretical* view of the working class which
conflicted with his observations. The English working class
were not internationalist, he argued in his essay on the Spanish
Civil War, they were far more interested in the day's football
match than events in Madrid or Berlin, but yet 'this does not
alter the fact that the working class will go on struggling against
Fascism after the others have caved in'. Orwell's socialist vision
led him against his own practical knowledge to ascribe a positive
function to a working class which had accepted capitalism. This
crucial contradiction is important for understanding many of
the ambiguities of *Nineteen Eighty-Four*. For Orwell maintained
that the working class historically are the only class which can
defend democracy:

One feature of the Nazi conquest of France was the astonishing de-
fections among the intelligentsia, including some of the left-wing
intelligentsia. The intelligentsia are the people who squeal loudest
against Fascism, and yet a respectable proportion of them collapse
into defeatism when the pinch comes.

* The Labour government of 1929–31 which, as a minority government,
depended on Liberal Party support in Parliament, had cut unemployment
pay in 1931 in order to safeguard the pound internationally. For the mass of
unemployed, the fact that the Labour Government had not solved the economic crisis, combined with its pro-capitalist policies, could only undermine
working-class optimism.
† Curiously, Orwell, in all his writings on the working class, never discussed
the trade unions but looked at the working class in isolation from the
Labour movement. At both the annual Labour Party Conferences and the
Trades Union Congress working-class political opinion was voiced during
the 1930s. The fact that the official leadership of the Labour Party and the
Trade Unions tended to ignore it is never discussed by Orwell.

Workers will always fight fascism, Orwell maintained, because fascism, of its nature pro-capitalist, cannot provide a better standard of living for the working class: 'The struggle of the working class is like the growth of a plant. The plant is blind and stupid, but it knows enough to keep pushing upwards towards the light, and it will do this in the face of endless discouragements.'* Orwell's experience in the Spanish Civil War (1936–8) as a volunteer fighting in the front lines† had convinced him that socialism was more than theoretically possible. In Spain in the workers' militias he experienced the practice of genuine equality: there was no sense of status, of hierarchy, and although there were many shortages, 'no privilege and no bootlicking'. The Spanish militias, wrote Orwell, were a microcosm of a classless society, a foretaste of what life under socialism would be like:

Many of the normal motives of civilized life – snobbishness, money-grubbing, fear of the boss, etc. – had simply ceased to exist. The ordinary class-division of society had disappeared to an extent that is almost unthinkable in the money-tainted air of England . . . The effect was to make my desire to see Socialism established much more actual than it had been before.‡

But socialism would not be possible through the self-styled middle-class left-wing intelligentsia. In Spain socialism *was* the working class. In England it was in the hands of 'cranks' and the 'Europeanized' intelligentsia. Orwell believed strongly in patriotism, in the 'English culture', encompassing dank weather, suet pudding, and the rights of the individual, and his most savage criticism of the middle class was directed against its 'severance' from this common culture. The middle-class intelligentsia, he wrote, 'take their cookery from Paris and their opinions from Moscow'.§ Unlike the ordinary person, the in-

* *Collected Essays*, pp. 200–201.
† Orwell went to Spain in 1936 and joined the P.O.U.M. militia, through his membership of the Independent Labour Party. The P.O.U.M. was a semi-Trotskyist group advocating proletarian revolution. The Spanish Communist Party, on the other hand, urged a democratic and not revolutionary settlement to Spain's problems.
‡ G. Orwell, *Homage to Catalonia*, London, Secker & Warburg, 1951, pp. 111–12. See also his essay, 'Looking Back on the Spanish War' (1943), where his belief in socialism and the working classes' roles in achieving it are again stated.
§ G. Orwell, 'England Your England', in *Selected Essays*, London, Penguin Books, 1957, pp. 85–7.

tellectual worshipped power, 'the new religion of Europe', and accepted totalitarianism.

But the middle class of Orwell's early novels is, in any case, 'done for' since 'capitalism is finished'.* The middle classes function as 'shock absorbers' between the ruling classes and the working class. They are doomed, Orwell says, but they resist their seemingly anachronistic situation with an exaggerated sense of status:

Practically the whole family income goes in keeping up appearances. It is obvious that people of this kind are in an anomalous position, and one might be tempted to write them off as mere exceptions ... Actually, however, they are or were fairly numerous. Most clergymen and schoolmasters, for instance, nearly all Anglo-Indian officials, a sprinkling of soldiers and sailors and a fair number of professional men and artists fall into this category.†

In the early novels Orwell portrayed this hopeless struggle to maintain status in a world increasingly indifferent to these groups. There is the continual worry over money. In *A Clergyman's Daughter* Dorothy feels sick at the sight of the unpaid butcher's bill, saying to her indifferent father, 'It's so dreadful to be always in debt! Even if it isn't actually wrong, it's so *hateful*. It makes me so ashamed.'‡ Gordon Comstock, in *Keep the Aspidistra Flying*, finds his whole existence bound up by the 'money God'. In this novel Orwell links artistic creativity with the leisure money can buy:

Money and culture! In a country like England you can no more be cultured without money than you can join the Cavalry Club ... And the money that such refinement means! For after all, what is there behind it, except money? Money for the right kind of education, money for influential friends, money for leisure and peace of mind, money for trips to Italy. Money writes books, money sells them. Give me not righteousness, O Lord, give me money, only money.§

Comstock is no socialist. He desires only the time and the money to write poetry; his work experiences in advertising, in the second-hand book trade, and finally, when virtually destitute, among bug-infested lodging rooms, do not turn him against the system of industrial capitalism. Like Dorothy he accepts it,

* *The Road to Wigan Pier*, p. 154.
† ibid., p. 156.
‡ G. Orwell, *A Clergyman's Daughter*, London, Penguin Books, 1964, p. 26.
§ G. Orwell, *Keep the Aspidistra Flying*, London, Penguin Books, 1962, p. 13.

and the novel ends with his suffering girl-friend made pregnant
and Comstock applying for his safe middle-class advertising job
again. Money dominates the structure of this novel absolutely:
its only romantic moment, for example – the trip to the countryside – is ruined by Comstock's inability to pay for his girl-
friend's hotel meal and for a contraceptive to consummate their
love. Like Nathanael West, Orwell denies his characters their
right to sexual pleasure. Comstock remarks that without
money 'no decent relationship with a woman is possible', and
when finally he and Rosemary make love in his dingy room it is
done without 'much pleasure'.* Dorothy, too, leads a joyless
life, terrified of men and the sexual act. Both these heroines are
cold, sexless women, one a virgin who shudders at the 'monstrous things' which follow the kissing and the 'mauling', '*all
that*' as she calls the act of love; Rosemary is described as
'sexually immature', thirty years old, and frustrating poor
Comstock in his simple quest for pleasure. Indeed, her ambition
is that he should abandon poetry for advertising, settle down,
and be *conventional*.

The atmosphere which Orwell conveys in these two early
novels is of a middle-class environment, seedy, pathetic, and
clearly doomed. Dorothy loses her faith and the novel ends with
her desperately looking for a substitute, for a belief which will
give a meaning to her life, but failing to find it. Instead she absorbs herself totally in the everyday routine of the vicarage:

The problem of faith and no faith had vanished utterly from her
mind. It was beginning to get dark, but, too busy to stop and light the
lamp she worked on, pasting strip after strip of paper into place, with
absorbed, with pious concentration, in the penetrating smell of the
gluepot.†

Comstock conforms and buys the aspidistra, the symbol of
respectability.‡ George Bowling, the middle-aged, overweight
insurance agent of *Coming Up for Air*, has, when the novel starts,
already accepted fate. In this novel, written after his experiences
in Spain, Orwell communicates a less oppressive, pessimistic

* *Keep the Aspidistra Flying*, p. 236.
† *A Clergyman's Daughter*, pp. 262–3.
‡ The aspidistra originates in Comstock's mind as a symbol of middle-class
respectability from his reading of Robert Tressell's *The Ragged Trousered
Philanthropists*, in which a starving carpenter pawns all his possessions except
his aspidistra.

atmosphere, largely through Bowling's idealized reminiscences of his life before the First World War, yet the same themes predominate: Hilda, his wife, is the sexless, 'lifeless, middle-aged frump', the daughter of two ex-colonials, concerned with status, and a 'ghastly glooming about money', indifferent to politics and culture; the middle-class milieu is conceived as wholly depressive, as *joyless*.

3

After the outbreak of the Second World War, Orwell tried unsuccessfully to enlist in the Army and found great difficulty in obtaining adequate employment. Judged medically unfit except for the Home Guard, he eventually spent four frustrating years broadcasting to India for the B.B.C. His world vision had crystallized into a complete rejection of anything other than democratic socialism, but his pessimism had grown so powerful that this perspective seemed hopeless. During the war years and those immediately following, Orwell wrote his two masterpieces within an intellectual vision which contained a number of contradictory elements. *Nineteen Eighty-Four* is a fictional structure dominated by these unresolved contradictions.

Firstly, Orwell retained a stubborn belief in socialism, and he saw in the war the catalyst of revolutionary change; the working class is the only class capable of effecting the transition from capitalism to socialism. Secondly, the main enemy was Russian communism whose methods of political indoctrination and control led irresistibly to totalitarianism. Shortly after the end of the war he wrote:

Exactly at the moment when wealth might be so generally diffused that no government need fear serious opposition, political liberty is declared to be impossible and half the world is ruled by secret police forces. Exactly at the moment when superstition crumbles and a rational attitude towards the universe becomes feasible, the right to think one's own thoughts is denied as never before.*

Totalitarianism was penetrating even England, with its old traditions of political liberty and freedom of expression. In 1943 *Animal Farm* was turned down by at least eight publishers on

* *Collected Essays, Journalism and Letters*, vol. 4, p. 249.

the grounds that it attacked Russian communism; in 1938 Gollancz, before seeing the typescript, had refused to publish *Homage to Catalonia* because he knew that Orwell would be critical of the Stalinists in Spain.* It is true that *Animal Farm* is a savage satire on Stalinism and that Orwell's purpose in writing it was propagandistic: 'It was of the utmost importance to me that the peoples of Western Europe should see the Soviet régime for what it really was.'† *Animal Farm* is not an attack on socialism nor on revolution,‡ but on the specific totalitarian features which Russian socialism had developed in its denial of the genuine socialist ideals of the 1917 Revolution. In Spain Orwell had experienced what socialism might be like and he wrote later that this period of his life was so different from anything that had gone before, it possessed 'a magic quality which, as a rule, belongs only to memories that are years old'.§ Orwell believed passionately in a society which was planned and *humane*, which neither Western capitalism nor the Soviet Union were. But already in *Animal Farm* there is an element absent from the novels of the 1930s: the obsession with *power*.

Totalitarianism is a system of tightly organized power; the

---

* Orwell's experience of left-wing journalism and publishing after he had returned from Spain must have further convinced him of the inherent weakness of the left intelligentsia towards communism and totalitarianism. The *New Statesman* refused to publish an article written by him on the suppression of the P.O.U.M. by the Spanish communists, and his review of Franz Borkenau's anti-communist *The Spanish Cockpit* was rejected on grounds that it 'controverted editorial policy'. Orwell wrote that Gollancz, the publisher of all Orwell's early books, from 1933–37, was 'part of the Communism-racket' and as soon as 'he heard I had been associated with the P.O.U.M.' refused to publish *Homage to Catalonia*. Orwell, op. cit., vol. 1, pp. 278–81 especially. *Animal Farm* was also turned down by Gollancz on political grounds, and when Secker & Warburg agreed to publish it, a year elapsed before they felt the political climate had changed enough to allow its publication.

† Introduction to the Ukrainian edition of *Animal Farm*, in op. cit., vol. 3, p. 402.

‡ Thus Jenni Calder in her study of Orwell claims that in *Animal Farm* Orwell 'presents a compact and detailed statement of the corruption of revolution' (*Chronicles of Conscience*, London, Secker & Warburg, 1968, p. 225). The line should have read 'of *a* revolution' for Orwell was convinced of the necessity for revolution, if a truly humane society was to emerge, but the revolution had to be a democratic one. See his comments on the English revolution he expected to develop from the Second World War, in op. cit., vol. 3, especially pp. 374–5, 424–5.

§ *Homage to Catalonia*, p. 112.

animals revolt to throw off an oppressive régime only to find themselves at the mercy of the pigs, a cohesive power group; the revolution turns into its opposite and instead of a democratically diffused power structure, political authority becomes tightly concentrated. Power corrupts, Orwell seems to say, if not tempered by democratic institutions. And the chances of a democratic form of socialism seemed remote.

In his essay on James Burnham's *The Managerial Revolution* (1946) Orwell, although critical of Burnham's actual analysis, accepted some of the conclusions, especially Burnham's political predictions on the rise of a new managerial class which would replace the old capitalist ruling classes. The managers will 'crush the working class, and so organize society that all power and economic privilege remain in their hands'. Private property rights will be abolished but without instituting common ownership; the world will be divided into three super states in Europe, Asia and America, each internally stratified 'with an aristocracy of talent at the top and a mass of semi-slaves at the bottom'. This is already the world of *Nineteen Eighty-Four*; power is separate from property, has become a thing in itself. Burnham went on to argue that capitalism as a system was 'clearly doomed' but that socialism was no more than 'a dream'. Orwell remarked that Burnham's conclusions on an irresistible world-wide movement towards planned economies controlled by repressive oligarchies were both 'plausible' and 'difficult to resist'. He seems to accept Burnham's argument that the seeds of totalitarian power in the Soviet Union were sown by the 1917 revolution itself, in the form of the Bolshevik party with its core of dedicated, full-time revolutionaries and theory of 'democratic centralism'.* Orwell's vision of the world, then, was now totally political and thoroughly pessimistic. In *Nineteen Eighty-Four* he created a significant dynamic structure precisely because his vision was deeply felt and compounded of these diverse contradictions.

* *Collected Essays*, pp. 352–76. Lenin's conception of 'democratic centralism' implied a professional group of revolutionaries who would act as the directors of revolution. The masses' natural revolutionary activity against the ruling classes had to be coordinated from a revolutionary centre. Orwell believed that Stalinism in part developed from this conception.

4

Nineteen Eighty-Four is the most savage of anti-utopias, a direct satire on the Soviet Union as well as on certain aspects of Western capitalism. Some critics have argued that Orwell based his novel on an earlier Russian anti-utopia, Zamyatin's *We*, which was written in 1920 as an implied attack on the Bolshevik's party's control of all aspects of social and political life in Russia. In 1946 Orwell had reviewed Zamyatin's novel, comparing it favourably with Aldous Huxley's *Brave New World* (1930), which he thought was partly derived from it. Zamyatin, Orwell argued, had grasped the essence of totalitarianism, the notion of 'cruelty as an end in itself, the worship of a Leader who is credited with divine attributes'. Huxley's vision of the future, Orwell went on, was weakened by his inability to explain the rigid system of social stratification which characterized his society – there were no economic or psychological reasons why it should exist: 'The aim is not economic exploitation . . . There were no economic or psychological reasons why it should exist: . . . There is no power-hunger, no sadism, no hardness of any kind. Those at the top have no strong motive for staying on the top, and though everyone is happy in a vacuous way, life has become so pointless that it is difficult to believe that such a society could endure.' In Zamyatin's society, by contrast, social stratification and its system of inequalities exist precisely to satisfy the 'power-hunger, sadism, and hardness' of the ruling élite.*

In Orwell's vision the world has become divided into three super states of Oceania, Eastasia, and Eurasia, organized for total control of their populations and for permanent warfare. In Oceania technology has developed to such an extent that material inequality is no longer functionally necessary, yet a rigid system of stratification divides the population into the 85 per cent working class (the 'proles'), a middle class of administrators, and a ruling élite of bureaucrats. The proles are kept under permanent control by the mass media with its mechanically manufactured films 'oozing with sex', sentimental songs, and newspapers full of sport, astrology, and crime, the products of the 'Ministry of Truth'. The 'Thought Police' periodically weed

* *Collected Essays, Journalism and Letters*, vol. 4, pp. 72–5.

out from the working class any potential leaders and the 'proles' lead lives which are wholly non-political. The motive for the domination of the Party (INGSOC) and the authority of its leader, Big Brother, is power itself.

Oceania is thus a society in which the individual as an individual has ceased to exist. Telescreens keep a relentless check on the behaviour of all members of the Party, at work, in the streets, at home; BIG BROTHER IS WATCHING YOU bears down from countless street hoardings and telescreens. Social life is thoroughly regimented. The Thought Police operate through terror, torture, and the manipulation of language; revolt becomes impossible if there are no words to express dissent. 'Newspeak' replaces English: words change their meaning, lose some of their ambiguity, or are simply removed from the language itself. At the same time the past is continually rewritten so that Big Brother and the Party never make mistakes. Individuals periodically disappear, 'vaporized' for 'thinkcrime', that is, for nonconformist thought. The family unit exists, but the children are encouraged to spy on their parents and report them for any signs of unorthodoxy:

Nearly all children nowadays were horrible. What was worst of all was that by means of such organizations as the Spies they were systematically turned into ungovernable little savages, and yet this produced in them no tendency whatever to rebel against the discipline of the Party. On the contrary, they adored the Party and everything connected with it ... All their ferocity was turned outwards, against the enemies of the State, against foreigners, traitors, saboteurs, thought criminals. It was almost normal for people over thirty to be frightened of their own children. And with good reason, for hardly a week passed in which the *Times* did not carry a paragraph describing how some eavesdropping little sneak – 'child hero' was the phrase generally used – had overheard some compromising remark and denounced its parents to the Thought Police.*

Nineteen Eighty-Four describes the revolt of one individual against this all-pervading conformism. Winston Smith is Orwell's 'hero', thirty-nine years old, separated from his wife, a member of the 'Outer Party' and employed in the Records Department of the Ministry of Truth to rewrite the past in conformity with the present policies of Big Brother and the Party.

* G. Orwell, *Nineteen Eighty-four*, London, Secker & Warburg, 1950, p. 27. All further references are to this edition and are included in the text in parentheses.

As a character Winston Smith is similar to Comstock in his general depressive passivity, and the way in which his surroundings dominate him. Like Comstock, who hated the conformity of the middle classes, Winston finds himself increasingly critical of the Party and its rigid system of discipline, but unlike Comstock he finally rejects the Party, only to be crushed utterly by its overwhelming power.

The novel is built around the conflict which develops between Winston Smith's humane individualism (in newspeak, 'ownlife' which takes the form of a nostalgia for a dimly remembered past, when life may have been better) and the collective, inhuman values of the Party and Big Brother. Winston is portrayed as an anomaly within a totally organized society: he recalls, for example, that only four years previously 'Oceania had been at war with Eastasia and in alliance with Eurasia. But this was merely a piece of furtive knowledge which he happened to possess because his memory was not satisfactorily under control' (p. 36). Winston is on the way to 'thinkcrime', the moment he begins a diary, a private activity outlawed in Oceania, in which he struggles to recall the past: was life always so dreary and so regimented? His rebellion is further strengthened when he finds proof that the Party has deliberately falsified the past knowing it to be false and that the Great Purges of the sixties were fabricated to leave Big Brother entirely in control of the Party and the Party in control of the State. Winston accidentally finds a photograph from *The Times* of three convicted spies, Jones, Aaronson, and Rutherford, attending a Party delegation meeting in New York at the very moment when, according to the confessions at their trial, they were conspiring the downfall of Big Brother and the Party in enemy territory (pp. 76–7). Winston consigns the damning photograph to the incinerators, the 'memory hole', but he knows it existed and that the Party is not always right.

Winston begins an affair with Julia, who operates a fiction-writing machine in the Ministry of Truth. Julia embodies an *instinctual* revolt against the Party; her rebellion is wholly private, aimed at the denial of pleasure which functions as an integral part of the Party's repressive authority. It complements Winston's *intellectual* revolt against the Party's deliberate and systematic perversion of history. They make love irregularly until Winston rents a room over a junk-shop in the proletarian area of Airstrip One (London). Their act of rebellion leads them to contact O'Brien, a member of the Inner Party, who Winston mistakenly believes is a member of the outlawed opposition, led by the reviled Goldstein, the recipient of the daily two-minute *Hate*. Emmanuel Goldstein is the 'Enemy of the People', 'the renegade and backslider, who once . . . had been one of the leading figures of the Party, almost on a level with Big Brother himself, and then had engaged in counter-revolutionary activities, had been condemned to death and had mysteriously escaped and disappeared' (p. 15). All acts of sabotage, treachery, doctrinal deviations, are ascribed to Goldstein's teaching summed up in his book, *The Theory and Practice of Oligarchical Collectivism*, and his organization *The Brotherhood*. Clearly Goldstein is Trotsky and the Brotherhood is his revolutionary anti-Stalinist Fourth International.* O'Brien meets the two rebels and asks for unconditional commitment. They agree except for one demand – never to see each other again – they would commit murder and sabotage for the opposition, but not this. O'Brien gives Winston Goldstein's book and he has read the first few chapters when the lovers are arrested by the Thought Police and taken to the Ministry of Love.

Winston had once said to Julia that the Party could control an individual's life externally, but it could not 'get inside you'. This is precisely what the Party, embodied by Winston's torturer interrogator, O'Brien, strives and succeeds in doing. Totalitarianism can destroy both the external freedoms *and* the freedom of the spirit; it was this illusion, that under the most repressive governments man could still retain his inner freedom, which Orwell attacks in the final part of his novel. The purpose of the torture is to get inside Winston's mind, to make him 'sane', to 'cure' him. He must believe his own confession of guilt and he must renounce his individual love for Julia. His submission must be of his own free will. O'Brien tells him, 'We do not destroy the heretic because he resists us: so long as he

---

* After his expulsion from the Soviet Union by Stalin (1929), Trotsky believed at first in reactivating the Communist International but gradually came to see the International, the Third founded by the Bolsheviks to coordinate world revolution, as a reactionary tool in the hands of the counter-revolutionary Russian Communist Party. In 1938 he founded the Fourth International. Two years later Stalin's agent in Mexico murdered him.

resists us we never destroy him. We convert him, we capture his inner mind, we reshape him' (p. 256). Winston resists: the Party is not all – there is the 'human spirit' – but Winston has been tortured out of all recognition and when he looks at his shattered body in the mirror, he breaks down and weeps. In his cell he comes to realize that the Thought Police have watched his every move during the previous seven years; they have photographs of Julia and himself, they knew of his diary, of the incriminating photograph – he is *alone*: he has not even the comfort of the Brotherhood, for O'Brien claims part authorship of Goldstein's book. The party is invincible. The Party must always be right. He writes: FREEDOM IS SLAVERY and TWO AND TWO MAKE FIVE. He is almost cured. In room 101 a cage is strapped to his face. Inside are two rats; Winston cannot stand rats. They are ready to devour his face when the spring which holds down the door which separates them from Winston is pulled. He cannot stand this final torture. He screams:

'Do it to Julia! Do it to Julia! Not me! I don't care what you do to her. Tear her face off, strip her to the bones. Not me! Julia! Not me!' (p. 287)

Thus the novel closes with Winston sitting alone in the same café as the three 'enemies of the people', Jones, Aaronson, and Rutherford had done earlier, sipping gin and waiting for his execution. One day he meets Julia; each of them has betrayed the other. They have both lost their inner freedom, for they know that what they screamed was true. The novel closes with Winston's acceptance of Big Brother: 'He had won the victory over himself. He loved Big Brother' (p. 298).

5

Most commentators have accepted *Nineteen Eighty-Four* as an attack on the Soviet Union and its ideology of Stalinism. There can be no doubt that this was Orwell's intention. He was not attacking socialism, but only, as he himself expressed it, 'the perversions to which a centralized economy is liable and which have already been partly realized in Communism and Fascism'. He did not believe that totalitarian society was historically

inevitable, only that it was possible 'if not fought against'.*
Orwell's characterization of totalitarianism, his 'sociology of
power', however, has serious weaknesses which relate to his
misunderstanding of the nature of Russian communism.

Oceania is a society in which political rule is not legitimated
by ideology but simply functions through total repression and
physical force. Orwell had criticized Huxley for misunderstanding the nature of power in a society of plenty, but his own anti-
utopia operates on the non-sociological basis of sheer terror.
O'Brien's justification for power was simply power itself. But
this is not a sufficient explanation for the persistence of Oceania.
The telescreens operate to whip up nationalistic feelings, the
public executions and parades of captured prisoners together
with mass rallies promote a frenzied, irrational atmosphere – but
nowhere is there any awareness that for any society to function
properly there have to be symbols and myths which justify the
rule of the few. Every ruling group in history justified its rule in
terms other than mere private gain or advantage. Political rule
is possible only if those groups which govern do so with a belief
that its policies are in the good of the nation. Russian communism in its Stalinist phase justified its vast system of political
terror and repression on the grounds that its policies were in the
interests of the communist future as well as for Russia itself.
The Communist Party called for sacrifices in the interests of the
future. The Stalinist State took care, for example, to cultivate
the writer and the artist, to win them over for nationalistic
communism. And through a perverted form of Marxism, turning
it into a dogma, the Russian bureaucracy could claim advantages
over the capitalist West and, through the public ownership
of all property, that Russia was moving towards communism.
The masses could not be left simply to vegetate, as is the case
with Orwell's 'proles'. Russian communism had to win them
to its side, both with terror and ideology.

Oceania is a totalitarian society: but what type of social structure is it? Orwell fails to make this clear. In the past there has
been a civil war and if the parallel with the Soviet Union is pursued, then the power structure of the Party is the equivalent to
the *counter-revolutionary* bureaucracy of the Stalinist period.
As in the Soviet Union capitalism has been abolished, but

* *Collected Essays, Journalism and Letters*, vol. 4, p. 502.

what has taken its place? Is the working class employed in factories, in productive work for profit, and if so, who controls and organizes the work units? What kind of economy does the Party administer: is it bureaucratic collectivism, state capitalism, or simply production for perpetual warfare?* In the Soviet Union a proletarian revolution destroyed capitalism only to end in a society rigidly stratified, in which Party functionaries were increasingly recruited from the middle and not working classes. It is not clear if Orwell intended the Oceania bureaucracy as a counter-revolutionary force opposed to the achievements of an original revolution. On the contrary, from the portrayal of the working class in *Nineteen Eighty-Four* as essentially passive and non-revolutionary, concerned solely with consumption rather than with political change, the bureaucracy was probably not a counter-revolutionary force, but something which grew naturally out of civil war, international wars, and the total mobilization of the population to fight these wars.

Thus power in Oceania does not flow from the collective ownership and bureaucratic control of property, as is the case in the Soviet Union, but from the fact of power itself. In the past, totalitarian states, such as the Soviet Union and Nazi Germany, have used power to subdue the possibility of working-class militancy and to this end the trade unions became part of the State and not distinct from it as is the case in capitalist societies. Power here hinges on the organization of work: a collectivized economy demands a high degree of worker, management, trade-union collaboration for the ultimate goal – economic efficiency. In Oceania, however, power is pure sadism, the irrational domination of man by others. Its point is not economic efficiency in production, but simply the psychological satisfaction of controlling others. O'Brien tells Winston that it is not sufficient for man to obey authority, he must *suffer*:

Power is in inflicting pain and humiliation. Power is in tearing human minds to pieces and putting them together again in new shapes of your own choosing. Do you begin to see, then, what kind of world we are creating? ... A world of fear and treachery and torment, a world of

* State capitalism is a system of production in which the State appropriates profit for its own purposes; it usually has nothing in common with socialism, which is a system of production in which workers' control of production determines that profit is socially useful, that is, in the interests of the masses, not a caste of bureaucrats or capitalists.

trampling and being trampled upon, a world which will grow not less but more merciless as it refines itself. Progress in our world will be progress towards pain. The old civilizations claimed that they were founded on love or justice. Ours is founded upon hatred ... If you want a picture of the future, imagine a boot stamping on a human face – for ever. (pp. 267–8)

By contrast, Gletkin, the interrogator of the old Boshevik, Rubashov, in Arthur Koestler's *Darkness at Noon* (1941), believed in the necessity for violence and terror and the Purges if the revolution was not to be subverted; he tortured out of a conviction in the future. O'Brien tortures Winston as part of the Party's policy of destroying the world of humane values. He claims triumphantly that the Party is destroying feelings between parents and their children, between friends, and finally individual love:

... in the future there will be no wives and no friends. Children will be taken from their mothers at birth ... The sex instinct will be eradicated. Procreation will be an annual formality like the renewal of a ration card. We shall abolish the orgasm. Our neurologists are at work upon it now. There will be no loyalty, except loyalty towards the Party. There will be no love, except the love of Big Brother. (p. 268)

In these passages Orwell is stating his dominant political belief: a revolution which socializes property will not effect a truly humane society, as many Marxists had assumed, unless the collectivization of property is carried through democratically. If the revolution is left in the hands of the middle-class intellectuals who usually form the hard core of any oppositional party, then it will bring only tyranny: the socialist revolution must be the task of the working class – this had been his political credo since 1936, for the middle-class intellectual, unlike the proletarian, worships power. In Spain, Orwell had experienced socialism, and this vision of the future, of the necessary future, never left him. The problem was always the working class – in England they were not revolutionary. Thus how was socialism to be achieved?

This problem constitutes the basic structure of *Nineteen Eighty-Four*. Orwell's pessimistic vision is more total here than in his earlier novels; he has written from within a vision of the world which demanded that socialism replace a bankrupt 'finished' capitalism, but a vision which became increasingly a utopia. In his diary Winston Smith writes that the only hope 'lay in the proles' and before he completes Goldstein's book he knows Goldstein's message is proletarian revolution. In the interrogation O'Brien tells him that the conception of proletarian rebellion is absurd: 'The proletarians will never revolt, not in a thousand years or in a million' (p. 262). *Nineteen Eighty-Four* is Orwell's testimony to his declining optimism in the possibilities of democratic socialism. The working class is not the revolutionary agent of social change; society will change through a total mobilization of power concentrated in the hands of a small, middle-class, intellectual, and technical élite.

Thus throughout the novel the physical presence of the working class is counterpointed to Winston's desperate search for understanding. 'I understand HOW: I do not understand WHY,' he had written: the 'proles' are the only hope for they constitute a majority and would thus need only 'to rise up and shake themselves like a horse shaking off flies [to] blow the Party to pieces tomorrow' (p. 71). But they do not. For Orwell's vision of the working class in *Nineteen Eighty-Four* was no different from his conception of them in the 1930s, defeated by the general strike and years of mass unemployment. In the novel Winston (Orwell) makes this observation, on proletarian women:

They were born, they grew up in the gutters, they went to work at twelve, they passed through a brief blossoming period of beauty and sexual desire, they married at twenty, they were middle-aged at thirty, they died, for the most part, at sixty. Heavy physical work, the care of home and children, petty quarrels with neighbours, films, football, beer and, above all, gambling, filled up the horizon of their minds. (p. 73)

This is the Orwell of *The Road to Wigan Pier*, who now observes, through Winston, 'two bloated women' arguing ferociously over tin saucepans (p. 72), another wrangle over the correct number of the weekly lottery winner, noting that 'the Lottery was the principal if not the only reason for remaining alive' (pp. 86–7). The working class is simply stupefied by the control exerted upon it by the Party and the Thought Police. It is a passive, undifferentiated mass, in which prostitution, drug addiction, and criminality of all kinds thrive. Deviance is ignored by the Party presumably since it functions as a social control. And the proletariat are outside the rigid, sexual ethic of the Party too, living instinctual lives, breeding in dirty profusion. It is this class which Winston must have faith in if there is to be any hope:

But if there was hope, it lay in the proles. You had to cling on to that. When you put it in words it sounded reasonable: it was when you looked at the human beings passing you on the pavement that it became an act of faith. (p. 87)

He says later, when he is with Julia, that only the 'proles' had remained human; they were spontaneous, instinctual – 'The proles are human beings. We are not human.' (p. 167) Here we have the typical Orwellian theme of middle-class deadness (the novels of the thirties) contrasted with genuine working-class spontaneity. The Oceania bureaucracy is middle-class and inhuman. And there is no hope: the proles will always be *integrated* into this inhumane society and they will never revolt. This is the message of Orwell's novel: socialism is mere utopia.

This is, however, a one-sided view of the working class. Orwell at no point discussed trade unions; he seems to believe that working-class social solidarity can never extend to political consciousness. In his works before 1945 he stressed the potentiality of the working class for socialist revolution. In his last years the vision becomes totally bleak: the working class will never be the agency of social change, for they accept bourgeois society. It was just one step to his view that they would accept totalitarian society also.

Thus the revolt of Winston and Julia takes on a special significance if seen from this class standpoint. In his earlier novels Orwell failed to portray genuine sexual love; his females are frigid and status-conscious. Julia is his one exception. She desires sexual love, she strives to fulfil herself erotically, to break away consciously from the Party's puritanical ethic. Orwell had grasped the sexual dynamics of totalitarian organization, for the sexual energy can better be directed to political values and activity:

Life as she saw it was quite simple. You wanted a good time; 'they', meaning the Party, wanted to stop you having it; you broke the rules as best you could ... Unlike Winston, she had grasped the inner meaning of the Party's sexual puritanism. It was not merely that the sex instinct created a world of its own which was outside the Party's control and which therefore had to be destroyed if possible.

What was more more important was that sexual privation induced hysteria, which was desirable because it could be transformed into war-fever and leader-worship. (pp. 133-4)

Julia, although uninterested in politics and depicted as instinctual rather than intellectual, is remarkably conscious of the Party's reasons for sexual control: 'They want you to be bursting with energy all the time. All this marching up and down and cheering and waving is simply sex gone sour' (p. 134). Julia is Orwell's first real woman because her rebellion, consciously sexual, must place her in opposition to the dominant Party norms; her relationship with Winston must develop towards socialism, towards understanding the nature of totalitarian society. In Oceania society a genuine human relationship is possible only in opposition to the prevailing values of the Party. In the earlier novels, written from the standpoint of the middle class, Orwell depicted women as part of that class, their horizons limited by its values, and desirous of remaining within it; they accepted its norms. But in *Nineteen Eighty-Four*, Orwell's vision was far richer, and more completely pessimistic, for his grasp of what socialism could be informs the hopeless quest of Winston and Julia for understanding and for humane values. Their defeat is a total defeat; humanity is defeated in Room 101. Only the middle classes were beaten in Orwell's early novels.

6

In his essay on Swift, Orwell concludes by arguing that no matter whether a writer is 'progressive' or not, the ultimate test for a work of literature lies with the writer's sense of conviction, for 'if the force of belief is behind it, a world view which only just passes the test of sanity is sufficient to produce a great work of art'.* *Nineteen Eighty-Four* is the vision of a man for whom socialism remains as the only hope for humanity and which itself is defeated by bureaucratic collectivism and totalitarian politics. Orwell was not a member of any political party; he had left the Independent Labour Party in 1940 when it adopted a pacifist attitude towards the Second World War. He remained an individual, criticizing the Russophile left, the Labour Party and, of course, the Conservatives, from the standpoint of demo-

* *Collected Essays*, p. 398.

cratic socialism. Unlike others of his contemporaries, Orwell spoke out fearlessly against any infringement on democratic freedoms. His style embodied his personal commitment: he was not *frightened*, as he himself had written of Henry Miller. His style and his vision are one: capitalism is finished, the middle classes are done for, all orthodoxies, political and religious, are suspect, totalitarianism is a menace and the working class is the last hope. He wanted socialism; he thought that the working class did not. Ultimately, this political pessimism, the consequence of a one-sided view of the English proletariat, is the strength of *Nineteen Eighty-Four*.

Select Bibliography

1. *General: Literature and Sociology*

M. C. Albrecht, 'The Relationship of Literature and Society', *American Journal of Sociology*, vol. 59, no. 5, March 1954.

Z. Barbu, 'Sociological Perspectives in Art and Literature', in J. Creedy, *The Social Context of Art*, London, Tavistock, 1970.

J. H. Barnett, 'The Sociology of Art', in Merton, Broom, and Cottrell (eds), *Sociology Today*, New York, Basic Books, 1958.

R. Bastide, 'Sociologie et littérature comparée', in *Cahiers Internationaux de Sociologie*, Paris, 1954, no. 17.

A. Bloch, 'Towards the Development of a Sociology of Literary and Art Forms', *American Sociological Review*, 1943, no. 3.

L. Coser, *Sociology Through Literature*, New Jersey, Prentice-Hall, 1963.

D. Daiches, *Literature and Society*, London, Gollancz, 1938.

—— 'Criticism and Sociology', ch. 18 of his *Critical Approaches to Literature*, London, Longmans, 1956.

H. D. Duncan, *Language and Literature in Society*, Chicago, University of Chicago Press, 1953.

R. Escarpit, *Sociologie de la Littérature*, Paris, 1958; 'The Sociology of Literature', in *International Encyclopaedia of the Social Sciences*, New York, Macmillan, 1968.

——*Le Littéraire et le Social*, Paris, Flammarion, 1970, contains a number of essays by Escarpit's pupils.

R. Hoggart, 'Literature and Society', in N. Mackenzie, (ed.), *A Guide to the Social Sciences*, London, Weidenfeld & Nicolson, 1966.

—— 'The Literary Imagination and the Sociological Imagination', *Speaking to Each Other*, vol. 2, London, Chatto & Windus, 1970.

F. R. Leavis, 'Sociology and Literature', *The Common Pursuit*, London, Chatto & Windus, 1952.

L. Lowenthal, *Literature and the Image of Man*, Boston, Beacon Press 1957.

—— *Literature, Popular Culture and Society*, New Jersey, Prentice-Hall, 1961.

—— 'Sociology of Literature', in W. Schramm, (ed.), *Communications in Modern Society*, Urbana, University of Illinois Press, 1953.

G. Lukács, 'The Sociology of Modern Drama' (1911), in E. Bentley, *The Theory of the Modern Stage*, London, Penguin Books, 1968.

J. P. Sartre, *Literature and Existentialism*, New York, The Citadel Press, 1962.

B. Slote (ed.), *Literature and Society*, Lincoln, University of Nebraska Press, 1964.

I. Watt, 'Literature and Society', in R. N. Wilson, *The Arts in Society*, New Jersey, Prentice-Hall, 1964.
R. Williams, *Culture and Society*, London, Chatto & Windus, 1958.
R. Wellek and A. Warren, 'Literature and Society', *Theory of Literature*, third edition, London, Peregrine Books, 1963.

COLLECTIONS
'Sociology of Literary Creativity', *International Social Science Journal*, UNESCO, vol. XIX, no. 4. *Littérature et Société. Problèmes de méthodologie en Sociologie de la Littérature*, Brussels, L'Institut de Sociologie, 1967.
Sociologie de la Littérature: Recherches récentes et discussions, Brussels, L'Institut de Sociologie, 1970.

2. *The Social Theories of Literature*

E. Auerbach, *Mimesis: The Representation of Reality in Western Literature*, Princeton, University of Princeton Press, 1953.
A. Ferguson, *An Essay on the History of Civil Society (1767)*, Edinburgh, University of Edinburgh Press, 1966.
G. W. F. Hegel, *Philosophy of Fine Art*, London, Allen & Unwin, 1920.
S. J. Kahn, *Science and Aesthetic Judgment: A Study in Taine's Critical Method*, London, Routledge & Kegan Paul, 1953.
H. Levin, *The Gates of Horn*, New York, Oxford University Press, 1963.
F. Schiller, *On the Aesthetic Education of Man (1795)*, ed. E. M. Wilkinson and L. A. Willoughby, Oxford, Oxford University Press, 1967.
A. Smith, *Lectures on Rhetoric and Belles Lettres (1751)*, ed. J. M. Lothian, Edinburgh, Nelson, 1963.
G. de Stael, *De la Littérature (1800)*, Paris, Minard, 1959.
H. Taine, *History of English Literature*, London, Chatto & Windus, 1906.
R. Wellek, *A History of Modern Criticism*, London, Jonathan Cape, 1955-66, 4 vols.
—— *The Rise of English Literary History*, Chapel Hill, University of North Carolina Press, 1941.
—— *Concepts of Criticism*, New Haven, Yale University Press, 1963.
E. Wilson, 'The Historical Interpretation of Literature', *The Triple Thinkers*, London, Penguin Books, 1962.
G. Vico, *The New Science (1744)*, New York, Cornell University Press, 1948.

3. *Marxism and Literature*

T. W. Adorno, *Prisms: Cultural Criticism and Society*, London, Neville Spearman, 1967.
H. Arvon, *G. Lukács ou le front populaire en littérature*, Paris, Seghers, 1968.
W. Benjamin, *Illuminations: Essays and Reflections*, London, Jonathan Cape, 1970.
C. Caudwell, *Illusion and Reality (1937)*, New York, International Publishers, 1967.
P. Demetz, *Marx, Engels and the Poets*, Chicago, University of Chicago Press, 1967.
E. Fischer, *Art Against Ideology*, London, Allen Lane The Penguin Press, 1969.

E. Fischer, *The Necessity of Art*, London, Penguin Books, 1963.
L. Goldmann, *The Hidden God* (1956), London, Routledge & Kegan Paul, 1964.
—— *Recherches Dialectiques*, Paris, Gallimard, 1959.
L. C. Knights, *Drama and Society in the Age of Johnson*, London, Chatto & Windus, 1937.
V. I. Lenin, *Tolstoy and His Time*, New York, International Publishers, 1952.
G. Lukács, *Goethe and His Age*, London, Merlin Press, 1968.
—— *The Meaning of Contemporary Realism*, London, Merlin Press, 1963.
A. Lunacharsky, *On Literature and Art*, Moscow, Progress Publishers, 1965.
D. N. Margolies, *The Function of Literature*, New York, International Publishers, 1969.
S. Morawski, 'The Aesthetic Views of Marx and Engels', *The Journal of Aesthetics and Art Criticism*, vol. XXVIII, no. 3, Spring 1970.
—— 'Lenin as a Literary Theorist', *Science and Society*, vol. XXIX, no. 1, Winter 1965.
K. Marx, *Economic and Philosophic Manuscripts of 1844*, ed. T. B. Bottomore, London, Watts, 1963.
—— *A Contribution to the Critique of Political Economy* (1857–9), New York, Charles Kerr, 1904.
K. Marx and F. Engels, *The German Ideology* (1845), Moscow, Progress Publishers, 1964.
—— and —— *Literature and Art*, New York, International Publishers, 1947.
—— and —— *Selected Works*, 2 vols., Moscow, Foreign Languages Publishing House, 1958.
R. Mathewson, *The Positive Hero in Russian Literature* (New York: Columbia University Press, 1958).
G. H. R. Parkinson (ed.), *Georg Lukács: The Man, His Work, His Ideas*, London, Weidenfeld & Nicolson, 1970.
G. Plekhanov, *Art and Social Life* (1912), London, Lawrence & Wishart, 1953.
G. Steiner, 'Marxism and Literature', *Language and Silence*, London, Faber & Faber, 1967.
G. Thompson, *Aeschylus and Athens: A Study in the Social Origins of Drama*, London, Lawrence & Wishart, 1946.
—— *Marxism and Poetry*, New York, International Publishers, 1946.
L. Trotsky, *Literature and Revolution* (1925), New York, Russell & Russell, 1957.

4. Structuralism and Literature

R. Barthes, *Writing Degree Zero*, London, Cape Editions, 1967.
—— *Elements of Semiology*, London, Cape Editions, 1968.
C. Bouazis, 'La théorie des structures d'œvres: problèmes de l'analyse du système et de la causalité sociologique', in R. Escarpit, *Le Littéraire et le Social*.
V. Erlich, *Russian Formalism*, The Hague, Mouton, 1955.
L. Goldmann, 'The Sociology of Literature', in *International Social Science Journal*, vol. XI, no. 4.
—— 'Micro-Structures dans les vingt-cinq premières répliques des "Nègres" de Jean Genet', and '"Les Chats"': both articles in *Sociologie de la Littérature*, Brussels, 1970.

J. Garson, 'Literary History: Russian Formalist Views, 1916–1928', *Journal of the History of Ideas*, vol. XXXI, no. 3, July/Sept, 1970.

R. Lane (ed.), *Structuralism: A Reader*, London, Jonathan Cape, 1970.

L. T. Lemon and M. J. Reis, *Russian Formalist Criticism: Four Essays*, Lincoln, University of Nebraska Press, 1965: essays by Victor Shklovsky, Boris Tomashevsky, and Boris Eichenbaum.

J. Leenhardt, 'Sémantique et Sociologie de la Littérature', in *Sociologie de la Littérature*, Brussels, 1970.

C. Lévi-Strauss, *Structural Anthropology*, London, Allen Lane The Penguin Press, 1968.

F. Saussure, *Course in General Linguistics*, London, Peter Owen, 1960.

L. Sebag, *Marxisme et Structuralisme*, Paris, Payot, 1964.

T. Todorov, 'Structural Analysis of Narrative', *Novel*, vol. 3, no. 1, Fall, 1969.

COLLECTIONS

A Prague School Reader on Aesthetics, Literary Structure and Style. Washington, Georgetown University Press, 1964. (ed.), P. C. Garvin 'Structuralism', *Yale French Studies*, nos 36 and 37.

5. The Sociology of the Writer

R. D. Altick, *The English Common Reader: A Social History of the Mass Reading Public 1880–1900*, Cambridge, Cambridge University Press, 1957.

—— 'The Sociology of Authorship', *New York Public Library Bulletin*, 1962.

M. Arnold, *Culture and Anarchy*, ed. J. Dover Wilson, Cambridge University Press, 1960.

A. Beljame, *Men of Letters and the English Public in the Eighteenth Century 1660–1774*, ed. with an introduction by Bonamy Dobrée, London, Kegan Paul 1948.

C. Bell, *Old Friends*, London, Chatto & Windus, 1956.

W. Besant, *The Pen and the Book: Advice to Authors*, London, Thomas Burleish, 1899.

M. Bradbury, *The Social Context of Modern English Literature*, London, 1971.

V. W. Brooks, *The Writer in America*, New York, Dutton, 1953.

A. S. Collins, *Authorship in the Days of Johnson*, London, R. Holden & Co., 1927.

—— *The Profession of Letters*, London, Routledge, 1928.

C. Connolly, *Enemies of Promise*, London, Routledge & Kegan Paul, 1938.

M. Cowley (ed.), *Writers at Work – The Paris Interview Series*, London, Secker & Warburg, 1962, 1965.

A. Cruz, *The Victorians and Their Books*, London, Allen & Unwin, 1963.

M. Dalziel, *Popular Fiction a Hundred Years Ago. An unexplored fact of literary history*, London, Cohen & West, 1957.

L. Edel, *The Psychological Novel*, New York, The Universal Library, Grosset & Dunlap, 1964.

R. Escarpit, *The Book Revolution*, London, Harrap, 1966, and U.N.E.S.C.O.

L. Fiedler, *Love and Death in the American Novel*, New York, Criterion Books, 1960.

L. Fiedler, *Waiting for the End. The American Literary Scene from Hemingway to Baldwin*, London, Penguin Books, 1967.

R. Findlater, *What are writers worth?*, London, Society of Authors, 1963.

R. Findlater, *The Bookwriters, Who Are They?*, London, Society of Authors, 1966.

B. Ford (ed.), *The Pelican Guide to English Literature*, vols. 4–7, London, Penguin Books, 1961.

B. B. Gamzue, 'Elizabeth and Literary Patronage', New York, *Proceedings of the Modern Language Association*, XLIX, 1934.

W. Gaunt, *The Aesthetic Adventure*, London, Cape, 1945.

V. and W. Goertzels, *Cradles of Eminence*, London, Constable, 1965.

J. Gross, *The Rise and Fall of the Man of Letters* – English Literary Life since 1800, London, Weidenfeld & Nicolson, 1969.

A. Hauser, *The Social History of Art*, 4 vols., London, Routledge & Kegan Paul, 1962.

J. D. Hart, *The Popular Book – The Social Background of our Popular Readings*, Oxford, Oxford University Press, 1950.

R. Hingley, *Russian Writers and Society*, London, Weidenfeld & Nicolson, 1967.

M. Hodgart, *Satire*, London, Weidenfeld & Nicolson, World University Library, 1963.

G. Hough, *The Last Romantics*, London, Duckworth, 1947.

H. House, *The Dickens World*, Oxford, Oxford University Press, 1941.

A. R. Humphries, *The Augustan World*, London, Methuen University Paperbacks, 1961.

L. James, *Fiction for the Working Man, 1830–1850*, Oxford, Oxford University Press, 1963.

J. K. Johnstone, *The Bloomsbury Group:* a study of E. M. Forster, Lytton Strachey, Virginia Woolf and their circle, London, Secker & Warburg, 1954.

D. F. Laurenson, 'A Sociological Study of Authorship', *British Journal of Sociology, 1969*.

Q. D. Leavis, *Fiction and the Reading Public*, London, Chatto & Windus, 1932.

Jenny Lee, *A Policy for the Arts*, CMND 2601, London, H.M.S.O., 1965.

P. Macherey, *Pour une Théorie de la Production Littéraire*, Paris, Maspero, 1967.

E. H. Miller, *The Professional Writer in Elizabethan England: A Study of non-dramatic Literature*, Cambridge, Massachusetts, Harvard University Press, 1959.

F. Munby, *Publishing and Bookselling*, London, Cape, 1956.

M. Plant, *The English Book Trade. An Economic History of the making and sale of books*, London, Chatto & Windus, 1932.

E. K. Rosengren, *Sociological aspects of the Literary System*, Stockholm, 1968.

J. W. Saunders, *The Profession of English Letters*, London, Routledge & Kegan Paul, 1964.

P. Sheavyn, *The Literary Profession in the Elizabethan Age*, Manchester, Manchester University Press, 1909.

S. H. Steinberg, *Five Hundred Years of Printing*, London, Penguin Books, 1961.

L. Stephen, *English Literature and Society in the 18th Century*, London, Methuen University Paperbacks, 1966.

A. Symons, *The Symbolist Movement in Literature*, London, Constable, 1908.

C. Tanzy, 'Publishing the Victorian Novel. A Study of the Economic Relationships of Novelists and Publishers in England 1830–1880', unpublished Ph.D. thesis, Ohio State University, 1961.

J. M. S. Tompkins, *The Popular Novel in England 1770–1800*, London, Methuen, University Paperback, 1969.

A. Walbank, *Queens of the Circulating Libraries: selected from Victorian Lady Novelists 1800–1900*, London, Evans, 1950.

G. Watson, *The Study of Literature*, London, Allen Lane The Penguin Press, 1969.

R. Williams, *The Long Revolution*, London, Chatto & Windus, 1962.

L. B. Wright, *Middle Class Culture in Elizabethan England*, Chapel Hill, University of North Carolina Press, 1955.

6. The Sociology of the Novel

D. Daiches, *The Novel and the Modern World*, Chicago, University of Chicago Press, 1960.

I. Deutscher, 'Georg Lukács and "Critical Realism"', *The Listener*, 3 November 1966.

U. Eco, 'Rhetoric and Ideology in Sue's "Les Mystères de Paris"', *International Social Science Journal*, vol. XIX, no. 4.

R. Girard, *Desire, Deceit and the Novel*, Baltimore, Johns Hopkins Press, 1965.

L. Goldmann, *Pour une Sociologie du Roman*, Paris, Gallimard, 1964.
—— 'Criticism and Dogmatism in Literature', in D. Cooper (ed.), *The Dialectics of Liberation*, London, Penguin Books, 1968.
—— 'Introduction aux premiers écrits de Georges Lukács', in G. Lukács, *La Théorie du Roman*, see below.
—— 'Marx, Lukács, Girard et la sociologie du roman', *Médiations*, no. 2, 1962.

I. Howe, *Politics and the Novel*, New York, Meridian Books, 1957.

G. Huaco, 'Sociologie du Roman: Le Roman Mexicain, 1915–1965', in *Sociologie de la Littérature*, Brussels, 1970.

E. Knight, *A Theory of the Classical Novel*, London, Routledge & Kegan Paul, 1969.

H. Levin, 'Toward the Sociology of the Novel', *Refractions*, New York, Oxford University Press, 1966.

G. Lukács, *The Historical Novel*, London, Merlin Press, 1962.
—— *Essays on Thomas Mann*, London, Merlin Press, 1964.
—— *La Théorie du Roman* (1920), Paris, Gonthier, 1968. (Eng. trans. Merlin Press, 1971.)
—— *Studies in European Realism*, New York, Grosset & Dunlap, 1964.
—— *Solzhenitsyn*, London, Merlin Press, 1971.

G. Mouillard, 'Sociologie des Romans de Stendhal', *International Social Science Journal*, vol. XIX, no. 4.

J. Ruhle, *Literature and Revolution*, London, Pall Mall Press, 1969.

J. P. Sartre, 'La Conscience de Classe chez Flaubert', *Temps Modernes*, vol. 21, no. 240, 1966.

D. Spearman, *The Novel and Society*, London, Routledge & Kegan Paul, 1966.

L. Trilling, *The Liberal Imagination: Essays on Literature and Society*, London, Secker & Warburg, 1964.

I. Watt, *The Rise of the Novel*, London, Peregrine Books, 1962.

COLLECTION

Problèmes d'une sociologie du Roman, Brussels, L'Institut de Sociologie, 1963.

DATE DUE

GAYLORD			PRINTED IN U.S A